Praise for
The Chimpanzee Chronicles

"Debra Rosenman has gathered up real life stories that will, collectively, sadden, anger, and inspire all who read them. Once I had looked deeply into the eyes of a chimpanzee in the concrete prison cell of a bad zoo, those of a bewildered, terrified, and hurting infant tied up for sale in an African market, those of a nervous juvenile forced to dress up and perform to entertain us, and—for me, the most significant experience—those of a thirty-year-old adult male who had lived in solitary confinement in a tiny cage along with many others in a research laboratory, I knew I had to try to help. Thank goodness for the dedicated, passionate, and often very courageous people whose work is recognized in this important book, one that will, I am sure, inspire all who read it to do their bit to improve the lives of the animals with whom we share, or should share, our planet. On behalf of the chimpanzees whose lives they changed, I thank and honor them."

—JANE GOODALL, PhD, DBE
Founder of the Jane Goodall Institute and a United Nations Messenger of Peace

"The deep suffering that human beings can inflict on chimpanzees because of their legal status as things, not persons, is made plain in *The Chimpanzee Chronicles*. As one compelling story follows another, readers viscerally experience what these cognitively and emotionally complex beings lose in captivity and what the fortunate few are able to regain thanks to their resolute human champions. Before these magnificent beings are gone forever, they need us to imagine a world in which their autonomy is respected and protected so they may live freely, with peace and dignity. This remarkable book will certainly help us get there."

—STEVEN M. WISE
Founder and president of the Nonhuman Rights Project and author of *Rattling the Cage*

"There is no doubt in my mind after reading the astonishing stories in *The Chimpanzee Chronicles* that chimpanzees are people. They are different from us, of course, but deserving of the same rights. After reading this compelling and completely convincing book, you will understand why chimpanzees deserve freedom from any harm, including lives in laboratories, circuses, and zoos. Debra Rosenman has done an excellent job in proving to the world that chimpanzees deserve to be held in the same regard as humans."

—JEFFREY MOUSSAIEFF MASSON, PhD
Author of *When Elephants Weep* and *Beasts*

"This is a book about hope. It is not always easy to read—being about children snatched from their mothers' arms and abused in sometimes shocking ways—but it chronicles the efforts of good people working to right wrongs. The fact that the children in question are of another species almost pales, given their equal capacity to suffer, anticipate harm, and welcome love and their gestural and vocal ability to reach across the species barrier and melt hearts. Unfortunately that ability is why some people want to acquire baby apes, stimulating the illegal capture and commerce that shatters chimpanzee families and endangers them as a species. *The Chimpanzee Chronicles* is a riveting compilation of twenty-five powerful stories that will grip you, inform you about our zoological kin, and inspire you to support those who fight for their survival."

—IAN REDMOND, OBE
Ambassador, UNEP Convention on Migratory Species; chairman, Ape Alliance and The Gorilla Organization; and ambassador and consultant, www.vEcotourism.org

"Debra Rosenman's riveting collection of stories clarifies the moral imperative of caring for the thousands of chimpanzees currently suffering in villages, zoos, and laboratories throughout the world. Reading *The Chimpanzee Chronicles* ensures that we see chimpanzees as the sentient and intelligent beings they are and acknowledge that their lives matter, too. Such a change in perspective is crucial if we are to have any hope of slowing or stopping our reckless assault on the natural world."

—CLEVE HICKS, PHD
Primatologist, lead researcher of the Bili Chimpanzee Project, DRC, and author of *A Rhino to the Rescue*

"From the frontlines of the war against wildlife, *The Chimpanzee Chronicles* is a unique collection of memories from some of the most courageous people on earth. In these pages are those who endure civil and international wars, who fight in either the most familiar or far-flung places on earth, and who often risk their lives for the chimpanzees they so dearly love. These are stories of strength, inspiration, and hope. This is perhaps the first time we have heard such extraordinary truths written by those who have witnessed firsthand how close we are to our chimpanzee relatives and how we must save them at all costs."

—VANESSA WOODS, *New York Times* best-selling author of *Bonobo Handshake*

"Debra Rosenman has collected stories that are surprising, heartbreaking, and heartwarming. Every page is astonishing. A compelling read that will leave you wondering if chimpanzees might well be more human than we are."

—NANCY MERRICK, MD, author of *Among Chimpanzees*

"From around the globe, *The Chimpanzee Chronicles* tells inspiring and heartbreaking stories of casualties and survivors of a long war on these sensitive, strong, and resilient beings. Their stories, told by humans battling for justice on their behalf, show how visible and invisible wounds can begin to heal with freedom, safety, love, and respect. Their urgent plight and our response provide invaluable lessons on how humans can change the lives of other animals—for better or worse."

—HOPE FERDOWSIAN, MD, MPH, FACP, FACPM

Physician, human and animal rights advocate, and author of *Phoenix Zones*

"Rosenman's *Chronicles* gives the reader an up-close understanding of the atrocities we have perpetuated against our closest genetic relatives, as well as the miracles that individuals have achieved for and through them. If you long for heroes, both human and other animal, and want to better understand humankind's place among all creatures, this book is the right place to start. It is a celebration—of chimpanzees and humans, the important connections between us, and the bridge chimpanzees provide us to all other species."

—THEODORA CAPALDO, EdD

President emeritus, New England Anti-Vivisection Society

"*The Chimpanzee Chronicles* is a collection of poignant firsthand accounts of the ways in which chimpanzees overlap with our own species in intellect, emotions, and psychological needs. Even more so, it is the story of how terribly we have mistreated chimpanzees in captivity, and of the people and animals who give us hope for a more humane future."

—CRAIG STANFORD

Professor of biological sciences and anthropology, University of Southern California, and author of *The New Chimpanzee* and *Significant Others*

"Rosenman's *Chimpanzee Chronicles* is a moving and important contribution to the growing understanding of our moral obligation to primates, our next of kin. Here history is written by leading primatologists, ethologists, activists, artists, and sanctuary staff, who share their experiences with heart, insight, and understanding. The point driven home through their poignant observations about chimpanzees is: we have exploited and wronged them, and this chapter in history must now close, never to be repeated."

—JO-ANNE MCARTHUR

Photojournalist, activist, and author of *We Animals* and *Captive*

"If captive chimpanzees chose to write their own books for humans, *The Chimpanzee Chronicles* might well be one of them. This anthology is an impassioned call for a new generation of human ethical treatment of chimpanzees—our own veritable kin—as well as all other species on this fragile planet."

—MICHAEL CHARLES TOBIAS, PHD
Author, global ecologist, animal activist, filmmaker, and
president of Dancing Star Foundation

"The stories told in this wonderful book will open up a whole new world to anyone who reads them. The writing is powerful, emotional, entertaining, and funny. What can't be denied is the strong connection that people from different countries and backgrounds share once they spend time with a chimpanzee. I urge everyone to read about these extraordinary individuals, both human and chimp."

—JOCELYN BEZNER, VMD, senior veterinarian, Save the Chimps

"*The Chimpanzee Chronicles* is a well-crafted collection of touching and sometimes startling vignettes from people whose lives have been irrevocably altered through their interactions with our closest living relatives—chimpanzees. Readers will be genuinely touched by these stories and ultimately inspired by the emotional journeys experienced by chimpanzees and humans alike."

—STEPHEN ROSS, PHD
Director, Lester E. Fisher Center for the Study and Conservation of Apes

"Our closest cousins deserve to be treated with dignity and respect whether in captivity or in the wild, something *The Chimpanzee Chronicles* demonstrates exceptionally well. Debra Rosenman inspires a call to action, both locally and internationally, to stop the inhumane treatment and improve the lives of all chimpanzees."

—DR. GLADYS KALEMA-ZIKUSOKA
First wildlife veterinary officer of the Uganda Wildlife Authority and
founder of Conservation Through Public Health and Gorilla Conservation Coffee

"Most people who work with great apes find it impossible to leave their hearts at the door. That is certainly true of this collection of essays about chimpanzees in captivity. But this book is not so much about chimpanzees as it is about relationships. These heartfelt and, at times, heroic stories will stay with you—and perhaps change the way you view our coexistence with our closest relations."

—BRENDA SCOTT ROYCE
Former chimpanzee caregiver and author of *Monkey Love* and *Monkey Star*

"Chimpanzees are subject to equal parts fascination and abandonment in our culture. Although things are slowly improving, these animals have yet to be granted a voice. *The Chimpanzee Chronicles* does just that. This book exposes the often heartbreaking histories of chimpanzees who were lucky enough to end up in sanctuary, while offering a rare glimpse into the lives of those who care for the cast-off apes of our society. They have suffered enough—we owe it to the chimps, now, to listen and learn from our mistakes."

—ERIKA FLEURY, program director at North American Primate
Sanctuary Alliance and author of *Monkey Business*

"*The Chimpanzee Chronicles* is a fascinating read for anyone seeking a deeper understanding of chimps and our relationships with them. In acknowledging that humans have wronged chimps and looking at how we try to rectify these abuses, it delivers passionate stories filled with perseverance and renewed respect for life."

—LAURA BONAR, RN
Chief program and policy officer, Animal Protection of New Mexico,
and advisor, Chimpanzee Sanctuary Fund

"Debra Rosenman has introduced us to our big chimpanzee family like no one else ever has. The stories will crack your heart wide open and inspire you to embrace all species. I'm grateful to all the caring humans who have stepped up to the job of being guardians for these incredible beings, and to Debra for pulling it all together."

—RAE SIKORA
Animal and environmental activist, educator, author, and
co-founder of The Institute for Humane Education, Plant Peace Daily, and Vegfund

To Learn From Animal Being

Nearer to the earth's heart,
Deeper within its silence:
Animals know this world
In a way we never will.

We who are ever
Distanced and distracted
By the parade of bright
Windows thought opens:
Their seamless presence
Is not fractured thus.

Stranded between time
Gone and time emerging,
We manage seldom
To be where we are:
Whereas they are always
Looking out from
The here and now.

May we learn to return
And rest in the beauty
Of animal being,
Learn to lean low,
Leave our locked minds,
And with freed senses
Feel the earth
Breathing with us.

May we enter
Into lightness of spirit,
And slip frequently into
The feel of the wild.

Let the clear silence
Of our animal being
Cleanse our hearts
Of corrosive words.

May we learn to walk
Upon the earth
With all their confidence
And clear-eyed stillness
So that our minds
Might be baptized
In the name of the wind
And the light and the rain.

—John O' Donohue
To Bless the Space Between Us:
A Book of Blessings

The Chimpanzee Chronicles

Stories of Heartbreak and Hope from Behind the Bars

Debra Rosenman

Foreword by Marc Bekoff

wild soul
P·R·E·S·S

Santa Fe, New Mexico

Published by: Wild Soul Press
3466 Cerrillos Road, Suite K-2, Santa Fe, NM 87507
www.chimpanzeechronicles.com

Volume editor: Debra Rosenman
Copyeditor: Ellen Kleiner
Book design and production: Janice St. Marie in collaboration with Debra Rosenman

FIRST EDITION

Printed in Canada

Publisher's Cataloging-in-Publication Data

Names:	Rosenman, Debra, editor. | Bekoff, Marc, writer of foreword.
Title:	The chimpanzee chronicles : stories of heartbreak and hope from behind the bars / Debra Rosenman ; foreword by Marc Bekoff.
Description:	First edition. | Santa Fe, New Mexico : Wild Soul Press, [2019] | Includes bibliographical references and index.
Identifiers:	ISBN: 978-1-7324651-0-7 (paperback) | LCCN: 2018907219
Subjects:	LCSH: Chimpanzees. | Captive chimpanzees. | Emotions in animals. | Cognition in animals. | Human-animal relationships. | Animal rights. | Animal welfare. | Animal intelligence. | BISAC: NATURE / Animals / Primates. | NATURE / Animal Rights. | SCIENCE / Life Sciences / Zoology / Primatology. | PHILOSOPHY / Ethics & Moral Philosophy.
Classification:	LCC: SF408.6.P74 R67 2019 | DDC: 636.9885--dc23

A portion of the proceeds from the sale of this book will benefit chimpanzee conservation programs and sanctuaries.

1 3 5 7 9 10 8 6 4 2

To Casey,

the chimpanzee who captured my heart and changed my life,

and to all chimpanzees who have suffered at the hands of humans

Figure 1. Burrito

On the Cover

Burrito, the chimpanzee portrayed on the cover of this book, personifies the transformative journey from captivity to sanctuary. He was born into the world of biomedical research on January 6, 1983, at the White Sands Research Center in Alamogordo, New Mexico. At birth he was taken from his mother, moved to the laboratory nursery, and named #67—Raj. Before Raj was even two years old, he was used as a test subject in a hepatitis B vaccine safety trial. Then on August 1, 1986, he was sent to the Buckshire Corporation in Perkasie, Pennsylvania, where his name was changed to Burrito and where he lived as a "house chimp" for six months before being leased out as part of an animal act at Jungle Larry's Safari Caribbean Gardens. Burrito returned to Buckshire a year later. After February 1988, there are no available records of him until his rescue from Buckshire on June 13, 2008, by Chimpanzee Sanctuary Northwest, which simultaneously rescued six female chimpanzees. Burrito was the youngest of the group.

Learning how to be a chimpanzee has been an ongoing education for Burrito because he was deprived of his mother's emotional and psychological nurturing, as well as the opportunity to develop species-appropriate social skills necessary to function in the chimpanzee world. Over time, Burrito has found the courage to face new situations, receiving reassurance from his chimp friend Foxie when he is uncertain or when conflict arises within the group. Burrito's confidence continues to grow, as does the bravado of his morning dominance displays. As he expresses his newfound influence and power, his female group members have begun to treat him more respectfully. Playful and, at times, mischievous, he exhibits many personality traits, perhaps the most salient of which is a series of delightful food vocalizations, showing he derives profound joy from every meal, special treat, and food enrichment activity at the sanctuary.

CONTENTS

Figure 2. Connie (left) and Max (right) at Liberia Chimpanzee Rescue & Protection sanctuary

FOREWORD

Captive chimpanzees are on the threshold of legally becoming persons. This new status will be a game changer for them. When their day in court arrives, chimpanzees will have legal rights to bodily liberty and ethical considerations that will hopefully ensure them safety and peace in a bona fide primate sanctuary, free from physical, emotional, and psychological harm. The abuses inflicted on these deeply feeling, cognitively evolved sentient beings for many decades in biomedical research laboratories, zoos, and for entertainment, are appalling. I'm astounded that it has taken so much work, and so long, to free captive chimpanzees from their pain and suffering. The lack of respect with which they are treated in the name of "science" and "entertainment" is indefensible.

The Chimpanzee Chronicles: Stories of Heartbreak and Hope from Behind the Bars is an extremely important book that reveals many facets of the world of captive chimpanzees and the incredibly dedicated people who selflessly care for them. The stories assembled by Debra Rosenman, each an emotionally penetrating thread of insight and compassion, invite us to reflect on our relationship with these intelligent and sensitive beings. Perfectly poised to have compiled such a collection, Debra has spent more than a decade advocating for captive chimpanzees. She has written and published articles about their plight, and is the developer of an elementary school program that helps children bridge a compassionate world among different species so that they and others can more effectively close the "empathy gap" that currently exists.

For *The Chimpanzee Chronicles,* Debra set her sights on twenty-five contributors' firsthand experiences that reflect the capacity chimpanzees have to feel and to express a wide variety of emotions. In this landmark book, you will experience close up how chimpanzees perceive their world through self-awareness, empathy, and joy, as well as how they cope with depression, isolation, and fear. You will come to know chimpanzees

Figure 3. Jackson (left) and Herbie (right) at Chimps Inc.

who understand illness and death and grieve for the loss of loved ones. You will even find out what chimpanzees communicating through American Sign Language (ASL) have to say to each other and to us. The narratives, from around the world, are eye-opening in their honesty, inspiring rage, deep compassion, and ultimately hope. Reading them makes it impossible to reject the book's foundational message that chimpanzees care about what happens to them, their families, and their friends—that they rejoice when "good" things occur and suffer when experiencing themselves or others treated as disposable objects.

Every story in this book is a gem. I was particularly moved by Gloria Grow's chronicle of Jeannie and all she endured as a medical research subject, including an emotional collapse before leaving the lab and embarking on a trajectory of love and healing. I was heartbroken to find out what Bruno, imprisoned at the same lab, asked contributor Mark Bodamer as they communicated in ASL, an appeal Debra first learned of when she met Mark in 2007 and that now rocks my own heart and soul.

I also loved Patti Ragan's story about Knuckles, a chimpanzee with cerebral palsy, who, despite playing a bit rough when first introduced to a new group of chimpanzees, was welcomed; they instinctively knew he was different and treated him tenderly. And I will long remember Rosa Garriga's narrative about Kouze, who caringly assisted chimps in need while the dominant male in the group threw stones at him. This shows the understanding, kindness, and empathy chimpanzees are capable of and how they will sometimes go to any length to help family and friends.

Some readers may criticize the stories for ascribing human attributes to the primates they profile. However, such a viewpoint—playing what I call the anthropomorphism card—is seriously outdated given all that we now know about the emotional lives of a wide range of nonhuman species. It has been extensively documented that chimpanzees are fully feeling individuals who express the same broad spectrum of emotions as humans. Whether they are feeling happy, fearful, sad, or angry, they are always communicating their emotions through facial expressions, body language, and vocalizations.

When we attribute rich and deep emotional lives to other animals, we're not inserting something human into them, as is sometimes—though today less often—claimed. Rather, we are applying Charles Darwin's well-accepted arguments about what is called "evolutionary continuity," the idea that differences among species are differences in *degree* rather than kind, and are measured in shades of gray rather than black and white. There is no reason to establish humans as a template against which other species are compared. In fact, large differences also exist among members of the same species.

A person would have to be severely out of touch with chimpanzees and themselves to claim, as do a dwindling number of denialists, "We really don't know what they are feeling" or "They don't really know what's happening." The important point is that other animals share with us many aspects of our emotional lives. It's high time to recognize this well-established scientific fact and stop quibbling about whether chimpanzees *really* do feel contagious joy and happiness and deep heart-wrenching pain and suffering. There is no doubt they do and the denialists are simply wrong.

I hope the experiences recounted in this book "rewild" readers' minds and hearts to appreciate chimpanzees and what they have lost in captivity. It's impossible to read these stories and not want to help current and future generations of captive chimpanzees who are dependent on us for their very lives. Let's expand our circle of compassion and help these animals live as they were meant to live. We must do no less. If *The Chimpanzee Chronicles* doesn't move readers toward some type of action, I'm not sure what will.

MARC BEKOFF

Department of Ecology and Evolutionary Biology, University of Colorado, Boulder,
and author of *Rewilding Our Hearts* and *The Animals' Agenda*
marcbekoff.com

Introduction

A SHORT LOOK AT THE LONG HISTORY OF CHIMPANZEES IN CAPTIVITY

There is no easy way around the truth: chimpanzees have been exploited, violated, and killed in the name of science, medical advancement, and financial gain. Forced to exist in our world with little, if any, consideration or respect for who they are, chimpanzees have lost their families, their land, and their culture. Human beings have broken their bodies and their spirits. The lucky ones have found refuge and healing in sanctuaries, but countless others have not. The suffering of captive chimpanzees has deeply affected my psyche, changed my worldview on captivity, yet also deepened my compassion and seeded the idea for this book.

The Chimpanzee Chronicles: Stories of Heartbreak and Hope from Behind the Bars presents a behind-the-scenes look at the physical, emotional, and psychological lives of captive chimpanzees who have been used in biomedical research, the entertainment industry, and the exotic pet trade. Spanning Africa, Australia, the Middle East, Argentina, Canada, and the United States, the book introduces twenty-five narratives written by people who have had the privilege of knowing and caring for captive chimpanzees, and who are in the best position to be a voice for them: primatologists, sanctuary founders and directors, caregivers, veterinarians, lawyers, a primate communication scientist, a wildlife documentary filmmaker, and a psychology professor. Also included are stories by a musician and by a young boy and his mother, all of whom are active in advocacy work for captive chimpanzees. Together, these chronicles bear witness to the unjust and heartless treatment of captive chimpanzees and the suffering they endured; the healing many of them experienced once retired into sanctuary; and the life-changing transformations of the contributors themselves, each of whom was committed to a single mission—improving the lives of captive chimpanzees.

Figure 4. Young chimps at LEMSIP

ᐠᐠᐠ ᐠᐠᐠ ᐠᐠᐠ

A century ago there were between one and two million chimpanzees living in about twenty countries across Central and West Africa. Today, it is estimated that less than three hundred thousand chimpanzees remain in the wild. The forces driving their demise are bushmeat hunting, wildlife trafficking, habitat loss from deforestation, and zoonotic disease.

Chimpanzees in the wild are commonly killed or captured for food and profit. Large numbers of people hunt bushmeat for survival, as they have for centuries; however, hunting for commercial purposes is the bigger problem as chimpanzee meat is highly valued and sold for human consumption in rural marketplaces, as well as through the black market, which has supported expatriate communities living in cities as far from Africa as London, Paris, and New York.

Baby chimps, whose meat has no value, are taken from the wild and sold as house pets, performers, or exhibit attractions in poor-quality zoos. Poachers seeking to acquire baby chimps have to slaughter the mother and other family members who would otherwise never let the babies be taken, resulting in the death of approximately five to ten chimpanzees for every confiscated baby, many of whom are unable to survive the separation from their mothers. The ones who do often undergo long, harrowing travels in small wooden crates or even suitcases to China, the Middle East, or Europe. Those strong enough to survive transport across the world with little or no hydration or nourishment arrive weak and ailing. The others die of shock, malnourishment, and heartbreak during the traumatic journey.

Wildlife trafficking of baby chimpanzees is not only illegal but also a lucrative business with strong ties to drug cartels that are smuggling arms and baby chimps alongside drugs. Middlemen who buy baby chimps from poachers can resell them for a handsome profit. The highest demand for chimpanzees these days is from China, Malaysia, and the Gulf States. Wealthy clientele from these countries pay to have permits and illegal documents at their disposal to support the intercontinental transport of chimpanzees from Africa. However, they don't know how to properly care for them; the young chimps are invariably treated like profit-making merchandise as they are paraded in costumes and put on exhibit in amusement parks and zoos. [1, 2]

Equally devastating are the consequences of deforestation, leaving wild chimpanzees without most of their food sources, such as flowers, fruits, nuts, and seeds; places to build night nests and sleep; and access to the leaves and bark used to self-medicate when combating illness. Without their usual food sources, chimpanzees have to roam until they find the sustenance they need for survival, often trespassing onto privately owned land, resulting in problems for landowners and harm to themselves.

Just as troubling are the huge populations of great apes being decimated by infectious diseases such as anthrax and Ebola.[3, 4, 5] These and other zoonotic diseases pose an increasing threat to chimpanzees, who are susceptible to transmittable diseases from other wild animals and from humans, whose activities are encroaching with greater frequency into their home-range territories.

꧅ ꧅ ꧅

Sharing an estimated 98.6 percent of DNA with humans, chimpanzees, because of their many similarities with us, have been exploited as science subjects, characters in films and other forms of entertainment, pets, and often, zoo displays. It is important to remember that chimpanzees are their own distinctive beings, a highly sensitive, intelligent, and cognitively complex species with the capacity for self-recognition, altruistic behavior, and expressing many feelings, including sadness, grief, fear, excitement, anger, depression, joy, and love. Highly social beings hardwired for physical connection, chimpanzees hold hands, kiss, embrace, and groom each other. In their natural habitats, they live communally in social groups where touch, part of their daily routine, is critical to their well-being—a way of life that abruptly ceases when they are abducted from the wild and forced into captivity, or bred in captivity without the company of other chimpanzees.

Because of their similarities with humans, chimpanzees have a long history of being used for scientific experimentation without regard for their physical, emotional, or psychological well-being. In 1916, primatologist Robert M. Yerkes published an article in *Science* magazine in which he proposed the use of monkeys and anthropoid apes for "systematic and continuous observation" and for "experimental investigations from every significant biological point of view."[6] Yerkes went on in 1923 to purchase a young chimpanzee and bonobo, both of whom died within a year. Over the next two years he acquired four more chimps—Bill, Dwina, Pan, and Wendy—the first to be used in his early behavioral and cognitive research. In 1930, with the financial support of the Rockefeller and Carnegie Foundations and Yale University, he opened the Yale Laboratories for Primate Biology in Orange Park, Florida, ushering in the long and abusive history of using chimpanzees in biomedical research.[7, 8]

In the 1950s, the US Air Force captured sixty-five young chimpanzees in Africa and brought them to Holloman Air Force Base in Alamogordo, New Mexico, to begin a breeding colony for its Air and Space Research program. For many years, these researchers carried out barbarous experiments on chimpanzees to test gravitational forces and high-speed travel for future space flights. The chimps were spun in centrifuges to see how long it took them to lose consciousness; submerged in water for g-force tests; crashed at supersonic speeds while strapped in sleds; and hurled out of missiles moving at supersonic speeds while anesthetized. These and many other experiments scorched, mutilated, and killed the chimpanzees.[9]

On January 31, 1961, a captured US Air Force chimpanzee called #65, who had been born in the wild in 1957 and should have been living in the comfort of his mother's arms in a forest in Cameroon, was strapped into a space capsule and propelled 157 miles over the earth, traveling at 5,857 miles per hour. Renamed Ham, an acronym for Holloman Aero Medical, he perfectly executed the tasks he had been trained to do on land, despite the extreme pressure of g-forces and the 6.6 minutes of weightlessness he experienced on the flight. After 16.5 minutes in space, his capsule touched down in the Atlantic Ocean sixty miles from the recovery ship, causing Ham to spend almost three hours in the locked capsule bobbing in the water until he was rescued.[10] The documentary *One Small Step: The Story of the Space Chimps* shows that when Ham was finally released from the capsule he displayed his upper and lower teeth in a huge fear grimace, an expression exploitatively misinterpreted as a smile. The US Air Force, wanting to prove to the world that Ham loved the capsule he had been strapped in, arranged a press gathering and tried returning him to the capsule for photographs, but the brawn of four grown men could not get him back inside.[11]

Ham's flight determined the safety of space travel for Alan Shepard Jr., the first American to go into space. Unlike Shepard, who upon his return received a NASA Distinguished Service Medal from President Kennedy at the White House and a ticker-tape parade in New York City, Ham was rewarded with an apple and then moved to the National Zoo in Washington, DC, where he lived alone for seventeen years.

In 1980, Ham was moved to the North Carolina Zoological Park, where he was finally able to live with other chimpanzees until his death three years later at the age of only twenty-six. The Air Force Institute of Pathology used his skeleton for further testing; the parts of his body that remained were placed in a grave outside the International Space Hall of Fame in Alamogordo, New Mexico.[12]

Ten months after Ham's flight another chimpanzee, five-year-old Enos, was launched into space, orbiting the earth twice and paving the way for astronaut John Glenn to orbit the earth the following year. While Enos was in space, malfunctioning electrical equipment sent a shock to the bottoms of his feet every time he responded correctly to his tasks, which, remarkably, did not stop him from completing his assignments. Sadly, despite Enos's remarkable achievement in space he remained a prisoner of the US Air Force until his death eleven months later at the tender age of sixteen.[13]

The US Air Force stopped experimenting with chimpanzees in the 1960s but, instead of retiring all the chimps, leased many of them to biomedical laboratories for testing. The majority went to toxicologist Fred Coulston, who later established the Coulston Foundation in Alamogordo, New Mexico, the largest biomedical research laboratory in the world, housing over six hundred chimpanzees and hundreds of monkeys, and subsequently known for committing continuous Animal Welfare Act violations of negligence and inadequate care. While a few of the chimpanzees at Holloman Air Force Base were rescued and sent to sanctuaries, the rest languished there for decades.

The biomedical research industry exploited chimpanzees as test subjects on an even more massive scale. Thousands were forced to endure cruel vivisection practices that entailed being prodded, poisoned, stunned, tranquilized, irradiated, and infected with HIV, hepatitis C, malaria, typhoid, Creutzfeldt-Jakob, Ebola, and many other infectious diseases, carcinogens, and viruses harmful or deadly to humans. The experiments on chimpanzees' bodies and minds were brutal. Early experiments included removal of significant portions of their brains to test brain function; injection of brain tissue from humans with schizophrenia and multiple sclerosis; injection of brain tissue from patients with kuru, a neurological disease with symptoms resembling those of a stroke or Parkinson's disease; and castration followed by removal of pituitary glands for hormone studies. Chimpanzees were killed so their organs could be harvested for use in human liver, heart, and kidney transplants. The invasive research procedures also included poisoning chimpanzees with high levels of radiation and administering addictive drugs like cocaine and morphine to test the effects on their bodies.[14] During the many years of experimentation, researchers had free rein to advance whatever protocol they wished, regardless of its devastating effects on the chimpanzees.

While it was standard practice to take newborn chimpanzees away from their mothers at birth, research laboratories went one step further: they isolated many of the newborns for years so researchers could test the effects of maternal separation on their bodies and psyches—a cruel and unnecessary procedure still practiced on other species. This egregious experiment caused irreparable physical and psychological trauma to both mothers and babies.

Even simple blood draws for routine examinations caused extreme anxiety and fear because they required that anesthesia be delivered by blowgun or a dart system, otherwise known as a knockdown. There are many accounts of chimpanzees in laboratories enduring more than three hundred knockdowns, each requiring numerous blowgun hits. The signs of distress chimpanzees exhibited while being anesthetized were consistently disregarded, as were their severe reactions to the experiments themselves. The testing continued until chimpanzees involved in the protocols either died or outlived their usefulness to researchers.

Compounding the ravaging effects of experimentation, most chimpanzees in biomedical laboratories had to endure deplorable living conditions. Whether residing alone or in groups, thousands of research chimpanzees were confined for decades with few, if any, ways to keep their keen minds busy and their bodies active. Little consideration was given to their emotional health even though the 1985 amendment to the Animal Welfare Act required laboratories to promote and enhance their psychological well-being. Many research chimpanzees lived solitary lives in tiny steel cages measuring 5' x 5' x 7', the minuscule size required to legally house a chimpanzee. (A large percentage of chimpanzees currently awaiting sanctuary have spent at least some portion, if not all, of their laboratory lives in cages of this size.) Many chimpanzees in active protocols lived alone for decades in cages so small that an adult male or large female could not fully lift their arms. Nor were they given so much as a blanket or other material with which to build a nest—a ritual that wild chimpanzees, high in the treetops, engage in every night. Only a fortunate few had access to the outdoors. Living without natural light, fresh air, and enrichment, the chimpanzees were confined behind bars with nothing to do but wait, their only crime being their similarities to humans.

As a consequence of their decades-long exposure to biomedical experimentation and inhumane living conditions, thousands of chimpanzees experienced stress levels that would have driven any human to madness. Many, if not most, exhibited symptoms reminiscent of those suffered by human prisoners of war and other survivors of abuse—the unrelenting anxiety, panic attacks, and depression characteristic of post-traumatic stress disorder (PTSD). The chimpanzees managed their extreme levels of stress, anxiety, and fear in the only ways they could: by self-mutilating (pulling out their hair, biting themselves, pulling their fingernails off), rocking back and forth day and night, and dissociating from their bodies. Some had complete nervous breakdowns.[15]

Yet despite so much suffering and death, many experiments performed on chimpanzees have not been medically beneficial to humans.[16, 17] And while some researchers may argue that medical advances were made using chimpanzees as test subjects, the ethical issues surrounding their use are of far greater significance.

Chimpanzees used in movies, television commercials, print ads, and as photographic props have also experienced cruelty and neglect. Actions that chimpanzees perform in the entertainment industry are not natural behaviors but tricks and routines they are forced to learn. Violent teaching methods, such as subjecting chimpanzees to beatings, cigarette burns, and electric shocks, have been used since the inception of circuses to train chimpanzees and keep them fearful so they will obey trainers' demands. Many performing chimpanzees have had their teeth knocked out in compliance with the erroneous assumption that the chimps would then be safer to work with, a conclusion that discounted their superhuman strength and ability to crush human bone in their mouths with or without teeth. Even so, the public perceives them as happy chimps because, as occurred with Ham, their fear grimaces are mistaken for smiles. Typically, chimpanzees purchased or bred by the entertainment industry perform only until age six or seven, after which they become too strong and dangerous to handle and end up being sold to substandard zoos or, in past decades, research laboratories.

Fortunately, the use of primates in the entertainment industry has been declining. Movie studios are increasingly turning to sophisticated computer-generated imagery (CGI) for lifelike portrayals of animals, eliminating the need to use live animals. Such movies as *Dawn of the Planet of the Apes, Rise of the Planet of the Apes,* and *War for the Planet of the Apes* demonstrate how far CGI technology has come in rendering chimpanzees, orangutans, bonobos, and gorillas so lifelike that they easily engage the viewers' emotions. These films and others like them have had profitable runs at the box office, proving that the use of CGI imagery can be commercially successful.

Chimpanzees kept as pets have experienced the same cruelty and neglect as those in the entertainment industry. As pet chimpanzees age, they are capable of innocently causing great bodily harm and physical damage due to their immense muscular strength, so by about age six most end up living solitary lives in small, inadequate cages on a family's property or being sold to unregulated roadside zoos or research laboratories. These chimpanzees can never again enjoy the freedom they had growing up. Abandoned by the family with whom they shared a deep identification and bond, they become traumatized and depressed. Then, too, having been raised like human children, they have no knowledge of their species' social behaviors, which in many cases makes it impossible to successfully integrate themselves into a chimpanzee group.

The well-being of chimpanzees in zoos has been compromised as well. Wild-caught young chimpanzees were first brought to the United States to be exhibited in zoos more than a century ago. Keeping wild animals in cages, especially animals who naturally roam large expanses of land, can never fulfill their needs. Although some zoos do everything in their power to ensure that their chimpanzees receive the best care possible in a confined setting, many zoos fail to meet even minimum standards, leaving their chimpanzees lonely, hungry, and sick. While it is best for chimpanzees, like all other animals, to be left in their wild habitats, those living in zoos should at least be helped to live active, social, and healthy lives in species-appropriate environments.

Because of the long-term abuse and severe hardships chimpanzees have suffered in recent decades, retiring them to sanctuaries that provide high standards of lifetime care is crucial to their well-being. These refuges, which are not open to the public, offer peaceful environments with natural sunlight, grass, trees, and communities of chimpanzees with whom to live. Amidst the ample room in which to play, climb, and socialize, chimpanzees in sanctuary settings enjoy delicious fruits, vegetables, nuts, and other healthy foods; the finest medical care; daily social and cognitive enrichment; and loving caregivers who attend to their needs.

In addition to imparting a greater understanding of the lives of captive chimpanzees, the stories in this book are intended to awaken a deeper awareness of our own human nature. We have put chimpanzees behind bars because we ourselves are living behind bars, locked away from our hearts. When we are not able to feel our own sorrows and those of others, we become physically, emotionally, and spiritually numb, as evidenced by the hundreds of researchers who, while experimenting on chimpanzees, were incapable of responding to their observable terror, grief, and despair.

The stories here were written by individuals whose work with captive chimpanzees helped to transform their own lives. It was the chimpanzees themselves who catalyzed the expanded perspectives on their sentience and the urgent need to protect their fundamental rights.

Part I of this book presents fifteen stories that explore chimpanzee captivity and rescue in the United States and Africa, including illegal wildlife trafficking; the physical and psychological trauma chimpanzees have endured in biomedical research laboratories; the suffering of chimpanzees used in entertainment or kept as pets; caregivers' experiences; and the retirement of research, entertainment, pet, and orphaned chimpanzees into sanctuaries, together with the healing they find there. Interwoven throughout these stories are common elements, demonstrating just how extensive the disruptive impact of trauma has been on captive chimpanzees and how much is at stake.

Part II features three stories that focus on the chimpanzees' use of American Sign Language (ASL) as a mode of communication, including how they talk with their caregivers, to other chimps, and to themselves. It also highlights how ASL has allowed chimpanzees to directly express their thoughts and emotions in a human language, giving us insight into their rich, complex mental, emotional, and psychological lives. These stories invite an intimate understanding of chimpanzees as they share feelings and thoughts about their world.

Part III contains four stories that offer a glimpse into the lives of chimpanzees in zoos in the United States, Australia, Argentina, and the Middle East, and the conditions, enrichment activities, and care provided in these facilities. The stories are told from the perspectives of a chimpanzee zookeeper, an animal welfare specialist who works with zoos around the world to free chimpanzees from isolation, and two volunteers responsible for collecting data on chimpanzee behavior.

Part IV introduces three stories about people doing extraordinary things to help improve the lives of captive chimpanzees. Whether through collecting enrichment items for chimpanzees in zoos or serenading chimpanzees with live guitar music, these individuals make a world of difference to chimpanzees in captive settings.

While the chimpanzees profiled throughout this book can never go back to the forests of their beginnings, they and other survivors can be permanently retired to sanctuaries to heal, live more in accordance with their true nature, and gain a modicum of sovereignty over their lives. Such sanctuaries (see "Chimpanzee Sanctuaries in North America and Africa" on page 337) welcome additional support for their chimpanzee residents, all survivors of the nightmares our species has put them through.

Hopefully, the narratives in this book will prompt reflection on humankind's dominion over chimpanzees versus their right to freedom; on compassionate choices in science; and on recognition of the sacredness of *all* animals. It is time to accept the ethical challenges posed by chimpanzees' emotional, behavioral, social, and cognitive similarities to humans, and end our exploitation of them. Chimpanzees have the inalienable right to live free of oppression, and to be safe and respected for who they are. We owe them the dignity and freedom that is their birthright. They deserve nothing less.

PART I

RESEARCH, ENTERTAINMENT, THE EXOTIC PET AND BUSHMEAT TRADES, AND SANCTUARY FOR THE LUCKY FEW

We must fight against the spirit of unconscious cruelty with which we treat the animals. Animals suffer as much as we do. True humanity does not allow us to impose such sufferings on them. It is our duty to make the whole world recognize it. Until we extend our circle of compassion to all living things, humanity will not find peace.

—ALBERT SCHWEITZER, *The Philosophy of Civilization*

Figure 5. Jeannie

KNOWING JEANNIE

Gloria Grow

In 1981, the pharmaceutical company Merck Sharpe & Dohme sent Ch-562—Jean—to the Buckshire Corporation research facility. Seven years later Buckshire sent her to the Laboratory for Experimental Medicine in Primates. There Jeannie was subjected to years of research, including being inoculated with HIV and given continual vaginal washes and cervical biopsies. She had often been treated for self-inflicted wounds—a sign of severe stress. Following a 1995 experiment, Jeannie had a "nervous breakdown." No longer of use to research, for the next two years she had been left alone, heavily medicated, in her slightly less than 5' × 5' × 7' cage. The drugs had done little to prevent her from screaming continually, ripping her fingernails off, thrashing out of control, or huddling against the floor in the back of her cage. That is where I met her, sitting in a dark corner, looking more terrified than anyone else I had ever seen. Jeannie looked up at me with beautiful almond-shaped eyes that seemed to be pleading, "Will you help me?"

It's hard to know where to begin describing a relationship as special as the one Jeannie and I shared. Perhaps I should begin by saying that we saved each other's lives: Jeannie desperately needed my help, and I needed to find a deeper meaning in my life. From the day we first met, Jeannie inspired me, motivated me, and helped me discover my purpose in life. Her shattered life represented the shattered lives of all the chimpanzees who had been used for decades in biomedical research in the United States. Although Jeannie died at my sanctuary, the Fauna Foundation, she had long before that experienced a loss of life in the harsh concrete and steel of a laboratory.

This is the heartbreaking situation that those of us who care for chimpanzees have to bear—and try to set right.

Animals had always been important to me, but at age forty I felt a need to do more to help them. As a young adult, I had opened a dog-grooming salon. Even the most suspicious and hostile dogs had felt loved and comforted by me. I had rescued dogs from backyard hoarders; provided for dozens of feral cats; liberated carriage horses from the streets of Montreal; and saved potbelly pigs, cows, and injured geese and ducks. They all had a home at my Fauna Foundation sanctuary. But I was frustrated because things weren't improving for animals in the world. I joined animal rights groups and learned all I could about as many issues as my head and heart could hold. I wanted to be a voice for the animals and make a difference.

In an issue of *Earthwatch Magazine,* I found what I had been looking for and immediately enrolled in a seminar entitled Caring for Chimpanzees at the Chimpanzee and Human Communication Institute (CHCI) in Ellensburg, Washington. At the end of the seminar, I announced, "I'm going to open the first chimpanzee sanctuary in Canada." To this day I don't know where that voice came from, but it rang with conviction. I left Ellensburg with great determination and a copy of the plans that had been used to construct the chimp building at CHCI.

Needing to surround myself with people of like mind, I subsequently attended a national animal rights conference in Washington, DC. The list of speakers was impressive—Dr. Peter Singer, Dr. Roger Fouts, Dr. Theodora Capaldo, Cleveland Amory, Dale Peterson, Gene Bauston, and Dr. Jane Goodall. It was one of the most inspiring weekends of my life. Dr. Goodall explained why there was a need for sanctuaries for chimpanzees; Roger Fouts, cofounder of CHCI, spoke about how chimpanzees bridge the gap between animals and humans. Roger and Deborah Fouts introduced me to Dr. Goodall, telling her that I was going to build a sanctuary for chimpanzees in Canada. Suddenly my intent to build a sanctuary seemed real. I returned home committed to following through with my plan.

After the conference, I spoke with Dr. James Mahoney, head veterinarian at the Laboratory for Experimental Medicine & Surgery in Primates (LEMSIP) in New York. The lab was closing, and I offered to take five older chimpanzees to prevent them from being transferred to another lab. Somehow five chimpanzees seemed manageable. I knew very little about caring for chimpanzees and did not yet have a facility in which to house them, but I had committed to making a miracle happen in seven months. Not for one moment did I doubt that this was what had to be done. I was being led by something more powerful than logic. I had to do whatever I could to make this happen—for the chimpanzees and for myself.

On a cold February day in 1997, in the middle of a New York winter rivaling Canada's, I visited LEMSIP for the first time. I'll never forget that initial visit: the echoing screams, clanging metal, pungent smells, and the faces of chimpanzees behind endless rows of bars broke my heart. I met chimps who had been captured in the wilds of Africa and thrown into that hellhole of a lab, youngsters and teenagers who had been born and raised in the barren lab, and older chimps who had known no reality but lab life. I had agreed to make a home for five LEMSIP chimpanzees; little did I know I was destined to take fifteen! While I did not meet Tom, Yoko, or Pepper on my first visit, I did meet the rest of the soon-to-be Fauna family of chimpanzees—Sue Ellen, Billy Jo, Pablo, Donna Rae, Annie, and the youngsters Rachel, Jethro, Regis, Binky, Chance, Petra, and Jeannie.

The youngsters were supposed to go to Florida's Lion Country Safari because they were the "clean chimps," the ones not yet infected, who still had the youthful appeal desired by those who planned to exhibit them. However, they were already troubled youngsters who had been born and raised in the lab without the benefit of adult chimpanzees to teach them the "ways of life" and, even at their young ages, had been used repeatedly in research and were showing signs of emotional stress.

From that first day, my life, and the lives of these chimpanzees, has never been the same. I feel profound love and respect toward every one of them and receive the same from them. It's easy to fall in love with chimpanzees; they steal our hearts and give us theirs. When those who have been so abused forgive us, they humble us. I have wonderful and inspiring relationships with all the chimpanzees who live at Fauna and others I have spent time with over the years. So how did Jeannie come to live so deeply in my heart? I think that will be clear as I share more about what it was like the first time we met.

Escorted around the lab with two other people, I was unprepared for what I saw. We were told not to react or cry and not to mention the size of the cages. What I saw left me speechless and immobile. It was surreal and unbelievable, too cruel to be true. There was not one right thing about the way the chimpanzees were living. No one should ever have to live that way.

The buildings were long windowless trailers—white, sterile, and efficient. There were doors at either end with two rows of cages that were suspended off the ground to make cleaning easier. The chimps ate, slept, urinated, defecated, and were knocked down (shot with anesthesia-laced darts) in those small cages. Many babies were born in the cages, grew up in them, and were destined to die in them. The cages were their entire world, with only a rubber tire hanging in the middle from which to view the endless boredom of their days.

Covered in a Tyvek suit from head to toe, I approached the chimps. It was hard to feel like a real person behind such protective gear. I could see the terror and alarm in their faces. I saw a figure on the right—tall, slim, muscular, and hairless—that looked like a naked man in a cage. He was a chimpanzee, although he looked like a tragic crossbreed, human and yet so chimp-like. I was in shock, recognizing him as kin but reduced to something nature never intended. "Oh my God, what happened to you?" I asked. My question was answered with his screams, an honest answer to that question about his desperate condition. His name was Melilot, and his life in research had left him looking like this. Born in the wild, Melilot had been caught in Sierra Leone and lived alone in his tiny cell for more than thirty years. Separated from all physical contact, Melilot had no one to touch him, groom him, or hug him when he was scared or alone. He was completely pale because he had been deprived of sunlight. Melilot had pulled out every single hair on his body, one by one, day after day, year after year until all that was left was his primal naked body, his man self. Of even greater disgust to me was that this dear soul had been given the nickname "Melilot Smells a Lot."

The intensity of the chimpanzees' screaming and banging was unbearable. Suddenly, all hell broke loose. I wanted to run. The cages were shaking and rocking. Many chimpanzees were spitting large mouthfuls of water. As the other people in my visitor's group walked away, I walked in, ignoring the chimps' fear and anger. I stood motionless at the door, feeling that to do so was better for them and for me. When I realized that we were the cause of this chaotic reaction, I backed up. I felt sad and embarrassed to be a human, part of a species that threatened and controlled these powerful beings. In the cage closest to me, a chimpanzee was spinning and banging herself against its steel bars, sending piercing sounds that reverberated throughout the building, shaking her cage and all the others in the long row. She was defecating. Saliva was spewing out of her mouth. Her eyes were rolling back in her head as she continued to spin. I felt like I was in hell—which was most certainly what she felt, too. That was how I met Jeannie: alone in her living hell.

We were told to back out of the area. Dr. Mahoney closed the doors and called for Mike, a technician, on the loudspeaker. He came quickly, knowing right away what was happening when he heard Jeannie's name. Mike quietly went into the unit while we remained outside. Through a small window in the steel door, I watched Mike walk over to Jeannie's cage and wrap his arms around it as though embracing Jeannie. In utter amazement, I watched as Mike reached his hands into the small openings in her cage and pressed himself against Jeannie and the bars. In turn, Jeannie pressed herself into him with her belly against the bars, her head turned to the side, as she screamed in fear. She wasn't a small chimpanzee and could have seriously injured him, but she didn't—Jeannie always hurt herself instead. Mike hugged her, and she hugged him back, through the terror and steel of the cage that could not separate these two friends. My heart broke for Jeannie and for Mike.

After it was over, I stood in the doorway and looked at Jeannie. I pulled my mask off because I could not bear the distance it put between us. I then pulled off my gloves and dropped to my knees in the doorway. Jeannie appeared as if an exhausted calm had come over her. She wasn't looking at me; she was looking *into* me. A look of despair filled her beautiful almond-shaped eyes, that seemed to be saying, "Help me. Get me out of here, please." Mike came over to me and whispered, "She needs to get out. Help her."

꙰ ꙰ ꙰

I learned that Jeannie and some of the other chimps I met in her unit that day were HIV positive. I was asked if this would present a problem for my sanctuary. The question seemed ludicrous to me. "Not at all," I answered. This was going to be the first time an HIV-positive chimpanzee would be released to a sanctuary. I cried the entire six-hour ride home. I could not imagine walking away from Jeannie, or any of them. My love for Jeannie made me work harder to get her out.

Before Jeannie could come live at Fauna, a great deal had to happen. We had to build her a special space where she had the choice to live alone or in a social group. As it turned out, building a home for the chimps in less than seven months was much easier than what Jeannie had to do.

"

A look of despair
filled her beautiful
almond-shaped
eyes, that seemed
to be saying,
"Help me.
Get me out
of here, please."

Figure 6. Jeannie in
her cage at LEMSIP

On my second visit to LEMSIP, I couldn't find Jeannie. When I asked where she was, I was told she had a throat infection and wasn't doing well, so they had moved her. I believed them. Jeannie still wasn't back by my third visit.

As time passed, the list of chimps to be relocated to our sanctuary kept changing. Two other chimps had been put in the group to replace Jeannie and Melilot. Pepper was to replace Jeannie. Yoko was swapped for Melilot and Tommie for Yoko. Everyone was being switched around; their vulnerable lives were in limbo every day. As the list kept changing, I didn't quite understand what was going on and didn't know what was likely to happen to Jeannie and Melilot. Decisions were being made about their futures depending on how they worked out socially on any given day. If they had a bad day or a fight, they could be pulled from the Fauna list and sent to another research lab. Chimps were chosen based on age, durability, character, sex, or health. This arbitrary, cold, and clinical shuffling meant a life of hell or a life of safety.

Then I received horrible news: LEMSIP, deciding Melilot could not socialize, had sent him to the Coulston Foundation in Alamogordo, New Mexico, one of the most notorious research breeding facilities for chimpanzees and monkeys, for use in more research. Workers at Coulston told me that Melilot wanted to remain on his enclosure's perch; he could not bring himself to step onto the concrete floor of his new cage after having spent his life on the bars of his cage flooring at LEMSIP. Melilot's fear was so strong that he would not go to the front of the cage, even for his food. The lab insisted he be "like everyone else." In this new world with its callous demands, Melilot died.

On my fourth visit, trying harder I snuck off to search for Jeannie. I found several abandoned trailers. Many chimpanzees had already been transferred; some had been sent to sanctuaries, most to other research facilities. I feared LEMSIP might have moved Jeannie. Then I heard horrible screams that sounded like her. I found my way to the trailer and waited for the screaming to stop. When I knew no one was around, I quietly went in. Jeannie was lying on the floor of her cage, as she always did, her face pressed against the bars. Completely alone in the unit, with the other five cages empty, she was eating a carrot, something in the years I knew her she never did again. Jeannie was not stressed because she had been heavily medicated. I told her that everything was going to be okay and that I would get her out of there.

Later that day I was told of LEMSIP's true plans for Jeannie—to euthanize her. The efforts the lab had made to socialize the chimps into groups before releasing them to Fauna weren't working for her. Jeannie's nervous breakdown had made her incapable of tolerating others. Unable to bear what was happening to her or to witness what was happening to others, Jeannie was not considered a good research or sanctuary candidate. I begged Dr. Mahoney to let her come to Fauna. The lab equivocated about Jeannie, but I held firm and said that if Jeannie didn't come I wouldn't take any others, praying that the lab wouldn't call my bluff. Dr. Mahoney felt the most humane thing was to end her life. I felt the most humane thing was to not let that happen. I was in love, and I couldn't let Jeannie down. Between my jumping through hoops to make special arrangements for her and Mike's pleas, Dr. Mahoney finally agreed to let Jeannie come to Fauna. In the end, he came to believe what Mike and I already knew: Jeannie would be all right once she was out of LEMSIP.

It takes something stronger than courage to do primate rescue work with those who are damaged beyond recognition in body, soul, and mind. It takes an open heart, nerves of steel, and extraordinary strength of body and mind. I don't know where it comes from, but I am glad I was blessed with the gifts required to do this type of work.

⚘ ⚘ ⚘

Sue Ellen, Billy Jo, Pablo, Donna Rae, Annie, Tom, Yoko, Pepper, and the kids Rachel, Jethro, Regis, Binky, Chance, Petra, and Jeannie all came to Fauna in the fall of 1997. I thought it would be joyful for them to be reunited with other chimps. I could never have imagined that the damage that had been done would prevent them from being able to socialize with others of their own kind.

Jeannie's new home was quiet, comfortable, and offered many choices. It was a place in which she could recover peacefully. Her space was close to the fireplace, the kitchen, and to me so she could see me, and everything going on, at all times.

During the initial phase of testing Fauna, the chimps created a lot of noise, threats, and bedlam while Jeannie huddled in a corner. There was no miraculous moment that changed everything for her. Jeannie's healing was a long, slow, painful process. I watched her suffering, her confusion, her fear. The bizarre and sad behaviors she had adopted to survive the realities of the lab—holding the bars and spinning herself around—were the only ways she could soothe herself and release her panic. I stood by helplessly for hours as Jeannie entered a trancelike state of dissociation where the mind and heart

Figure 7. Jeannie looking out of her Fauna Sanctuary enclosure

and body are separated from each other in a desperate attempt to be free from pain. I was powerless as I watched Jeannie build her inner sanctuary, a space inside that offers victims of abuse the only place where they feel safe, if only for a moment. I watched and prayed and tried to find ways to comfort Jeannie and help her learn that her world was different now, safe from the pain and trauma she had suffered at LEMSIP. I often collapsed in frustration, but I never gave up despite the slow progress. I knew in my heart that Jeannie had not given up either. Our relationship was an important part of Jeannie's journey, and we would do this together no matter what. But first Jeannie needed to find the broken, scattered pieces of her life and gingerly put herself back together so she could trust again.

Jeannie responded with anxiety and agitation whenever something new was introduced to her. Most of the chimps wrapped themselves in soft fleece blankets given to them to build night nests, sleeping in comfort instead of on cold steel laboratory bars; but Jeannie could not tolerate one more change or invasion of her safe little world, including the touch of a soft blanket. She could only tolerate sameness, even if it was a barren floor.

Gradually Jeannie got better, and her ability to live a comfortable, even enjoyable, life became more of a reality. With time and the healing power that loving care brings, Jeannie had something to look forward to each day. Most importantly, she had people around her who cared deeply. Within months her outbursts became less frequent, and she was eventually taken off all medications. She now had a sparkle in her eyes that had not been there when they first met mine. Slowly, with great caution, and depending heavily on the support we were giving her, Jeannie was finally able to make decisions about her own life. This magnificent chimpanzee who had been stripped of everything was emerging as a peaceful and gentle soul.

As the years soothed her emotional pain, Jeannie became Buddha-like, drawing me into her quiet presence and helping me reach my own inner peace. This was the essence of Jeannie, whose given name could not have been more aptly chosen as in Hebrew *Jean* means "the Lord is gracious" and in English "God is forgiving."

Jeannie taught me about love and the wisdom of honesty, patience, and kindness, even in those excruciating moments when she was thrust back to her earlier years during horrible flashbacks. Jeannie never blamed me for all that had been done to her. Her capacity for forgiveness always left me wondering how she could forgive so much and we so little. Jeannie was not angry with all humans, but she could easily be reminded of the men in white coats—people from the lab who had scared or hurt her. Simple gestures by strangers, certain voices, shadows, or the body language of people insensitive to her fears could immediately set her off. Unlike Jeannie, I am not very forgiving, nor am I gracious when it comes to the ignorance of humans and the profit-driven crimes they commit against sentient beings.

It took one year before Jeannie would let me touch her toe and another before I could touch her fingers. I understood that I had no right to touch her body and that she did not owe me anything, but I also recognized that touch is essential to all living beings. Over the years, Jeannie would hold my hand through the larger cages, and one day she did something extraordinary—she gently took hold of my hand and lovingly placed it over her heart. This pivotal gesture spoke of her recovery and was something she continued to do until she died. As social beings, chimpanzees depend upon touch as their primary way to communicate their feelings, needs, love, friendship, and commitment to each other. Jeannie's exploitation and isolation had stolen all that from her, but because of hope, kindness, commitment, and love Jeannie was able to touch her heart and bring me with her on the voyage back to herself.

In hindsight, what I did to help Jeannie was simple: I sat quietly with her for days, months, years. Expecting nothing, I loved her unconditionally. The first three years I never missed a day with Jeannie (or the others). Then slowly she began to trust that things were different and better, allowing me into that sacred place called her heart.

Figure 8. Gloria and Jeannie sharing a tender moment

Figure 9. Jeannie relaxing in the sun

⬚⬚ ⬚⬚ ⬚⬚

I will never know exactly what we did that helped Jeannie heal. Was it the place, the choices, the privacy, the delicious food options, the relative control she had of her life, allowing her the freedom to sleep in until she wanted to get up or move only when and if she wanted to? Was it the choice of living alone or with others? Was it the unconditional love and understanding? Or was it because finally, and very simply, Jeannie could sit outside with her arms in the air, lifting her head to the sun and wind or misty rain, letting herself be embraced and soothed? No one but Jeannie will ever know.

Most days I would arrive at the chimp house and ask Jeannie, aloud, "What is my Jelly Bean doing? Where is she?" Given Jeannie's sense of humor, she would immediately be in a great mood. She was loving, spirited, and had an adorably unique play face. Many chimps who have been around humans have different play faces; and hers had a pursed top lip, trying to cover her teeth but not quite succeeding. Jeannie had a deep husky voice, and her happy vocalizations were expressive and loud. When happy, she could not contain herself, and sounds of joy would ring through the chimp house whenever she saw me. Jeannie's delightful, very distinctive food grunts were so contagious that they sent all the chimpanzees in the building into shrieks of happiness. Next to our love for one another, bananas were a close second. She also loved to lie on her tummy on the smooth, shiny, warm, and very slippery floor of her room. When her room had just been cleaned and emptied of all enrichment, including blankets and toys, Jeannie would slide across the floor and then lie on her back making what I can only describe as snow angels. Jeannie also enjoyed her daily ritual of drinking hot tea and spending special time with her human and nonhuman family.

Each day after everyone left I would go back to the chimp house and make tea and sandwiches for the chimpanzees, then lie on the floor beside Jeannie drinking hot tea with her, a peaceful ritual she loved. It was a pleasure to take a sip and hold hands, take another sip and hold hands. I would sometimes even lie beside her on the floor while she slept, just to be with her. The joy Jeannie found in being touched and loved was dear to my heart.

Then on New Year's Day 2007, as I walked from my house to spend time with Jeannie, I was near the small bridge just beside the chimp house when I heard strange sounds that I could not identify. At first, it sounded like fighting, but they were actually alarm calls from the chimps. Above the din I could hear Binky, who was in the room directly across from Jeannie. In that shattering moment my heart sank, for suddenly I knew the calls were about Jeannie. When I reached the chimp house, I looked for her in the spot where we met every night. She wasn't there. I ran upstairs to where she had been earlier in the day, and she wasn't there either. I glanced at Binky pacing back and forth, whimpering, and looking up. There Jeannie was, lying on the platform, her limp arm hanging over the edge. Jeannie had been coming down the stairs, heading toward our spot. I opened the door, climbed the stairs to reach her, and called her name, but when I got to her I knew she was in that place between two worlds. I lay with her, holding her close, wanting to smell her and be alone with her before calling anyone to say she was gone. I held Jeannie for a long time, sobbing and telling her I loved her and I was so sorry for all she had been through. I sobbed until there was nothing left of me.

I had to put my Jeannie outside on that cold January night until she could go for an autopsy. The chimps got upset when someone they loved left, and this loss was especially hard for them. The next day, we received the news that no one wanted to touch Jeannie because she had been infected with HIV years earlier. This meant she could not be sent for a thorough autopsy, which would have revealed the full extent of the damage done to her body during her research years, and that we had to perform the autopsy ourselves at Fauna. To protect myself from collapsing, I instinctively blanked out and did what I had to do. We put tissue samples into containers to be sent to the labs for analysis. I was handed Jeannie's heart to wash off and place in a container. Her heart had been destroyed not only emotionally but also physically: instead of the firm muscle of a healthy heart, it was soft, scarred, and discolored. Her heart was a mess for someone so young—only thirty-one years old, according to her records. I stood there holding Jeannie's heart in my hands, recalling the many times I had felt her heart beat while she held our hands together over it. Although her heart was no longer beating, it was more connected than ever to mine.

The day Jeannie was taken from Fauna for cremation a part of me died. I thought it would be the last time I'd see her, but two days later we got a call that Jeannie had not fit in the incinerator and would have to come back. I was horrified, thrown again into a surreal world with this being I loved so deeply. All the same I was happy because I could once again kiss Jeannie's beautiful face, smell her sweet scent, and have another chance to say goodbye.

I drove Jeannie to another crematorium. I helped lift her battered and worn body— cut from chest to groin, sewn shut, and frozen—onto the tray that would slide her into the oven. I made sure her arms and legs were placed gently and that no additional problems would occur. I kissed her and said goodbye. The door closed. This time she was really gone.

EVOLUTION

Allison Argo

My relationship with chimpanzees began in 1998, when I was asked by the executive producer of PBS's *Nature* series to make a film about the lessons humans have learned from wild animals. As I began searching for sequences to include in *Wisdom of the Wild,* I found two fascinating stories about chimpanzees that were very different from one another yet perfect for the film.

The first story was about the use of medicinal plants by wild chimpanzees in Tanzania and how local healers had observed and adopted the chimps' use of plants into their own practice of human medicine. We filmed this story in the gloriously untouched Mahale Mountains of Tanzania, a national park on the edge of Lake Tanganyika. In this remote area where there were no roads and rarely a tourist, the chimps had almost no contact with humans; only a handful of researchers had observed them over the years. These wild chimpanzees were remarkably unfazed by our presence. When we found them in the forest, they looked right through us as if we didn't exist. We were able to film them for twenty minutes at a time as they groomed in the afternoon sun, swung through the trees, and fed on termites and fruit. It was incredibly moving to witness chimpanzees living in the wild and traveling through the forest with such freedom, mothers with their babies and family groups intact. I consider those weeks in the Mahale Mountains among my most precious.

The second story I included in the film was about five chimpanzees who had been taken from the wild and used in medical research. Surprisingly, what we learned from them didn't involve medical breakthroughs but rather their capacity for resiliency and forgiveness. They had been subjected to decades of painful invasive experiments and yet, once retired, had been able to adapt to a new life with little anger or aggression toward the humans who cared for them.

These two stories marked the beginning of my journey into the world of chimpanzees and a turning point in my life. By the time *Wisdom of the Wild* was broadcast, I knew I had to make a full-length film about chimpanzees. The two stories in the film were merely the tip of the iceberg, and so much more needed to be said. I wanted to delve deeper, to document our checkered history with chimpanzees, to record how they had been treated by the human race, and to ensure that we would never forget how much they have sacrificed for us. Fred Kaufman, the executive producer of the *Nature* series, thought chimpanzees deserved an hour as well. It took us a few years to pull the funding together, but finally *Chimpanzees: An Unnatural History* was given the green light.

The subject turned out to be even more complex than I'd imagined, and I spent nearly a year researching and scouting. One of the first locations I visited was the old Coulston Foundation laboratory in Alamogordo, New Mexico. This biomedical research lab was notorious for its inhumane treatment of chimpanzees and for racking up numerous US Department of Agriculture (USDA) violations. Coulston had gone bankrupt in 2002, and in a legendary turn of events Dr. Carole Noon had managed to procure the funds to buy the laboratory, land, and buildings. As part of the deal, the 266 chimpanzees housed on the property were donated to Noon's new sanctuary, Save the Chimps. (Twenty-one retired US Air Force chimpanzees had already been moved from the Coulston facility to Noon's Florida sanctuary the year before.)

Dr. Noon used to say of her early years, "I was nothing but a good idea." But she was far more than that: she was a person with vision, an unwavering commitment to chimpanzees, and a passion to fight till the end. She had earned her doctorate in primatology late in life and was determined to make up for lost time. Dr. Noon was on fire.

Though the Coulston facility was no longer a functioning lab when I arrived, there were grim reminders everywhere of the horrendous existence the inmates had led. It was a hellhole, a ghost lab still inhabited by hundreds of chimps. Dr. Noon led me around the property, showing me the dismal remains of what life had been like for these chimps. She showed me the room where the medical procedures had been carried out and then led me to "the dungeon," a windowless concrete bunker where chimps had been held for the duration of a study in 5' × 5' × 7' cages. Then I followed her into a small shed where three chimps had literally been cooked to death because of a heater malfunction. It was the stuff of nightmares. I became faint, feeling the ghosts in that tiny, windowless shack.

But on this stark patch of desert in Alamogordo, the landscape was clearly changing. Dr. Noon and her team had added ropes and hammocks to the concrete cells; there were stuffed animals and blankets everywhere; and dozens of humans, under Noon's guidance, were working like army ants to enrich the lives of the chimpanzees who had endured horrendous conditions for so long. The most significant change to the old lab involved opening the concrete walls between cell blocks. Suddenly the chimps who had lived in solitary confinement for a decade or more were now in the company of other chimps. As I surveyed the scene, I saw hundreds of chimpanzees, a community of survivors, each one an individual with a personal story that would make anyone's skin crawl. I watched as the chimps groomed each other and explored their newfound freedom. Before I left, Noon gave me a chunk of concrete from a wall she had knocked down. I still keep it as a treasure, a reminder of this remarkable woman and her vision. Noon had done what was seemingly impossible—she snatched 287 chimpanzees from the jaws of the biomedical machine. And now, with every blow of the sledgehammer she was reclaiming their lives.

This was only the first phase of Noon's vision. Her ultimate plan was to move every chimpanzee across the country to set them free (or as close to free as possible) on three-acre islands in Florida. Noon's dreams were lofty, but her vision to retire these chimpanzees in dignity, to let them feel the grass and see the sky without the weight of steel bars, was going to come true—and our film crew would be there to capture this extraordinary moment in history so it could be shared with the world.

I carefully chose a cinematographer for the film; Andy Young had a background in primatology, and I knew he'd be extremely sensitive to the chimps. Prior to filming, we'd approach the chimps quietly—heads down, eyes averted—until they invited us to interact with them. Before we even put the camera on the tripod, we would spend at least half an hour just sitting with them so they would start to feel at ease. Andy would cradle the camera, show it to the chimps, and then put it up against the mesh so they could touch and smell it. I remember Andy talking quietly to Lou, an older chimp who had been a long-term subject of the space program. Andy explained that this was a really nice camera, a Panasonic SDX 900—the latest technology at the time—and this was such and such a lens. Lou listened intently, inspecting the lens and the camera. Finally, Lou reached through the mesh and very gently touched the camera with his finger.

Only when the chimps seemed comfortable enough to ignore us did we start to film. We always tried to be respectful because we were invading their space; this was their home, and we were only visitors. If a chimpanzee seemed agitated, we immediately put the camera down and moved away. Each day after shooting we returned to our hotel rooms. The first night I cried myself to sleep. It's impossible not to identify with these intelligent and clearly sensitive beings. The injustice was overwhelming. Lou had been kidnapped from his family in the wild and spent thirty-five years in a small cage, much of it in solitary confinement, regularly subjected to painful medical experiments. I kept wondering whether I would have had the strength to survive such circumstances.

While researching the film, I had assumed we'd be able to include the story of a working biomedical laboratory, but it quickly became clear that no laboratory would open its doors to us. The National Institutes of Health (NIH) would not even grant us a telephone interview. I was floored. We weren't making an exposé for *60 Minutes*—this was a *Nature* film for PBS. Our tax dollars were being used to keep these chimpanzees in research, and yet we could not get one interview with an NIH scientist or policymaker.

The filming took nearly a year. During the process, I met chimpanzees whom I began to consider friends—Lou, Tom, Thoto, Ron, Grub, Toddy, Suzi, Billy Jo, Bobby, and Pepper—each unique in personality, physical appearance, preferred foods, and favorite pastimes. I was constantly amazed that they had survived their various ordeals relatively intact, though of course there were scars. Billy Jo, a pet before becoming a lab inmate, could no longer live with humans but was unable to relate to chimps; he was caught in a social no-man's-land. Rachel had regular psychotic breakdowns. Bobby would self-mutilate. Many chimps would overgroom until their limbs were nearly naked. Had I been through what they'd endured, I'm sure I would have done the same, or worse. My heart ached for these individuals.

The deepest relationship I established was with Pepper, a chimpanzee at the Fauna Foundation sanctuary outside Montreal, Canada. Fauna had been founded by Gloria Grow and Dr. Richard Allen in 1997 as a bucolic country refuge for unwanted farm animals. Years later they heard that the Laboratory for Experimental Medicine & Surgery in Primates (LEMSIP) was going to close its doors. Unable to turn their backs on any animal in need, they offered to take in fifteen chimpanzees. Theirs was the first sanctuary to provide refuge to chimpanzees infected with HIV.

Pepper was one of the lucky chimps to be given a second chance at Fauna. She got along with other chimps but related in such a sophisticated way to human beings it was uncanny. I felt like I had a girlfriend at Fauna. Pepper loved to hang out, share food, and chat. In the mornings, she would spot me in the distance having my coffee and hoot to me until I came over. I would sit near the mesh with my coffee, and Pepper would reach out, take the cup from me, ever so gently, then sip a little coffee and give it back to me. Next she would take a bite of her banana, hand it to me, then I would take a bite and hand it back to her. That's when I began to feel that there was not a tremendous divide between us.

Figure 10. Pepper

Like all chimps, Pepper liked to groom. One day I had my arm against the mesh and she was grooming my wrist, but my watch was clearly in her way. I could tell that it was annoying her, so I unbuckled the strap, and before I knew it Pepper had the watch inside the cage. I've lost various items during my years of filming captive primates—hats, clipboards, microphones. In the wild, there is constant change and variety; in captivity, anything new is a dearly coveted novelty. So I accepted, with regret, that I had lost my watch forever. Pepper inspected the watch and then held it with her foot so she could continue to work on my wrist. While she groomed, I tried to remember where I'd bought the watch and how much it had cost. When Pepper finally finished grooming, she took the watch from her foot and handed it back to me through the mesh. Suddenly the gap between chimp and human seemed even smaller.

Pepper, although a petite chimp, had a uniquely deep, guttural voice. Sometimes she'd begin hooting, and I would join in. This would send her over the moon with excitement. One day when we were hooting together Pepper suddenly smacked me right on the mouth with a big, joyous kiss. Years after I'd come to know and love Pepper, I was in postproduction sorting through archival footage from the now-defunct LEMSIP lab when I came upon an awful video clip of a terrified chimpanzee cowering in the corner of a small metal cage, shrieking as men in lab coats anaesthetized her. While watching, I realized there was something familiar in the timbre of the chimp's voice—and then I recognized the distinctive face of Pepper, the beautiful, docile, generous being I'd come to know at Fauna. It broke my heart to see the pain and panic she had endured in the lab, and it struck me as remarkable that she could learn to trust humans again despite the horrors our species had inflicted on her. I'd wager that her willingness to trust humans again was not simply a survival tactic but rather a conscious choice.

Billy Jo was also willing to trust humans despite the years of trauma he'd been subjected to at LEMSIP. Billy Jo's history with humans was long and complicated. He had lived with people as a youngster, entertaining children at birthday parties and shopping centers. But when he'd become too large and difficult to handle, his owner had turned to the only solution he could think of: he gave Billy Jo to a nearby medical lab, LEMSIP. Here Billy Jo underwent countless knockdowns, liver biopsies, and invasive medical tests. After one surgery, while the anesthesia wore off, he bit off two of his own fingers.

While we were filming at Fauna, Billy Jo's former owner, Bob, came to visit him for the first time since delivering him to the lab decades earlier. It was a remarkable but

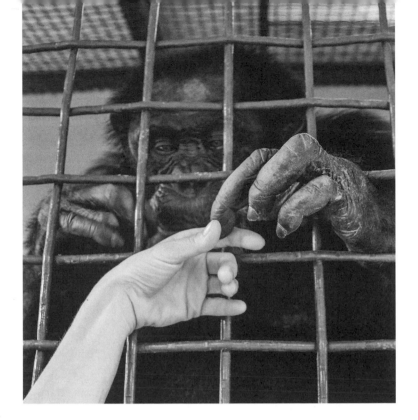

Figure 11. Left: Billy Jo and Allison touching fingers

Figure 12. Below: Billy Jo

bittersweet reunion. Billy Jo recognized Bob immediately and was ecstatic to see him again. Bob was delighted as well, but he'd come for only a brief visit; there was nothing Billy Jo could do to prolong it.

After an hour Bob said goodbye and walked away. Billy Jo reached with desperation through the cage, then his hand just dangled, as if the breath had been knocked out of him. For a long while he sat motionless, staring after Bob. I tried to imagine what it must have been like for him. In the edit, I lingered on the moment of silence after Bob's departure, because that's what Billy Jo was left with—a metal cage, memories, and a void that could never be filled.

Bob had told us that he used to take Billy Jo out for ice cream, so Gloria sent out for a vanilla cone to cheer him up. When Billy Jo spotted the ice cream, he began to hoot with joy. He was shaking as he took the little cone in his enormous hand and delicately began licking it like a well-mannered human. It had been at least twenty years since he'd held an ice cream cone, but he had not forgotten.

Gloria gives extraordinary care to all the chimps at Fauna. There's nothing she wouldn't do for them. She makes sure they have an endless supply of every imaginable food: fresh fruits and vegetables, eggs, juices, popcorn, even coffee and donuts if they choose. She believes that nothing she can do would ruin their health any more than it had been ruined in the lab. She makes sure that all the chimps have a trolley in front of their enclosure overflowing with their favorite goodies. Gloria gives them the company of other chimps, toys to explore, mattresses, blankets and pillows for their nests—even hoses if they feel like playing in water. But she can only do so much. One day while we were filming, Gloria shared her deepest frustration. She said that she'd had great intentions when the chimps first arrived, but nine years later they were still under lock and key, "Once the chimps moved in, I realized I was just the jail keeper. They were still living behind bars!" That's the reality Gloria and the chimps live with every day.

By the time the film was complete, I'd spent nearly three years with chimpanzees, and I'd become very comfortable around them—so much so that in hindsight, I think the boundary between human and chimp had begun to blur. One fateful day after filming, I was quietly sitting by a small group of chimpanzees. When a female chimp approached, I backed away, but not fast or far enough. She was able to grab my hand and in an instant prove that she was the alpha female. Since that encounter, I've had two surgeries on my left hand, and a couple of fingers are still noticeably disfigured.

The chimp gave me a warning; she could have done far worse. I consider my mangled fingers a reminder that I crossed a line. While I have been welcomed into their world upon occasion, I do not speak chimp, and I do not know their culture. For a brief moment I lost sight of that.

It's intoxicating to think we can communicate with a wild animal. We are thrilled when an individual from another species looks us in the eye and relates to us. But there are differences, and they are important ones. Chimpanzees are absolutely unique beings whom I will never fully understand. My blunder has deepened my respect for these remarkable beings.

During the three years I spent making *Chimpanzees: An Unnatural History*, I ate, drank, slept, and breathed chimpanzee. As a result, I became an even stronger advocate for protecting chimpanzees in the wild and for giving those in captivity the best lives possible. I also became less tolerant of speciesism. Although chimpanzees have a different culture and a different physiology, it doesn't mean that they are inferior because they don't speak English or Japanese, can't get a degree from Harvard or walk bipedally for great distances. We should be celebrating diversity and fostering respect for those who are different from us. I believe that we cannot learn to respect members of our own species if we're unable to respect others in the animal kingdom.

* * *

The reason I make films is to help people access information in order to make more informed choices in their lives. Nearly twenty years ago I was cast in a TV commercial shot in Los Angeles. The director wanted it to appear as if I were traveling around Africa shooting wildlife films. When I showed up on the set, I was surprised to find they'd hired a trainer with a baby chimp. I had no idea there would be live animals in the commercial. Whenever anyone on the set went goo-goo over the chimp, the trainer would bark, "The chimp is working. Don't distract it!" After ten minutes of doing tricks, she was whisked off, and I never saw her again. I was left with a growing sense of regret that I had participated in what I now know to be a damaging and inhumane industry. I've often wondered about that little chimpanzee. I hope she found her way to the Center for Great Apes, a sanctuary in Wauchula, Florida, created by Patti Ragan. This remarkable refuge takes in chimps and orangutans discarded by the entertainment and pet industries when they become too strong to manage. (This is where Bubbles, Michael Jackson's famous chimp companion, wound up when he grew beyond cuteness.)

We all evolve over time. One of my favorite examples of personal evolution is that of Carol Buckley. Before establishing an elephant sanctuary in Tennessee, she had performed for years in circuses with her elephant Tarra. In fact, I filmed Carol and Tarra performing at a circus over twenty years ago. Carol doesn't believe in circuses now; perhaps she had to come from that world in order to do her current work. Not only has she created two elephant sanctuaries and rescued numerous elephants from inhumane conditions in North America, she also works to improve the lives of captive elephants in Asia.

My personal evolution has been more subtle, but looking back on my films I can see that they reflect a growing awareness of other species and their needs in our human-dominated world. My greatest hope is that my films will help others evolve. In *Chimpanzees: An Unnatural History,* I included black-and-white archival footage of a baby chimp in a tutu walking across a tightrope; the look of fear on her face is deeply disturbing. Images like this should make us queasy.

I end my narrative the way I ended the film, with the story of Tom, the oldest chimp at Fauna, who had previously spent thirty years as a medical research subject. There was no information about Tom before his arrival at the lab, so no one knew when or where he had been born; Gloria wondered if he might have been wild-caught. When Fauna finished creating its outdoor islands and the chimps were gradually let out, most of them were frightened and stayed comfortably close to the building; Tom, however, bolted straight out, galloped across the entire island, leaped onto the trunk of a huge tree, and began to climb. When he was about sixty feet above us, he stopped and rested in the crook of a branch, looking out across the sanctuary. Gloria wept and said, "I think it's confirmed: this is a wild-caught chimp." I immediately knew that the image of Tom high above the cages would be the ending for the film. Now I needed the right words.

My deadline was looming, and I'd hit a block. I remember asking myself, "What was Tom thinking? What was he feeling?" Putting myself in Tom's place high in the tree, I imagined him musing, "I've been in a cage for as long as I can remember. And now I can finally see where I live. Look at this odd place—my home." The final words of the film then came easily: "We know so little about this old chimpanzee given the name Tom by someone, someplace. All we know is that he spent thirty years in a steel cage, far from the forests of Equatorial Africa. This old chimp can finally survey the strange

> **"**
>
> *We know so little about this old chimpanzee given the name Tom by someone, someplace.*

Figure 13. Tom

landscape that has become his home. His trials have come to an end, but his story will live on, a reminder of the thousands like him who are still waiting for a second chance."

Since the making of *Chimpanzees: An Unnatural History,* Billy Joe, Tom, Lou, Thoto, Carole Noon, and dear, sweet Pepper have all passed away. I will never forget those magnificent individuals who taught me volumes about resilience, forgiveness, determination, and selfless conviction. I stand in awe of what Carole Noon accomplished in her lifetime, but it would not have been possible without the willingness and collaboration of those she was trying to help. She and the chimpanzees worked as a team to achieve the unimaginable.

The little piece of concrete Noon gave me from the Coulston cell blocks still sits on my desk, rough and misshapen—ugly and yet beautiful in its significance. It serves as a powerful reminder to speak up for those who deserve better but have no voice, a reminder to never give up, no matter how daunting the road ahead might be. And it's a reminder that there are still baby chimpanzees in diapers, toddlers in TV commercials, and full-grown chimps in makeshift basement cages and backyard "zoos." Thousands like Tom have sacrificed everything so that we might live a little longer or laugh a little louder. They deserve so much more.

The Special Ones

Debby Cox

I was introduced to chimpanzees in 1986 while studying zookeeping in Sydney, Australia. My first class was at the Taronga Zoo. At the time, I was working as a veterinary nurse at the Royal Society for the Prevention of Cruelty to Animals (RSPCA) when an emergency case came in at the last minute, causing me to be late for my first class. When I arrived, the other class members had already chosen their projects for the year. As fate would have it, the only species left on the list were chimpanzees. My classmates were intimidated by the thought of having to identify each individual living in the large chimpanzee community at the zoo, so they had chosen other species. The head keeper for the chimpanzees, Paul Davies, was a great mentor who assisted me in learning to recognize all twenty-five chimpanzees, allowed me access to their records, and spent hours telling me about their life histories.

From the day I met the chimpanzees at the Taronga Zoo, I was mesmerized. As I sat in front of the viewing windows observing them, I was struck by how much like us they are, how aware they are of their world, and how affected they are by our actions, not only from a global perspective but also as individuals. Chimpanzees understand us better than we realize, and because of their cognitive abilities they are like human children, incredibly vulnerable. An unsettling feeling came over me at the thought of what chimpanzees are forced to go through in laboratories, circuses, and zoos, where some keepers are not as sympathetic to their needs and emotions as others. Like other animals in captivity, they are completely reliant on humans for fulfilling their needs, whether physical, behavioral, or emotional.

Since that initial encounter I have met many amazing chimpanzees. Fifi was my first and most influential chimpanzee mentor. She was one of those individuals I greatly admired and respected, not just as a chimpanzee but as a sentient being. Since Fifi had been captured in the wild, her mother had presumably been killed, as the only way to take an infant away from a mother is to kill the mother, who would never voluntarily give up her infant. Originally, Fifi was brought to Australia to be used in medical trials for polio vaccines. After the trials, Fifi, along with a few other chimps, had been donated to the zoo. One of the founding members of the chimpanzee community at the zoo, she lived there for over fifty years.

An elder in her community respected by both humans and other chimps, Fifi was a doting mother, grandmother, and great-grandmother, with an incredible gift for mediation—an ability to touch fighting individuals on the shoulder and instantly calm the situation. I was amazed at her gift of touch and impressed that she even took the time to intervene. She rarely took sides in such conflicts, unless, of course, they involved her family. Fifi died on July 26, 2007, at the grand old age of sixty, with her family and friends around her. We could not have asked for a better farewell for this extraordinary individual.

In 1993, I traveled to Burundi to volunteer at the Jane Goodall Institute's halfway house for orphaned chimpanzees. The government of Burundi had requested the assistance of JGI a few years earlier because it wanted to initiate a law enforcement program to counter the illegal trade of chimpanzees in the country but needed help taking care of the confiscated orphans. So in the late 1980s JGI set up a halfway house for the newly confiscated chimps while waiting for the government to find land it could use for a long-term sanctuary, along with funds to actually build the sanctuary. I went as a volunteer to see if I could handle working and living in Africa, and whether my last eight years of training and education would be of use in that environment. My previous experience had been with chimpanzees who had been raised by their mothers in captivity, but now I would be dealing with young wild chimpanzees who had been brutally taken away from their families and then either confiscated or surrendered to authorities.

In many African countries, especially in Central Africa, keeping infant chimpanzees as pets is still common practice, particularly among expatriates and influential individuals. Hunters use guns, spears, or nets to capture and kill the mothers, who are eaten as bushmeat; the infants are then sold to traders, who resell them as pets either locally or to other traders for export outside Africa. Infants are often kept as pets in the house, but once they reach juvenile or young adult age they are too strong to control and generally end up chained to a tree or inside a garage, where they stay until slowly dying of neglect. Most of these chimpanzees suffer for many years under terrible circumstances. The lucky ones are confiscated by law enforcement authorities in the early stages and then transferred to us when they are young.

In the 1970s and 1980s, it was customary for laboratories, circuses, and zoos to take chimpanzees from the wild. Laboratories, in particular, found it cheaper to purchase chimps from the wild than to breed them in captivity. However, once international regulations on endangered species were established through the Convention on International Trade in Endangered Species of Wild Fauna and Flora (CITES), a member of the International Union for Conservation of Nature (IUCN), things changed. In the United States, some states still allow the breeding and selling of chimpanzees as pets to the general public or for use in the entertainment industry. This practice has a negative impact on our ability to conserve and protect chimpanzees in Africa.

I was now witnessing the reality of chimpanzees living in the human world. I had not thought much about the larger implications of their fate in captivity when I had been a zookeeper, assuming that the exploitation of chimps was largely a thing of the past. So it was a huge shock to discover the cruelty that humans were still inflicting on these apes.

The big question for me was: could I help them recover? Chimpanzee recovery is complicated and involves both physical and psychological aspects. Physical recovery normally takes about three to four months, but psychological recovery takes longer, and some individuals never recover from the effects of their traumatic experiences. During my involvement with chimpanzee recovery, I held infants in my arms at 4:00 a.m., watching them lose their fight to live after many months of deprivation. I recovered infants who had been tied to a stake in boarded-up rooms with no sunlight, seeing the dullness in their eyes change and life instantly come back into their bodies when I made a pant grunt sound as a mother would do to an infant. After picking them up and hugging them, I could feel their initial resistance and fear shift to desperation to be held, afraid that I would let them go again.

Such infants were often in a state of depression, and I'd have to cajole them out of it with a lot of patience and willingness to hug and groom them for hours, prepared to eat, sleep, and even go to the toilet with the infant chimps clinging to me twenty-four hours a day. Little by little, as these baby chimps regained confidence, I initiated play with them, and slowly they became secure enough to return to the vibrancy they would have had with their mothers in the forest.

An example of this type of recovery occurred with Niyonkuru. He had been rescued from a Congolese hunter who had been trying to sell him in Bujumbura, the capital of Burundi. The staff at the halfway house and the local law enforcement authorities had worked together in a sting operation to recover Niyonkuru from the hunter. The authorities had escorted the hunter back to the border; however, he had returned and threatened to harm the staff members' families if they did not give him the chimp. In the end, the police and military arrested the hunter a second time, took him back to the border, and told him that if they found him in Burundi again he would be jailed. (A Burundian jail was not something a Congolese citizen wanted to experience.) In many countries, authorities turn a blind eye to such practices, but not in Burundi in the 1990s.

The staff decided to name this chimpanzee Niyonkuru, which means "gift from God" in Kirundi, because they felt God had given them Niyonkuru and had also protected them. Niyonkuru was still in a state of severe depression when I arrived. His coat was dull, which is normal, but so were his eyes. He would walk about the yard like a lost soul, not wanting physical contact with anyone—chimp or human. His eyes were blank, he did not play with anyone, and he expressed no emotion, which for a chimpanzee is unusual as they are the most expressive apes apart from humans.

Figure 14. Niyonkuru using a deflated football like a comfort blanket

“

Niyonkuru did not play with anyone, and he expressed no emotion.

Figure 15. Niyonkuru

Figure 16. Niyonkuru, the alpha male in his group, at Sweetwaters Chimpanzee Sanctuary

Soon after Niyonkuru arrived, an incident made us realize how traumatized he was. At the end of each day, the infants were placed into sky kennels to sleep, two together. One evening a volunteer returned to check on the infants and realized that one of Niyonkuru's fingers had been accidently caught in the door. This had to have been very painful, and yet Niyonkuru sat motionless, as if comatose. Not until more than four months after we rescued him did he begin responding, leaping into my arms for reassurance after something had frightened him. We all knew this was a crucial step for him, but we had to wait until he was ready for such physical contact.

Most people remember April 1994 as the beginning of the genocide in Rwanda. What most people do not realize is that violent incidents were also taking place in Burundi, which, while less dramatic, were just as devastating to people. In late 1994, we lost two staff members to this conflict, innocent men walking home from work who were killed by the military for no reason other than the fact that they were Hutu. By 1995, the situation in Burundi had deteriorated to the point where we could not guarantee the safety of the chimps or the staff. And although we had decided to relocate the chimps in June 1994, not until eight months later were we finally able to move the ten oldest chimpanzees to Sweetwaters Chimpanzee Sanctuary in Kenya. Sweetwaters was built by an agricultural company called Lonhro to provide refuge to orphaned chimpanzees in Central and West Africa. The CEO of Lonhro had met Jane Goodall in Kenya, asked what the company could do to help, and Jane had said, "Build a sanctuary!" So they did. Fortunately, it had been built to accommodate many more chimpanzees than were orphaned in Kenya at the time.

After months of planning, getting permission from the various governments, negotiating, and preparing, we arrived at Sweetwaters. At nightfall, after we had settled the chimpanzees into their new home, a group of us—including Elia Nkurikiye, our senior keeper from Burundi; Vince Smith, the sanctuary manager at Sweetwaters; Bill Walluer, our cameraman; and Don Buford, executive director of JGI USA—drove back to our accommodations. As you can imagine, everyone in the car was elated and talkative. Don noticed that I had grown silent, and as we got out of the car he said to me, "Whatever is wrong with the facilities, we will fix it." I told him nothing was wrong and then burst into tears. The poor man had no idea what was troubling me, so I explained that for the past twelve months I had lived with the knowledge that I might have to euthanize the ten chimpanzees we had just moved. The civil war in Burundi had been escalating with the possibility that Bujumbura could explode into a full-scale war zone and we would have to evacuate, with no other choice but to euthanize the chimps because we did not have transport boxes or a mode of transportation to move ten adult chimpanzees out of the city to a safe place. The realization that I no longer had to carry out that action had suddenly relieved my pent-up emotions. Many of the sanctuary managers in Africa have to live with this burden. Bala Amarasekaran of the Tacugama Chimpanzee Sanctuary in Sierra Leone, Graziella Cotman of the Tchimpounga Chimpanzee Rehabilitation Center in Congo, and Claudine André of the Lola Ya Bonobo in the Democratic Republic of the Congo have all lived through civil wars trying to not only stay alive themselves but also protect the orphaned apes under their care. Why do we do it? You just have to be hugged by one of these orphans to understand. You cannot turn your back on them; to do so would be inhumane.

After closing the halfway house in Burundi in December 1995, I moved to Uganda to help the Jane Goodall Institute set up Ngamba Island Chimpanzee Sanctuary. At that time there were twenty-four chimpanzees living in captivity in Uganda. Most of them were in what formerly had been called the Entebbe Zoo, now known as the Uganda Wildlife Education Centre. Ten of the oldest chimpanzees originally from the zoo were living on an island in Lake Edward in Queen Elizabeth National Park, a temporary solution until a permanent sanctuary could be built. My first duty was to improve the antiquated facilities (small barren cages) and care for the chimps at this center; my second duty was to help set up a sanctuary. With funds from USAID and the innovative expertise of the new director, Wilhelm Moeller, we were able to build a beautiful island enclosure with natural vegetation, large mature trees, and a very nice nighttime holding area for twenty chimpanzees. Any chimp in a Western zoo would have been happy to swap places for these digs!

In March 1996, we were tipped off about the sale of a primarily forested island that was only 23 kilometers from Entebbe. We purchased the island and then raised funds to build appropriate facilities for the ten older chimps from Lake Edward and the chimps from Entebbe. Fortunately, with the help of the Born Free Foundation, the International Fund for Animal Welfare, the Taronga Zoo, and many other private donors, we were able to do this.

The initial idea was that the island would house forty-five chimps, the original twenty (leaving behind the four oldest chimpanzees to live in the new facilities at the center) and then those who would later arrive, based on the assumption that the confiscation rate would be one chimp every two years. Unfortunately, we did not count on war in the eastern Democratic Republic of the Congo (DRC). After the Rwandan genocide in 1994, hundreds of thousands of refugees began moving into the eastern DRC. Along with the refugees came perpetrators of the genocide, who promptly seized territory and started terrorizing the Congolese villagers. At the same time, Mobuto, the aging dictator of the DRC, was overthrown by Laurent Kabila, who was killed not long after, and his son, Joseph Kabila, was installed instead. Joseph Kabila had the unsavory task of trying to appease a multitude of warlords, people in neighboring countries that wanted a piece of the DRC's natural wealth (diamonds, gold, coltan, timber) and the international community, which insisted on retaining the same peacekeeping forces that had failed in Rwanda. Since 1999, the DRC has had a UN peacekeeping presence, but after nineteen years and billions of dollars there has been no change. The civil war in the DRC resulted in a higher than usual illegal trade, as well as easy access to the Uganda market through the Uganda army, which was based in the DRC at the time. Over three years, Uganda confiscated more than twenty orphaned chimpanzees coming across the border from the DRC, including one named Ikuru, who has a heartbreaking story.

At about age two, Ikuru had been rescued in the DRC by a Ugandan military officer after the troops had raided a rebel camp and discovered her sitting beside the chopped-up body of her dead mother. The officer, overcome by this sight, had decided to keep her. He had gone to a nearby village and asked an old man to look after her while he continued with his duties, saying he would be back to get her soon. Six months went by before he was relieved of his post and able to return. During this time, while Ikuru had been kept alive she had not been well cared for, either nutritionally or psychologically. The Congolese had not treated Ikuru as a normal pet, so she was never held by anyone. When the officer brought her across the border, the authorities explained that it was illegal to have her and he would have to hand her over. JGI and the Uganda Wildlife Education Centre team had been informed and flew up to Arua to collect her, along with two other young confiscated orphans named Adiru and Mawa.

Ikuru became my housemate, along with Adiru, who was extremely sick and died about a week later. At the time, Ikuru had a potbelly and skinny arms and legs, with dull skin color and blank eyes; in a matter of days, most of her baby teeth fell out. The first evening, as I was preparing my dinner and getting a bottle ready for her, Ikuru disappeared from my hut. I found her behind the hut, trying to make a nest for the night, sitting all alone rocking backward and forward. (We have often seen post-traumatic stress disorder in orphaned apes who, like Ikuru, have endured prolonged deprivation.) In an attempt to break her cycle of rocking, every evening just before sunset we made sure that one of us lay down and held her as she went to sleep.

Many chimpanzees who have been alone for years suffer from various types of phobias. Some are afraid of open spaces, preferring to stay in small, cramped settings. Others have an aversion to being touched and jump when you try to groom them, often wrapping their arms around themselves, in what we call a self-clinging pose, to reassure themselves. Still other chimps clasp their thighs when they are afraid, their movements becoming stilted and jerky, and you are never quite sure if they will hug you or bite you. While I have seen most infants return to what I would consider a normal state, many older chimps retain some abnormal behavioral traits. It is especially important to ensure that the chimps do not develop or maintain behaviors that cause self-harm, such as biting themselves or banging their heads against walls, which happens in very adverse situations.

Even now, after all these years, Ikuru starts rocking if she is emotionally stressed. We always make sure that she feels safe, secure, and comfortable in the social setting of the sanctuary, along with the other orphans. This is what makes the sanctuary unique: we consider the needs of every individual while trying to build a social setting where chimps can live as normal a life as possible. We are mindful that we are looking after individuals who have had some of the most traumatic experiences anyone could possibly imagine. While most eventually recover, some, like Ikuru, who today resides in a community of chimpanzees on Ngamba Island, live with psychological scars forever.

Figure 17. Ikuru, as an adult, on Ngamba Island

Figure 18. Left to right: Ikuru, with friends Umutama and Kazahukire, on Ngamba Island

Today, my work is focused on ensuring that chimpanzees stay where they belong—in the wild—and do not fall victim to the bushmeat or live animal trade. In many countries around the world, including Africa, people eat bushmeat, which the conservation community defines as wild animal food harvested either illegally or unsustainably. Many countries in Central Africa rely heavily on bushmeat as their animal protein source. This presents a major problem because with diminishing habitats and the increasing human population, there is not enough wildlife to sustainably supply markets, and many countries in Central Africa do not have a cultural history of, or an environment suited to, raising domestic livestock. Also problematic is the fact that while in the past most people only hunted for their own needs, today they hunt bushmeat commercially, transporting it to capital cities and even overseas to destinations like London, New York, and Amsterdam.

Chimpanzees, who as infants are more robust than gorillas, are the animals most commonly seen being sold illegally across Central Africa. The DRC is a classic example of a country whose people, due to the chaos of civil war, are desperate to earn currency and are willing to risk going into a neighboring country to sell the only thing they can—their wildlife. Access to both modern weapons and forest regions that, once inaccessible, due to the arrival of logging roads are now open and unguarded, causing a massive die-off of wildlife in Central Africa. With the lack of support from governments to enforce wildlife laws, and the absence of awareness and suitable alternatives, the fight against the unsustainable harvesting of wildlife in Africa continues to be a tragedy.

Illegal live trade in endangered species (chimpanzees, gorillas, monkeys, elephants) is also still active and, if anything, expanding. The scary part is that it is connected to the illegal arms and drug trades, which, in turn, are often linked to organized crime networks. Illegal wildlife trade is frequently exacerbated by lack of compliance with laws, especially in countries where there is conflict. Illegal wildlife trade increases in such countries because individuals dealing in illegal weapons, drugs, and minerals are the same people participating in wildlife trade. With an increase in these trades, especially minerals and firearms in the DRC, it was only a matter of time before there was an increase in illegal wildlife smuggling across the borders. Only recently have international law enforcement agencies taken notice of the illegal live animal trade market.

We all must take responsibility to ensure that our closest living relatives have the opportunity to live as they evolved to live—in the forests of Africa. They deserve our respect and are entitled to live free of persecution and destruction. If we, as humans, cannot make the effort to respect and protect chimpanzees, what chance do we have of protecting the rest of our planet? No matter how hard we try to care for chimpanzees in captivity, we will always fail to provide them with what they really need—a dynamic environment with a large fission-fusion community that offers them the freedom to change their social groupings, a natural component of chimpanzee social behavior in the wild.

I feel privileged to have been in the company of chimpanzees. I have learned a lot from them, especially about motherhood, conflict resolution, and compassion. Chimpanzee mothers have a tolerance I have never seen in human mothers. They teach their infants in a compassionate, positive way, basically never saying no to them until they are at least five years old. Infants learn by observation what is right and wrong.

wrong. Mothers distract infants from doing something annoying or dangerous rather than use punishment or a negative response, such as saying no, as human mothers often do. Chimpanzee mothers aren't the only ones using these techniques; all community members engage in this positive teaching process, which I find fascinating and very productive if you want children who are confident and outgoing. In the sanctuary, I have seen chimpanzees demonstrate compassion on the same level as witnessed in human communities. When a chimp is sick or has an injury, another chimp will give support with an arm around the shoulder or a kiss on the injured part. They will show compassion not only to their own kind but to other species as well. Another reason chimpanzees are great to work with in captivity is exposure to their amazing ability to forgive. They are forgiving of us, as captors; they do not let arguments linger; and even when there is a fight between individuals they do not hold grudges as we often do in our society. In addition, chimpanzees, like all great apes, are incredible thinkers, something we should not forget as we keep them in captive settings.

Education is one of the major components of our work, along with habitat protection and community-centered conservation. We help communities develop appropriate sustainable livelihoods that will not damage chimpanzee environments or their future. We educate children, adults, and professionals, such as members of law enforcement agencies, about the importance of protecting endangered species and train local staff to take on the long-term task of caring for the chimpanzees we failed to protect the first time around.

I used to wear a chain around my neck with a small key that had been used to lock the chain around Amisero, a young chimpanzee rescued in Burundi. The local staff had named her Amisero, which means "hope" in Kirundi, because when she was ill they all hoped she would survive—and fortunately she did. When I was feeling depressed or overwhelmed by the tasks at hand, I only had to touch the key to be reminded not to give up, that there was always hope. I once lost the key and chain while rescuing a dog being beaten to death by a local security guard, and replaced it with another, which functions still as a symbol to help me stay focused on my mission and not lose hope.

THE EMPTY CAGE

Asami Kabasawa

Standing in front of the empty cage abandoned under the shade of a big mango tree in Rockel, a small West African town just outside Freetown, Sierra Leone, I realized that my journey had come full circle. The tiny cage used to hold orphaned chimpanzees who had been captured in the tropical forests of West Africa and shipped to the United States, Europe, and Japan was now empty.

My journey with chimpanzees had begun almost twenty years before, when I had held a baby chimpanzee in my arms for the first time. I was an undergraduate student at Hunter College in New York City majoring in anthropology, with an interest in primates. One of my classmates in primatology class announced that the Laboratory for Experimental Medicine & Surgery in Primates (LEMSIP), affiliated with New York University, was hiring volunteers to work with chimpanzees in its enrichment program, which had been started to improve the psychological well being of the chimpanzees, baboons, and other primates used in on-site medical experiments.

I had always been fascinated with primates but had never worked with them. I had a vague idea about medical laboratories but did know that the chimpanzees were confined in small cages and subjects of horrible experiments. Nonetheless, I was interested in participating in the enrichment program if it was going to improve the lives of the chimpanzees.

During my first day as a volunteer at the lab I was completely overwhelmed by the deafening noise and pandemonium in the adult chimpanzee units. As I walked past the cages with my supervisor, the chimps spat big mouthfuls of water on me, drenching me by the time I arrived at the end of the hall. I tried to keep calm and not show my fear, even though I was scared that the chimps would break out of their cages. Thinking back on the experience, I am sure the chimpanzees took great pleasure in impressing me, as I was a new and strange-looking woman, the only Asian at the lab.

All volunteers started out working with the babies. My first day, while in the chimpanzee nursery "playroom" with a few baby chimps, I was told to sit very still and not reach out to touch them until they came over to me. Baby Serena trotted toward me and then climbed right into my lap, looking directly into my eyes while clinging to me so hard that her tiny hands bruised my upper arms. I did not speak English very well at the time, but no one needed to explain anything to me. Clearly, Serena was starving for comfort and physical connection that would have happened naturally if she had been with her mother. I decided right then to continue volunteering as long as there were chimpanzees in the laboratory—not because I agreed with using chimpanzees, or any animals, for medical experiments but because I believed that we are all responsible for their well-being. I vowed to do my part until we found alternatives to experimenting on animals and all lab animals were retired.

When I met my special boy, Tequila, who had crooked eyes and an impish smile, it was love at first sight. I was working in the nursery, and a caregiver was holding three-year-old Tequila in her arms. I walked by them and just said hi to Tequila, and to everyone's surprise he immediately jumped into my arms. My supervisor told me to walk around holding him; Tequila was relaxed and calm in my arms the whole time. Despite being a sweet and affectionate chimpanzee, Tequila had been labeled a "problem child" because whenever he was taken out of his cage to play with the other chimpanzees he refused to go back into his cage and caregivers had to spend hours chasing and cajoling him to get him back in. Of course, it was normal for him to behave like that since no chimpanzee is happy confined in a small cage or being blamed for such conduct. But there were forty baby chimpanzees in the nursery at any given time, all with different schedules for feeding, medications, and special needs care. While Tequila was having great fun getting all the attention, the other chimps had to stay in their cages, deprived of their own playtimes.

Sadly, as Tequila got older and stronger he had a problem socializing with the other chimpanzees, so he lived alone in a tiny cage while the other young chimps lived in social groups. I would remove Tequila's feeder, allowing us to play and touch through the small squares of his cage, which were just big enough for me to put my arm through. Normally he was playful, pulling my hands into his cage through the squares and guiding me to tickle him until he laughed and kicked his legs in the air. Because he loved to clap his hands, we would both clap to see who could clap louder. I would also give Tequila long grooming sessions when he was on his belly, after which he would relax and drift off to sleep.

Some days Tequila did not want to play; he just wanted to put his arms through the squares and embrace my neck. We would sit with our faces touching through the grille of the cage for the entire session. When Tequila was like this, it made me so sad I would often cry. I felt his deep depression, immeasurable loneliness, and the sense of hopelessness crushing his tiny chimpanzee heart. After all, he was still a young boy who should have been within reach of his mother, family, and friends. In the wild, his mother would have cuddled Tequila to sleep every night, but born in a medical laboratory to be used in experiments Tequila had to adhere to lab protocol, which was to separate babies from their mothers so they would become accustomed to being handled by human caregivers.

Every time I left Tequila's cage for the day, my heart broke. He cried and threw fits until he choked. Thinking about him kept me awake at night as I imagined him coping alone in his tiny cage and feared he would die from depression and grief. I considered not returning to the lab so Tequila would not have to go through this every time I left, but then thought that if looking forward to seeing me even once or twice a week was a tiny light in his life I should go back. So I kept returning for two years until Tequila was retired, along with fifty other chimpanzees, to the Wildlife Waystation in Sylmar, California. After the babies left, I traveled to Guinea for a year then spent two years at the Wildlife Waystation caring for the ex-LEMSIP chimpanzees. By the time I left, Tequila was the alpha of his group of five boys and no longer cried when I was out of sight.

In 2001, I moved to Sierra Leone to work as a volunteer at the Tacugama Chimpanzee Sanctuary located in the Western Area Forest Reserve, about 9 kilometers from Freetown. Tacugama had been founded by Bala Amarasekaran in 1995 to rescue and care for confiscated pet chimpanzees. The sanctuary filled a great need because it was illegal to capture, trade, or keep chimpanzees as pets in Sierra Leone. Chimpanzees at Tacugama live in large forested enclosures with solar-powered electric fences. My duties, as the only volunteer back then, were to establish and supervise quarantine procedures for newly received chimpanzees and to help the local caregivers.

I spent four years at Tacugama as a volunteer and one more year traveling to many other parts of the country interviewing local people about chimpanzees, wildlife, and the forest. Upon my arrival at Tacugama, there were twenty-seven chimpanzees, and by the end of my stay the number had more than tripled. I went back again in 2006 to collect data for my PhD thesis and then completed my PhD studies at Kyoto University, Japan, on the history and issues of the chimpanzee pet trade and on people's perceptions about chimpanzees in both habitat and nonhabitat countries.

During my PhD studies, I met an old woman in Rockel who talked about the empty cage under the tree that had been used to transport and hold small orphaned chimpanzees. It was a hot, sunny day in the dry season of 2007. This woman's sun-weathered dark face, crowned with a colorful African print scarf, wrinkled with a smile as she explained in Krio, the pidgin English of Sierra Leone, how she had taken care of the chimpanzees, treating them like human babies. I imitated a baby chimpanzee cry, and she looked very surprised, laughed, and said, *"Eh, u sabi babou den? U get uown babou?"* which means "Do you know chimpanzees? Do you have your own chimpanzee?" I replied that I did not own a *babou* but had been taking care of them for many years.

After imitating chimpanzee vocalizations and gestures, she talked about how she had taken care of baby chimpanzees, giving them baths, and how it had been difficult to administer medications because they were smart and didn't want to take them. I always felt a camaraderie when talking with people who worked with chimpanzees; as she affectionately reminisced about those days, I could sense that she liked them. I asked her if she knew what had happened to the chimpanzees, and she said no, other than that they were going to "white man lands." She then added, "I know white men teach animals, like dogs and horses, to do things, so maybe the chimpanzees were trained to work for white men."

As we continued talking, I found out that she had been a servant for the family of Dr. Franz Sitter, and taking care of chimpanzees was one of her tasks. During this time, I had been tracing the history of the chimpanzee trade in Sierra Leone and other West African countries, so I knew about Sitter's role as a major exporter of baby chimpanzees from the 1950s to the early 1990s, before Sierra Leone had become a signatory of the

Convention on International Trade in Endangered Species of Wild Fauna and Flora (CITES), which aims to protect wild animals and plants by controlling international trade. But I believed that the old woman had no idea about Sitter's *babou* business or her boss's role in exporting chimpanzees. Sitter and his daughters had left Sierra Leone at the beginning of the decade-long civil war. His wife, a Sierra Leonean and daughter of an influential chief, had died long before and was buried in a tomb facing the back of the house where the old woman and her family were now living.

After hearing that Sitter was paying for baby chimpanzees, people from all over the countryside, as well as from neighboring countries, brought chimpanzees to Freetown. Sitter also had his people supply babies from chimpanzee habitats in Guinea and Liberia, and transport them through the northern part of Sierra Leone that bordered Guinea, where the Outamba Kilimi National Park is now, as well as the Gola Forest, a large forest bordering Liberia. Sitter collected the baby chimpanzees in his Freetown compound; a local vet checked their health; and then Sitter shipped the babies from Freetown to labs, zoos, and circuses in Europe, the United States, and Japan. He gained a reputation among those importing chimpanzees as a reliable supplier, having exported more than two thousand babies over the years.

Although records of past international chimpanzee trade are often incomplete since the papers have been forged, usually claiming the babies were not caught in the wild, recent genetic studies of captive chimpanzees in developed countries indicate that the majority of first-generation chimpanzees are from West Africa, most probably from Sierra Leone since there were no major exporters other than Sitter. While I was conducting interviews in remote villages near chimpanzee habitats, people still spoke of Sitter as "the white man with one arm from Freetown, coming to buy chimpanzees and other wild animals." It's been about twenty years since Sitter left the country, but his negative legacy lingers on.

It is deplorable that so many chimpanzees were exported by Sitter and that so many chimpanzees are sacrificed for just one baby. All chimpanzee orphans witness their mother and family members being murdered and have to endure being separated from their mother's dead body. Many babies do not survive the trauma of this separation or the poor handling during transportation.

In 2001, my first year at Tacugama, we received twenty-eight chimpanzees, doubling the number already in our care. This was due, to some degree, to the abundance of white people in the country working for peace-keeping organizations and humanitarian NGOs. The expats purchased many chimpanzees out of pity, in an attempt to save them, but then ended up not being able to properly care for them. At the end of my stay at Tacugama three years later, we had almost ninety chimpanzees. Except for four "accidental" births, all of them had been born in the wild, separated from their mothers, kept by humans, and, in most cases, mistreated in one way or another.

We didn't know the exact ages of many of these chimpanzees but could guess by the development of their teeth—if adult incisors are about to emerge, the chimp is close to five years old—and their body size. However, body size was often deceiving because many chimpanzees came to us extremely malnourished. And in the case of a chimpanzee named Tito we couldn't judge his age by his tooth development because he was missing most of his front teeth, from either a severe injury or being kicked in the face when he was very young.

All the chimpanzees at Tacugama were special to me, but I will tell the stories of Tito and Augusta—two chimpanzees with very different temperaments yet similar backgrounds—to illustrate how they were abused by their owners before being rescued. When I first met Tito, a ten-year-old with a serious-looking, expressive black face, he had been at Tacugama for five years. As a baby, while living with his owner, he had been forced to smoke and drink and had not been fed enough food. I am amazed that he survived and that despite the neglect and exploitation, he was good-natured, loved people, and was very forgiving. He was the only chimp who would tickle me back when being groomed; his weak spot was under his chin and neck. Often we would stand looking at each other face-to-face through the grille of his cage, tickling each other while Tito laughed with his mouth wide open, showing whatever teeth he had.

I loved to imagine all the things going on in Tito's head because he was always deep in thought. Endlessly plotting schemes that did not always work out well, Tito would often get into trouble with other chimpanzees, causing fights in his group. If caregivers were around, Tito would run to them, pointing at other chimps, as if to say, "It wasn't me!"

Augusta was the queen of Tacugama. She had come to the sanctuary at around twelve years of age, so she was an adult when I met her. She did not like people and

> "
> *I loved to imagine all the things going on in Tito's head because he was always deep in thought.*

Figure 19. Tito

did not hide it. All the chimpanzees at Tacugama loved and respected Bala, except Augusta. Bala, who was usually not afraid to go into the adult enclosures, feared Augusta and would not dare get too close to her. Despite Augusta's feelings toward humans, I greeted her every day, asking her how her day was going or if she had eaten enough, as I did with the other chimpanzees. But Augusta would either turn her head away, ignoring me, or vigorously shake her hand at me as if to say, "Bugger off!"

Before Augusta was rescued, she had been kept as a pet by a local soldier. When she had become too old to control—which generally happens as chimps reach five or six years of age—she had been drugged with Valium and kept chained by the neck in a cage too small for her to stand in. Had Augusta been able to speak, she could have given us plenty of reasons not to forgive us.

Not only did Augusta not like people, she also did not like chimpanzees, probably due to her lack of social experience with them during her first twelve years of life. She was very aggressive toward all the chimpanzees at the sanctuary, most of them too young to stand up to her fierceness. We did not want her to live alone, and fortunately there was one adult male chimpanzee, named Gorilla, who was social and tolerant enough to stay with Augusta without fighting. Though we did not have the luxury of asking Gorilla for his consent, he was the only chimpanzee friend Augusta ever had. Since the first half of Augusta's life had been filled with misery, I constantly hoped that she felt safe at Tacugama, knowing that no one was ever going to hurt her again. She died suddenly in 2008, at about age twenty-five.

I sometimes wished all the chimpanzees at Tacugama were more like Augusta, hating people for what we had done to them; I actually felt ashamed when those like Tito were so forgiving. I knew that no matter how hard I worked to improve the lives of the captive chimpanzees, I could never replace the parts of their lives humans had destroyed. We had killed their families, obliterated their communities, and taken away their independence and freedom. Once in captivity, no matter how good the conditions, every aspect of their lives had become dependent on human beings. We had made decisions for them as if genuinely knowing what was best for them and what they really wanted.

I first came to know chimpanzees as individual beings in the biomedical laboratory, where they were "reproduced," forced to be orphans, and then used as experimental subjects for the perceived sake of saving human lives. Today, as more and more people are discovering how similar chimpanzees are to us, and what intelligent, feeling beings they are, the inhumane use of chimpanzees in biomedical research is changing. The number

Figure 20. Augusta

of chimps used in research has greatly decreased, and in some countries the practice has been banned. In the last twenty years, many more people have become concerned about chimpanzee conservation, and, as a result, conservation activities such as environmental education and habitat protection are now being carried out in all habitat countries. To date, there are over eight hundred orphaned chimpanzees rescued from the bushmeat and exotic pet trades living in African sanctuaries. As many as sixteen sanctuaries in twelve African countries have been established to take care of them.

The small empty cage I saw in Rockel might have been used to carry members of Tequila's family, or maybe Tito's, or Augusta's. Perhaps it carried the parents of chimps I met at LEMSIP, as well as those in zoos in the United States, Japan, and Europe. That cage continues to be a reminder of all the baby chimpanzees who have been captured, all the chimpanzees murdered, and the extreme abuse and suffering they have each endured. I hope to see many more empty cages in my lifetime.

UNBREAKABLE SPIRITS

Jenny Desmond

When I was three years old, I told my mom that animals were more important than people. Many years later, when I was volunteering for Steven Wise, a lawyer fighting for legal personhood for chimpanzees and other sentient animals, she reminded me of my childhood statement and how it had evolved to my current belief that animals *are* people.

While growing up I took care of animals of every shape and size, all orphaned, injured, and unwanted. Though my parents insisted on cages for the animals, I continually refused, so our house, and our lives, were often chaotic. But while my parents didn't share my passion for animals, they lovingly nurtured mine.

Despite my passion for animals, at first life didn't take me in the direction of working with them. I once fainted at the vet's office, and I knew I would never be happy working in zoos, entertainment settings, or other places where animals were captive or treated as commodities. So I got my master's degree in social work from the University of Denver and began working with abused children, troubled teens, and runaways.

Then I moved to Boston, where I met my husband Jimmy, and in 2000 we went on a backpacking honeymoon visiting, among other places, the Sepilok Orangutan Rehabilitation Centre in Borneo, Malaysia. There we saw great apes in the wild for the first time, an experience that would change the course of our lives.

Later we came back to volunteer at the center. My job was to look after eighteen orphaned orangutans, all under the age of three. Though this seemed like a dream job, it was not as cute or cuddly as I imagined. The young orangutans' mothers had been killed; the orphans were skinny, sick, terrified, and depressed; and care and resources were minimal, with only a few untrained caregivers who had difficulty relating to the orangutans, so the orphans did not receive the love, nurturing, and medical attention they desperately needed. The babies' room was dark and dirty, and their outside enclosure small and devoid of enrichment. Three of the orangutans were infants who spent their days in baskets and were bottle-fed every few hours. One day an infant was left by her caregiver in the scorching sun for hours, and by the time we found her she was barely alive. A veterinarian who happened to be there doing research tried to resuscitate her, and I gave her CPR, but we couldn't save her.

Jimmy and I left the center two months later, after improving the lives of the orphans by providing daily enrichment activities; teaching the staff new ways to interact with them by implementing easy treatment and care protocols; and cleaning, painting, and buying new cages for their night room. Even though the situation still seemed dire, it inspired us to gain more experience so we could help other animals in need. We then visited Orangutan Foundation International, also in Borneo, run by renowned primatologist Dr. Biruté Galdikas. The facility was overflowing with orphans and had limited resources, yet it felt like a happy place for the orangutans because of the love and nurturing they received.

Next we decided to work with chimpanzees in Africa. I wrote to Jane Goodall, who put me in touch with her assistant, Mary Lewis, who in turn connected me to Debby Cox, the executive director of the Jane Goodall Institute Uganda. In spring 2000, Debby generously offered us volunteer positions managing the Rhino Fund Uganda, a Ugandan NGO helping to repopulate rhinos in Uganda's national parks. At the time, the Rhino Fund was based at the Uganda Wildlife Education Centre in Entebbe, along with the Ngamba Island Chimpanzee Sanctuary and the Jane Goodall Institute. We became involved in all four projects. That's where we met Matooke.

Debby asked us to rescue and temporarily care for Matooke, who had been living in squalid conditions. We found him in an abandoned room at Queen Elizabeth National Park headquarters in western Uganda, tied to a crate by a wire around his waist and sitting in his own waste. He had been there for many days and was sick; dehydrated; had dull, dry hair; and weighed nearly nothing. Matooke was only two years old and close to death. The gravity of what I was seeing hit me hard—Matooke had watched his mother and family be brutally murdered, then had been torn from his mother's dead body, kidnapped, sold on the black market, starved, and finally left to die. He was missing part of an index finger, which most likely had been chopped off to force him to let go of his dead mother.

Back at the sanctuary, I spent five days and nights lying outside the open door of the crate in which Matooke had been transported, offering him food and water, and talking softly to him in his language and mine. After one day, he ate a Ugandan food called *matoke* (thus his name) and drank a bit of water from a dish. After three days, he moved a little closer to me. On the fifth day when I greeted him, he responded by touching me, an intimate moment that was a turning point for both of us.

In the weeks and months that followed, Matooke grew stronger and healthier. For nine months, we spent nearly every minute together as I tried to help him feel safe and secure enough to regain trust and confidence. Matooke was then ready to be integrated into the family of chimpanzees at the center who had also been rescued from illegal hunters, traders, roadside zoos, and private owners and now lived in a seminatural area with trees, bushes, grass, and a night dorm. One of the happiest days of my life was when Matooke chose not to return to me but instead stay with his new chimpanzee family, the future I had envisioned for him. Matooke eventually became the alpha male in his family and is today a beautiful, big, strong boy.

One day, while watching Matooke climb a tree and talking with another caregiver about our fear of someone taking the baby chimps away to sell them again, I felt a depth of love for Matooke that I had not previously experienced, and suddenly I knew I would give my life to protect him. From that moment on, I became fully committed to the welfare of all the chimps.

Jimmy and I then made one of the most difficult decisions of our lives—to leave Uganda and go back to the United States to gain the expertise and legitimacy we needed to better fight for Matooke and others like him. In December 2000, after ten months at Rhino Fund Uganda, we left for the United States so Jimmy could go to veterinary school and I could work in various jobs honing the skills I needed for our future rescue, care, rehabilitation, and conservation work.

Jimmy earned his doctor of veterinary medicine degree in 2008, and between 2010 and 2015 we worked with many African wildlife centers and organizations as volunteers, consultants, managers, and vet/rescue professionals. We became involved with the Jane Goodall Institute and the Pan African Sanctuary Alliance, and were hired by the Dian Fossey Foundation and the Disney Conservation Fund to establish a rehabilitation center for Grauer's gorillas (a subspecies of the eastern gorilla) in the Democratic Republic of the Congo. We also worked in Uganda developing chimpanzee health and conservation protocols, and traveled as consultants throughout East Africa assisting rescue centers, rehabilitation projects, and conservation initiatives, including Colobus Conservation, a wild monkey rehabilitation center on the Kenyan coast.

In May 2015, while in Kenya contemplating our next move, we received a call from the Humane Society of the United States (HSUS) informing us of a situation needing immediate attention—assisting sixty-six chimpanzees living off the coast of Liberia who had been abandoned without food and water by the New York Blood Center (NYBC). These chimpanzees had been used as research subjects in hepatitis B vaccine, HIV, and other invasive studies for three decades before being retired to six different islands in 2006 and receiving minimal care since NYBC's withdrawal of funds. Though the NYBC had given notice of its intention to pull out of the project, it ended up suspending all financial ties and care for the chimps without arranging for their support, leaving them dehydrated and starving. The water supply on the islands was dependent on archaic water systems built by the NYBC that were broken. Local individuals were caring for these chimps without pay or support, desperately trying to keep them alive. The chimpanzees' dire situation was further exacerbated by the fact that they had only been fed every second day for ten years. Retiring these chimpanzees in such a manner had left them to die a slow death.

Jimmy and I couldn't say no, so we committed to a five-week crisis intervention. About a month after receiving the call from HSUS we set off for Liberia to put a care team in place ensuring that the short-term needs of the chimps would be met while other plans for their future could be made. Fortunately, we had sufficient financial support to get right to work. In a remarkable collaborative effort, after NYBC abandoned the chimps, animal advocates had called global attention to the crisis through grassroots protests, social media campaigns, and petition drives. A GoFundMe campaign was launched in May 2015, supported by a remarkable coalition of over thirty-five animal welfare, great ape, and conservation organizations, and to this day has raised close to $400,000. Having worked with hundreds of chimpanzees with traumatic histories, I thought that we were emotionally ready to handle what we were about to see. I was wrong.

Figure 21. Finn (left) and his mother Anita (right) receiving food from an arriving boat

Surrounded by mangrove trees, the islands—ranging in size from ten to eighty acres and only a few miles from the Liberian Institute for Biomedical Research, where the NYBC research had been conducted—were in an estuarine wetland with no fresh food or water, and no protection against predators, weather, or disease. As we approached one of the islands where many of the oldest surviving chimpanzees lived, we heard screams of desperation. When the island came into view, twelve chimpanzees stood before us emaciated, with protruding ribcages, skin hanging off their bodies, and extensive hair loss. They waded far out into the water desperately clambering to reach the boat and grab anything they could. It was a shocking sight that will forever be burned into my memory. Jimmy and I at first just sat there and cried but soon realized

Figure 22. Left to right: Doris, Samantha, and Bullet on the edge of the island waiting for food

we couldn't indulge our feelings of shock and sadness for long since we needed them to fuel our efforts to help the chimps during the weeks to come.

Two chimpanzees, whom I came to know as Samantha and Bullet, were standing at the front of the group. According to her files, discovered at the former research site, Samantha, the oldest remaining survivor, had arrived at the NYBC during the early days of research in 1976, at the age of one and a half. She had been sold to the center by a man from a nearby village, then collared and chained to a makeshift jungle gym outside the director's home along with about twenty other young chimpanzees. Involved in HIV, hepatitis B and C, and other research, Samantha had been anesthetized 350 times and undergone 50 liver biopsies. Also used as a breeder, she had given birth to her first baby without knowing how to care for an infant—a common occurrence among first-time chimpanzee mothers lacking role models as children—so she was tranquilized and her baby was taken from her, dying shortly thereafter. Her second baby, too, had been immediately taken from her then died. Her third and last baby had been found dead in the breeding colony enclosure, a death attributed to "unknown causes."

Bullet, the other chimpanzee at the front of the group, had been captured by the NYBC when he was only two years old. It is believed that when his mother was shot during his capture, a stray bullet had lodged in his right arm, which eventually became infected. Ultimately, the NYBC director decided that amputation was the only option to save Bullet's life. Afterward, Bullet had been caged, given the number 147, and immediately entered into research protocols. During his decades in research, Bullet had been anesthetized more than 400 times and endured more than 50 liver biopsies, as well as many hundreds of blood draws, resulting in chronic illnesses. He had also suffered frequently from severe bite wounds received from cagemates during fights in close quarters with no means for escape.

Chimpanzees like Bullet and Samantha had been supplied to the NYBC from various sources. NYBC routinely hired big game hunters to search for wild chimps in the forest, in addition to soliciting chimpanzees from local bushmeat hunters and people keeping chimps as pets. The demand for laboratory subjects had caused the death of many hundreds of chimpanzees.

There was much to do to help Samantha, Bullet, and the sixty-four other chimpanzees on the islands. Our top priority was to get sufficient good-quality food to them daily, along with water, since the water systems on every island were broken. We found a remarkable team of people who had cared for the chimps while they were in the NYBC research program and after their retirement. These caregivers, also abandoned by the NYBC, had been spending their personal time and resources to prevent the chimps from dying of starvation and dehydration. They collected and disbursed whatever food they could and brought water in buckets filled from wells on the mainland to distribute to the chimps in small cups.

The former NYBC caregivers had risked their lives providing food and water to the abandoned chimps, and some had been killed in the effort. Decades of corruption in Liberia had led to two civil wars between 1989 and 2003, resulting in 250,000 deaths and thousands of refugees. Most of the original research chimpanzees who had

Figure 23. A thirsty young Finn receiving a drink of water

been left in cages, therefore unable to escape, either were killed by soldiers or died of dehydration and starvation because caregivers couldn't reach them. Human survivors of these civil wars have terrible tales to tell: walking for weeks to reach refugee camps in Côte d'Ivoire or Guinea; loved ones killed or lost to disease; and the sadness of losing their chimpanzee friends. Liberia was still recovering when, in March 2014, it was struck with an Ebola outbreak requiring expert response teams from around the world to come and assist victims of the deadly virus. Stationed at the old NYBC research center, a few responders noticed people carrying buckets of food and water to boats on the river. When they found out what was happening, they helped with personal donations and sent out calls for help to animal welfare groups in their countries of origin.

⊡⊡ ⊡⊡ ⊡⊡

As we began caring for the sixty-six NYBC chimpanzees on the islands, I spent nights going through their medical records found at the site and creating a profile for each individual. It took hours to get through each file, and the process was emotionally draining. As I reviewed the files, I learned that the research protocols alone, such as weekly blood draws, biopsies, and injections of all kinds, had been extremely invasive; in addition, the chimpanzees had endured wounds and continual infections due to their compromised immune systems and poor living conditions. They had also been repeatedly darted with an anesthetic, not only for research protocols but to allow the staff to clean their cages, remove their infants so they could be sampled, and capture the chimps who escaped. They had watched cagemates scream while being darted then hauled away in wheelbarrows. While most chimps screamed when they were about to be darted, some, like Samantha, simply held out a leg, resigned to their fates.

Getting sent to the lab's breeding colony, which was small and confined, allowed the chimps to be in the company of others but often resulted in mothers having their babies taken away. The infants lived in a basic one-room structure that the NYBC staff called a nursery. In the daytime, caregivers occasionally took the young chimps outside to climb and socialize, but at night they were locked in cages, sleeping without their mothers or caregivers and often screaming in fear when their caregivers left. Infants were often used in research within their first weeks of life. Too young to be anesthetized, or perhaps because anesthesia was unnecessary, they were taken to the lab, where their arms and legs were held tightly by the staff to keep them from moving while blood was drawn or biopsies performed. The infants stayed in the nursery until they were toddlers, considered old enough to be moved to an 8' × 8' × 10' cage in which two or three adult chimps or a combination of adults and toddlers lived. These concrete cages contained, at most, a tire and a metal hammock.

⊡⊡ ⊡⊡ ⊡⊡

After our exhausting five weeks of work, the chimpanzees on the islands were receiving fresh fruit and vegetables, nuts, and supplemental vitamin balls every day. Land vehicles and boats had been repaired, ensuring regular delivery of food and other provisions. The chimps could now drink water any time they wished, thanks to repaired water systems. In addition, a birth control regimen had been put in place, and basic veterinary procedures established. The chimps gradually gained weight and became stronger. The most profound change was in their behavior—they were acting like chimpanzees again. It was exciting to have participated in making so many improvements in the lives of these chimpanzees over such a short period of time.

When our five weeks ended, it was time to return to Kenya, where our dog Princess, friends, sun, and sea awaited us. We still had in our care two orphan chimps, Guey and Sweet Pea, who had been taken from illegal captive situations and given to us by an expat upon our arrival. We had agreed to help these two young chimps get out of Liberia because there was no sanctuary in the country that could care for them. So before leaving for Kenya, we hired temporary caregivers for them, vowing to get them to a sanctuary somewhere else. We were profoundly aware that Guey and Sweet Pea's situation reflected a crisis facing all chimpanzees in Liberia.

In November 2015, six months after our arrival in Liberia to work with the former NYBC chimps, Jimmy, Princess, and I moved there permanently. Our experience with the former NYBC chimps made it impossible for us to not return even though we knew it would be a difficult path. Not long after our arrival, we discovered a chimpanzee named Portea, who had been rescued by the same expat who had rescued Guey and Sweet Pea. Despite having few resources, no accommodations for Portea, or any plan in place for her future, we took her into our care, joining Guey and Sweet Pea, who had not been moved to a sanctuary outside Liberia. It was now clear that we needed to help not only the former NYBC research chimpanzees but all the chimpanzees in Liberia.

About a year later Jimmy and I flew back to the United States to present a proposal to HSUS. We were already contracted with them to help the NYBC chimpanzees but wanted to go a step further and help all Liberian chimpanzees in need. We proposed establishing a sanctuary not only for the island chimps but for Guey, Sweet Pea, Portea, and others like them. At first, HSUS enthusiastically agreed, knowing that despite being a massive undertaking, it was the right thing to do and, with their help and resources, was feasible. HSUS ultimately decided to stay focused on the former NYBC research chimpanzees, which terrified us since we had already taken in many orphan chimpanzees. Nevertheless, we regrouped and, in November 2015, established

Orphaned chimps are coming to our sanctuary faster than we are able to keep up.

Figure 24. Ella at the police station before rescue

a sanctuary on our own called Liberia Chimpanzee Rescue & Protection (LCRP), in Charlesville, about one and a half hours from the capital city of Monrovia. We envisioned it as a model sanctuary that could be replicated throughout Liberia and beyond. We reached out for guidance; in response, an impressive network of individuals and organizations around the world provided the moral support we needed.

As a result of this commitment, our lives have changed dramatically over the past few years. Currently, we care for forty-four chimpanzees—with many more orphans likely to arrive—who are victims of Liberia's illegal bushmeat and pet trades, as well as international wildlife trafficking networks. Realizing the need to build the chimpanzees a proper home to secure their futures, we recently purchased a long-term renewable lease for approximately one hundred forested acres in a semi-wild environment not far from Monrovia, near the Farmington River in Liberia's Marshall Wetlands, a landscape targeted for protected status.

Liberia has the second largest population of western chimpanzees *(Pan troglodytes verus)* and the largest tracts of connected forests remaining in West Africa, extending to Sierra Leone to the west, Guinea to the north, and Côte d'Ivoire to the east. But chimpanzees in Liberia are critically endangered due to habitat destruction, the sale of their meat for consumption, and local and international trade of infants. Orphaned chimps are coming to our sanctuary faster than we are able to keep up, reflecting the magnitude of this tragic situation.

While our focus is on chimpanzees, we recognize them as ambassadors for all wildlife and conservation efforts. With this in mind, we helped launch a Law Enforcement Task Force that includes local and international wildlife protection and conservation organizations. In less than two years, the group has grown from a small coalition to a large and diverse collaborative force. International wildlife trafficking, animal protection, chimpanzee welfare, and conservation groups have already shown great interest in supporting these initiatives.

As a result, our sanctuary is now one of the primary driving forces for chimpanzee protection and conservation in Liberia. Its presence has enabled the government to better enforce existing wildlife protection laws leading to over twenty confiscations of chimpanzees from illegal sources in a two-year period. Prior to the existence of the sanctuary, Liberia's Forestry Development Authority, charged with protecting the nation's wildlife, would not confiscate illegally held chimpanzees and consequently allowed illegal hunting, killing, trading, and trafficking. The sanctuary and the establishment of the Law Enforcement Task Force have positively impacted chimpanzees and other species in Liberia. And we will continue to help ensure that the estimated seven thousand wild chimpanzees living in Liberia's forests stay there.

All the chimpanzees who come to us are traumatized, and many exhibit behaviors typical of post-traumatic stress disorder (PTSD), such as rocking, sucking their thumbs or fingers, pacing, and other repetitive behaviors that may never completely disappear. It takes a great deal of love and attention to help these chimpanzees recover; and while most of them do, we have to face the reality that some can't be saved. Michael came to us when he was very small and sick. He smiled and played but never fully recovered from the physical trauma he had endured. Months later he suddenly developed fluid in his lungs and, within hours, died in my arms.

LCRP's other orphaned chimpanzees share similar stories—the killing of their mothers and other family members for bushmeat, being kidnapped and sold—but the ways they end up with us vary. Gola, given to us in August 2016, not only witnessed the murder of her mother and family but watched the poacher chop up her mother's dead body and was then carried off in one of his arms, with her dead mother's body in the other. Sadly, the ranger who rescued Gola was not in uniform or accompanied or armed, and so was unable to make any arrests. Gola was the youngest infant I had ever had in my care, and I was terrified that I lacked sufficient skills to properly care for an infant so small she could fit in my hand. However, Gola, despite her fear, shock, and trauma, not only survived but thrived.

Young chimpanzees naturally cling to their mothers at all times and if separated will scream because they are terrified to be left behind or alone. Sadly, the way Mira's captors stopped her from following them was by chaining her up. While a chimpanzee infant will cry and scream for the first few days of this kind of confinement, eventually, like a human child, Mira would have given up—and lost hope of getting the nurturing she so desperately wanted. Our first encounter with Mira was seeing a photograph, sent anonymously by a local expatriate that showed her sitting behind a house with a heavy chain around her neck, the other end attached to an iron stake embedded in concrete. It took us three weeks to organize the right team to confiscate her, hoping in the meantime she would not be sold to someone else or moved to a new location. Once the plan was in place, I accompanied wildlife authorities and the police to the town where she was being kept. The ranger with whom we were working went ahead of us to find her exact location and then left someone there to stall the "owners," came back to where we were waiting, and said we had to hurry.

Figure 25. Gola giggling

My adrenaline was pumping as we drove up to the house, and when I caught sight of Mira I immediately jumped out of the truck and greeted her in chimp language. She leapt into my arms, squeezing me so tightly I later had bruises. I hugged her back and, with tears streaming down my face, whispered that she would be leaving with me that day and never be chained again. There were a lot of people crowded around us, some laughing, some shocked that Mira was sitting in my lap, and some tossing candy to see if she would leave me. The family had the key to the lock attached to the iron stake but had tellingly lost the key to the lock around Mira's neck, so we had to take her with the heavy chain still hanging from her neck. When officials arrived at the home of Mira's captor, only his wife was there, so they charged her with illegal possession of a protected animal. The rescue was chaotic, and the woman was not arrested, due to

Figure 26. Jenny meeting Mira on the day of her rescue

the complexities of the system. (In response to the forty-four confiscated chimpanzees brought into our care, only two perpetrators have been formally charged; however, a groundbreaking action this year ended with the first-ever successful prosecution of a chimpanzee trafficker in Liberia.)

Once back at the sanctuary, we had to use a hacksaw to remove the ten-pound chain, but Mira stayed very still throughout the long and stressful process. When the chain fell off, it felt as if a massive weight had been lifted from us all. Mira climbed down from my arms, moved around a little, then came back into my arms. She looked into my eyes, and I said, "Mira, you can go wherever you want." Then the day's fear, sadness, shock, anger, and frustration all melted away as she began swinging from place to place, climbing trees, and running with joy.

Maintaining hope for the recovery of these extremely traumatized chimpanzees supports our efforts. An orphan named Connie arrived with a broken wrist and a broken spirit. It was clear he had an immense fear of humans as he wouldn't let anyone touch him. He also wouldn't take food or water, which meant we couldn't give him medication to help ease the pain of his injured wrist. He lay on a mattress and blanket in the living room for hours, not daring to sleep. I felt a profound sadness, wondering if he could ever recover from such a traumatized state. I knew that to help Connie I would have to not only maintain hope myself but also work hard to help Connie find hope. On the first day, he began to move around just a bit, glancing toward us then drinking a sip of juice. When he felt comfortable enough, he moved a little closer. He ate a piece of a grape after I took a bite and gave the rest to him. He spent three days lying on the mattress or the couch, rarely sitting up or moving, and drinking and eating just enough to survive. But on the fourth day we knew we were gaining his trust after he sat up and began to eat, although I still had to eat first to get him to do the same. We learned to interact with him only when he engaged with us first, and let him do his own thing when he didn't. Then, one day when Connie was investigating the living room while we worked on our computers, he walked toward one of the rope swings in the house, stopped, and lightly stomped his foot, a sign that he wanted to play. Jimmy and I looked at each other and at the same time said, "Did you see that?" It was a very good day.

Supporting our recovery efforts, the local community has begun helping us rescue chimpanzees in need. For instance, not long ago a young Liberian man named Joseph, who works near our home, came to see me and said, "I have something to show you about a chimpanzee." He then showed me a video of an adult chimpanzee barely visible inside a small metal cage. It was clear the chimp had never been taken out and the cage had never been cleaned. The people who were keeping her told Joseph they didn't want her anymore because she was mean and they planned to sell her for food or as a pet. Joseph informed them that it was wrong to keep a chimp in a cage, to eat a chimp, and to sell a chimp, and that they must talk to us because this chimp needed to come to our sanctuary. Amazingly, someone who two months ago might never have noticed or cared that it was not okay to keep, kill, eat, or sell a chimpanzee had come to alert me about a chimp in distress, along with a solution—a remarkable sign that things are, in fact, changing.

Great change has also occurred among caregivers, many of whom have undergone life-changing transformations since our arrival. The caregivers who stayed with the chimps abandoned by NYBC, and had previously participated in darting them and assisting during invasive procedures, are now feeding and nurturing them on the islands or caring for the traumatized orphans at our sanctuary. Many say that through this work they have found personal redemption.

My life with the chimpanzees has taught me first and foremost that it is possible to survive against all odds; that broken trust is not a life sentence; and that, while it may not be possible to forget trauma, one can choose to *forgive* it. I have learned, too, that grief and sorrow transcend all differences between species; that love and kindness can help overcome suffering; and that gratitude and appreciation can open the door to joy where once it could not be found. Perhaps the greatest lesson I have learned from my chimpanzee family is that saving another's life can help save your own.

I am now part of the fabric of this beautiful country of Liberia, with its courageous people. While I continue to care for orphan chimpanzees who come into our home and sanctuary, I never stop wishing they were still with their true families in the forest and that my role was not necessary. And though I live with the sadness of knowing this is not the case, I dream of a day when our baby chimpanzees can form their own makeshift families, like Matooke did, but, instead of spending their lives in a sanctuary, can be reintroduced into a safe yet wild world, to live as they were meant to live—starting families, embarking on adventures, and creating memories together. Hope, which miraculously can pop up even in the darkest moments, just might help us realize this dream.

Hand in Hand: Remembering Rhett

Jacqueline Stewart

Rhett died after I left the lab. So much happened while I was there and so many chimps died after I left that I don't remember exactly when he passed away, but Rhett himself remains clear in my mind, including the moment when I first saw his bruised face—the moment that changed everything for Rhett and for me.

Rhett was a male chimpanzee who lived in a social group at a primate research center that conducted biomedical, cognitive, and behavioral research on nonhuman primates—monkeys and chimps, in particular. On the surface, the area where I worked seemed pretty benign. Most of the monkeys there lived in social groups. A little more than half of the chimpanzees who lived there were members of social groups that each had about a quarter of an acre of outdoor space, as well as indoor housing. The remainder of the chimpanzees lived in indoor/outdoor concrete runs. Such living conditions might be considered acceptable in a sanctuary, but no sanctuary would do the sorts of things that went on behind the scenes there: taking infants from their mothers, separating individuals from their families to conduct experiments, removing all or part of internal organs.

There was another area of the laboratory that I only entered occasionally, where the invasive biomedical research was conducted. The hundreds of monkeys in this area primarily lived alone in rows of tiny cages. The chimpanzees resided in barren two-hundred-square-foot concrete runs with no bedding, very little enrichment, and few toys. When members of the media or the public were invited to see the facility, they weren't allowed, to my knowledge, in the biomedical research area. It's my belief that visitors were never permitted to see what went on behind closed doors in that section because conditions there were far worse than in areas where the monkeys and apes were socially housed.

My experience in the lab changed my view of the rights of all beings—for the better. While a university student studying biology and primate behavior, I had concluded it must be necessary to use rats, mice, monkeys, dogs, and other nonhuman species in biomedical research to make advances in human medicine. I assumed these individuals were well cared for, believing researchers would not treat their subjects badly if they were trying to collect data from them. Having enjoyed a zookeeper internship while in college, I sought out a position in a primate research facility so that I could provide excellent care to monkeys and was hired as an entry-level animal care technician.

My first hint that things were not all that they seemed came when one of my supervisors talked about disciplining monkeys. There were several social groups of macaques, and the male macaques were particularly protective of their children. They would sometimes stand up to humans if they felt a baby in their group was being threatened. Disciplining the monkeys involved netting a male monkey who attempted to protect his group and dragging him around the compound to instill fear of humans. I never witnessed this being done, and I do not believe that it's a practice engaged in now, but it clearly had been not long before I arrived. I was stunned, and troubled, by this revelation. I had great respect for our fellow primates and would not have wanted to do anything to harm them.

Another practice that disturbed me was taking baby monkeys away from their mothers for research on the day they were born. The technicians would stick them in a light-tight black box and send them to the area where all the hard-core biomedical research was done. The babies were then fitted with prisms, contact lenses, or goggles to manipulate their sight and the input of light into their eyes to see how it affected eye development.

The lead investigator for this study presented findings that presumably indicated the importance of this work: there was a high incidence of nearsightedness in children in Thailand. The logic of his reasoning escaped me. I am nearsighted, and I have treatment for it. I thought that perhaps the money being spent on manipulating the vision of baby monkeys would have been better spent on providing eyeglasses for children in Thailand.

Malaria was one of the diseases studied in the chimps, whose spleens were removed before infecting them with the mosquito-borne disease. (Chimpanzees are resistant to malaria, but removing their spleens apparently eliminates the resistance.) The chimps were then sick for about a month, after which the researchers gave them medication to cure them of malaria. But the research had long-term consequences for the chimpanzees. For instance, a feisty female chimpanzee whom I loved and admired was traumatized by these procedures and, as a result, dug a deep hole in her side where her spleen had been. I never understood the point of this research as it was not conducted for purposes of finding a preventive or cure for malaria.

These are just a few examples of the troubling—and questionable—research that went on behind closed doors, all in the name of science and medical advancement. The more I learned about the research being done there and elsewhere, and the more I saw how the monkeys and chimpanzees really lived, the more I questioned it all. I was soon veering off the path of supporting biomedical research, having been completely derailed by the callous attitude of the powers that be at the research center.

Initially, I only worked with monkeys, and for a time I had no interest in working with apes. Then I met my first chimp and fell in love. I begged to work with them and nagged my supervisors until they gave in. I was thrilled to become one of their caregivers and quickly got to know their individual quirks, preferences, and unique personalities.

Rhett was a very quiet, mild-mannered male who tried to be friends with everybody. He was in a difficult position because the group's two other adult males were engaged in a power struggle at the time. Rhett, it seemed, was trying not to take sides or get caught in the middle. He was also kind to the females and, overall, a very nice, diplomatic chimp.

One day I noticed that Rhett's face, which was typically very light colored, appeared dark around his nose, as if he had a bruise. So began the saga of Rhett, which haunts me to this day.

I reported to the veterinary staff that Rhett had a bruised face, thinking that possibly he had been punched in the nose or had sustained some sort of injury, though nothing very dramatic. But then he would not eat his monkey chow (dried biscuits), the only staple food given to the chimps, along with one orange a day and food-based enrichment a few times a week. Rhett made food grunts and looked eagerly at the chow, seemingly hungry, but he wouldn't eat it. Chimps love to eat, so not eating raises alarm bells. Concerned that he would go hungry, I was pleased to discover that Rhett would eat his chow if I soaked it until it was soft. I suspected that there was something wrong with his teeth or jaw that made it painful for him to chew, and I reported this to the veterinary staff. Eventually, he was anesthetized and given a physical. It was discovered that he had liver problems. They never clearly explained the nature of his liver problems, and I didn't know the extent of his condition as I never saw the blood values or exam results. They just said there was something wrong with Rhett's liver that could affect his appetite.

The veterinarians decided to separate Rhett from his family to treat him. I was appalled by their decision because they had the capability to treat him in the building where he was living, so that he could at least hear and see his family. It was also a newer, well-heated building—an important consideration at that time of the year.

Overriding my objections, the veterinarians moved Rhett to a colder and draftier building in which he had never before lived, and put him in isolation. I was upset. Although I was just a care technician, in the past the veterinary staff had taken my input regarding the chimps' welfare into consideration. However, a new veterinarian had been hired, and the lead veterinarian, who was very restrictive and spent most of her time in the biomedical research section, had become more involved with the medical care of the monkeys and apes in the area where I worked. Neither of them appeared to value the input of care technicians, a fact that became increasingly clear as my struggle—and that of my fellow care technicians—to give Rhett proper care continued.

Rhett sat in his cage depressed, all alone, away from his family. We were not allowed to give the chimps blankets, but they could have burlap sacks, so I gave Rhett as many burlap sacks as possible. We also put a space heater in the building for added warmth. But he just sat there, dejected. Granted, he may have been feeling sick, but it was evident that this new location was not good for his well-being. And still he appeared hungry but would not eat hard chow, so I continued to soften it. Convinced by now that there might be something wrong with his jaw or teeth that made it painful for him to eat hard food, I asked the veterinary staff to take an X-ray.

He just very gently held my hand before pulling away. He had, at the very least, accepted me as a friend, but I was deficient in so many ways. I wasn't a chimp. Rhett needed his family.

The new veterinarian, who was also new to working with chimps, was upset with me for giving Rhett soft food and forbade it, only allowing me to give him hard biscuits, which went uneaten. When I questioned her instructions, she said that if Rhett didn't eat we would then have more information. I pointed out that we already had that information. Logic, however, was apparently not her strong suit. I did not follow her instructions and began sneaking in soft monkey chow, applesauce, and anything else soft I could get my hands on so that he would be able to eat. I wasn't about to let him go hungry, or watch him stare at food that he could not eat as hunger gnawed at him.

One day I was so distressed over Rhett that I crouched down in front of his cage and stuck my hand through the bars, holding it out to him. Rhett looked at my hand, then reached over without any enthusiasm and put his hand in mine. We sat there holding hands as I bawled. I had meant this gesture to be reassuring to him, but I felt that he had accepted my hand just to be polite or even to make me feel better in some way. I don't know if he derived any comfort from it. This experience was terribly sad but also amazing because Rhett did not bite me or become aggressive. He just very gently held my hand before pulling away. He had, at the very least, accepted me as a friend, but I was deficient in so many ways. I wasn't a chimp. Rhett needed his family.

I remained furious that the veterinarians were treating Rhett without any thought to his mental and physical well-being. During one of his follow-up physicals, they might have X-rayed his skull, but I'm not certain. I was cut out of his veterinary care and no longer allowed to give him his meds, which was unusual because the care technicians were always the ones to give the chimps their meds. One sympathetic veterinary technician told me what she could about Rhett's condition and treatment; the other veterinarians continued to be dismissive.

Finally, I filed a complaint with the Institutional Animal Care and Use Committee (IACUC) about Rhett's treatment. IACUCs are mandated at any institution receiving federal funding for animal research. Similar to institutional review boards (IRBs) that review human clinical trials, IACUCs are supposed to review all animal research protocols, prevent cruel and unnecessary research, and investigate complaints. The IACUC investigated the situation and found that there was no wrongdoing on the part of the veterinarians. The day I received their ruling they moved Rhett back to the original building to be near his family, claiming that he had recovered enough to go home, although nothing had changed in his health or demeanor during that period. He continued to stay separated from his group, but he was at least next to them, where he could interact with and even touch them—where I had wanted him to be treated in the first place. It's my belief, which may not be accurate, that someone with authority had determined that they weren't going to validate my complaint but did recognize that there was no reason not to treat Rhett in his home building. The coincidence of the findings and Rhett's move was certainly remarkable. Having gotten what I was looking for, I didn't push things further.

The complete lack of concern for Rhett's well-being has always stuck with me. I felt that pulling him from his family group had been unnecessary and forbidding his caregivers from giving him food that he would eat had been negligent and cruel. Sadly, it was not the first or the last time that chimps were treated like that during my employment at the research center.

The longer I worked in the lab, the less its operations made sense to me. I had an opportunity there to meet the chimps infected with HIV, who lived in an isolated area. To enter, I had to don a disposable coverall, mask, gloves, scratch-resistant sleeves, and a hood—basically a space suit—which was contrary to everything we knew about how HIV was transmitted and the work done by advocacy groups to get the public to stop fearing HIV-positive individuals. What I saw inside that building was something out of a horror film. The chimps were institutionalized, living indoors in dismal conditions with just a skinny window in each cage. I cannot even begin to describe the level of misery. One chimp showed no interest in life at all; the others clamored for anyone to notice them. Fortunately, the surviving chimps are now retired and living a much better existence at a sanctuary.

Then my epiphany: One day while hosing a cage I thought, "If some other species on this planet, or an alien species, tried to do to us what we're doing to these chimps and monkeys, we would be horrified and fight back. We would not find it ethical, or justified, to be imprisoned and experimented on even if it benefited the other species." And so I concluded that regardless of the justification for doing research, causing suffering was wrong, even in the name of alleviating suffering, which, frankly, did not seem to result from all these experiments. I began to expose what was going on behind closed doors and to speak out more within the confines of the lab. Of course, I was limited in what I could do; I had to be careful because I wanted to keep my job as an insider in order to get information.

Eventually, I left my position at the research center to pursue opportunities in the animal protection field. However, it was a struggle to decide if I should leave; I didn't want to abandon the chimps and monkeys because I feared that eventually there would be no one to watch out for them. Ultimately, I decided to change careers, recognizing that my ability to make a difference in the lives of the laboratory primates was limited and that I found some of the tasks I had to assist with morally reprehensible. It was time to move on and make a difference in the lives of other beings who had experienced the same suffering.

Rhett died of liver failure sometime after I departed. Despite the fact that a benign tumor was discovered on his liver, he lived much longer with his condition than anyone had predicted, as chimps often do. His final years were spent with his family, and he was never subjected to the harsh realities of biomedical research. Rhett had recovered the ability to chew hard food before I left, so I remain convinced that his liver problem had little to do with his bruised face and refusal to eat hard food. Regardless, he never should have had to experience the lack of empathy that is all too common in biomedical research labs. Fortunately for me, Rhett's own empathy did not waver as he held my hand.

A SANCTUARY OF MIRACLES

Patti Ragan

Establishing a great ape sanctuary was never my dream. Although I was always fascinated by great apes, as many people are, I never thought I could actually work with them. But a tiny four-week-old, four-pound orangutan infant named Pongo changed the course of my life.

During my careers as a schoolteacher and small business owner, I read everything I could about great apes and signed up to be a docent at our zoo in Miami. In 1984, I had an opportunity to volunteer with a group called Earthwatch and spent three life-changing weeks in Borneo at an orangutan rehabilitation project working with Dr. Biruté Galdikas, the world's leading authority on orangutans at that time. This led to a volunteer position the following year assisting on a long-term project tracking and observing wild orangutan behavior, as well as providing foster care for infant orangutans who needed rehabilitation to return to their forested homes.

My Borneo experience led to another opportunity: caring for Pongo, an infant orangutan who was living at a Miami tourist attraction. Pongo's mother was ill and could not nurse him, so I took this tiny orangutan and gave him round-the-clock care, as one would a human infant. After I had fostered Pongo for seven months, his owner told me that he planned to sell Pongo to a circus trainer. I was distraught. I had assumed Pongo would be returned to his mother or, because his owner was a zoo dealer, perhaps sent to an accredited zoo to grow up with other orangutans.

However, after appearing at a county fair for the tourist attraction, Pongo became very ill, and that changed everything. Over the course of several weeks, Pongo was examined, tested, and treated by pediatricians, neurologists, and veterinarians, who found that he had meningitis. As he had suffered high fevers and grand mal seizures for two weeks, his prognosis was grim. For fourteen days and nights, during which he had more than two hundred seizures, I held him close, trying to comfort him. Miraculously, Pongo survived, and his owner decided not to sell him to the circus trainer. Because of the care I had given Pogo through this difficult time, his owner said, "He's yours. You decide where he goes."

While I never imagined keeping Pongo personally, I did think I could find him a home in a zoo. But because he was considered a hybrid—a cross between Bornean and Sumatran orangutans—Pongo had little chance of being accepted by an accredited zoo at that time.

I searched for a sanctuary where Pongo might live. But in 1990 there were no true sanctuaries for orangutans and only one for chimpanzees. I kept thinking, "Someone should start an orangutan sanctuary," so I did it. A year later, when Pongo's former owner asked me to care for a twelve-week-old chimpanzee named Grub, my dream of an orangutan sanctuary materialized as the Center for Great Apes, a permanent sanctuary for orangutans and chimpanzees that is now located in Wauchula, Florida. Pongo, the catalyst for establishing the sanctuary, is today a handsome and healthy twenty-nine-year-old adult male weighing 240 pounds.

The Center for Great Apes encompasses 100 acres of orange groves and fields surrounding another 25 acres of lush green tropical woods where the apes' habitats are built. Eighteen large multistoried dome habitats are connected with over a mile and a half of treetop aerial trails so that the orangutans and chimpanzees can stroll through the woods when they choose to visit other groups or follow staff and visitors as they walk through the sanctuary. A creek runs through the forested property, and the primate residents can travel across the creek on the aerial trails to visit the veterinary clinic or watch through the windows while their meals are prepared in the nutrition center. Sixty-three rescued and retired orangutans and chimpanzees who had spent decades in the entertainment industry, research labs, or the exotic pet trade have found refuge at the center; nine chimpanzees and two orangutans subsequently passed on. The fifty-two remaining great apes continue to receive excellent nutrition, appropriate health care, enriching activities, tall spaces for climbing, and—most importantly—companionship with others of their own species.

My perspective on captive great apes has radically changed as my knowledge about their circumstances has grown. When I first began volunteering at the Miami tourist attraction, two of its baby orangutans were sold to a California trainer for use in movies and television shows in Hollywood. Not knowing anything at that time about the issues and challenges faced by captive great apes, my first thought was, "Oh, they're going to be famous and have a good life." But when I visited them a year later at their Los Angeles compound I was disappointed to learn that "working" apes have a short "shelf life." When infant chimpanzees become juveniles, they are not only vastly stronger than humans but very intelligent, willful beings with huge canine teeth. Their wild nature, coupled with their great strength, makes them capable of causing injury. Thus by the time they're seven or eight years old—still only juveniles in the great ape world—they are most often too dangerous to manage safely, and their Hollywood working days end. Today, the practice of using apes in entertainment has greatly declined due to computer graphic imaging (CGI) for movies and because of animal activists who have opposed the practice. Also, most private owners realize by the time their pet is six or seven years old that they cannot handle these apes.

By contrast, in the wild chimpanzee mothers raise their babies until they are eight or nine years old, nursing them for the first five or six years, during which time the babies acquire all the important behaviors of their species—communication, vocalization, and social gestures—knowledge vital for them as adults. Chimpanzees raised by humans, even chimps who are exceptionally well cared for, often have a difficult time integrating with their own species since they haven't learned how to deal with conflict or appropriately approach other apes.

The behavior of a young male chimpanzee named Chipper, whom we took in years ago, illustrates this predicament. Chipper had performed in a circus for the first ten years of his life. He had lived alone in a small cage and performed in several live routines a day, where he would go into the ring, do his comic shtick with the trainer, and then return to his small cage in the backstage area for the remainder of the day, with little or no chimpanzee companionship. This routine left Chipper in tremendous deprivation because chimpanzees are very social primates. In the wild they live in large communities of families, and everything they do—grooming, foraging for food, resting, and playing—is with others in their group. When Chipper arrived at our sanctuary, he was afraid of the other chimpanzees. Sixteen years later he has learned a lot but still has issues in his group, not knowing how to settle disputes and unsuccessfully challenging larger males because he never learned the importance of having females as backup. When enjoying apes in shows, the general public is not aware of how the apes' beginnings with humans affect the rest of their lives.

Another issue is what happens to them when they can't perform anymore. Sadly, pet owners and animal trainers rarely have a long-term future planned for their chimps, although today, with ten chimpanzee sanctuaries in North America, the fortunate ones end up in sanctuary care.

Most businesses that use chimpanzees for ads rarely, if ever, provide anything toward their future care. Many former entertainment apes in the United States have appeared on television shows; in advertisements, including Super Bowl ads; and in mainstream movies. Everyone involved with these ventures made money—well, *almost* everyone. The animals who performed made nothing. While the government may have funded sanctuaries that care for former National Institutes of Health (NIH) research lab chimps, ad agencies and production companies do not fund sanctuaries for great apes coming from the entertainment field. And previous owners rarely have the money necessary to provide help for them.

There are still many aging chimpanzees in private homes who are in difficult situations. People ask us to take them, saying they will help care for them financially but not realizing how much it actually costs. Providing a sanctuary resident with veterinary care and medications, a nutritious diet of fresh produce and other foods vital to their health, daily enrichment, a safe and spacious habitat, and dedicated caregivers who keep the habitat clean adds up to over $20,000 a year. Chimpanzees from entertainment come to the sanctuary at age seven or eight because they can't work anymore. If they live to be fifty or sixty years old, a financial commitment upwards of $1 million per ape is required for their care.

Each chimpanzee who arrives at the Center for Great Apes has a special background and history. A few have emotional, physical, and psychological scars from years of solitary living, neglect, or abuse. Others have special needs, including teenaged Knuckles, who has cerebral palsy, and an elder female, Toddy, who has motor and neurological issues stemming from bullet fragments that had become lodged in her brain as a baby in Africa when her mother was shot and killed while holding her. We also have chimpanzees with talents ranging from painting to mask making. Some people believe primates paint representationally, but I think they just love the colors. They finger-paint or use brushes to paint the walls, the floor, or their feet. If we're lucky, sometimes they paint on a canvas that we can auction to raise money for the sanctuary.

In addition to artistic talents, some of the chimpanzees exhibit a talent for humor, clearly playing jokes on the others and on us. For example, sometimes when Grub heard the staff coming to open up his night house first thing in the morning, he would put a hat or blanket on his head; cover his eyes, pretending not to see anyone; and wait for the caregiver to exclaim, "Oh, there you are!" before excitedly jumping up and down because we had understood his joke. No matter what their challenges, needs, and talents might be, all the chimpanzees require a great deal of thoughtful, loving care. Following are profiles of some of our chimps, reflecting their histories, the sorts of activities in which they engage, and the range of care they receive at the Center for Great Apes.

DENYSE

Denyse arrived at our sanctuary in her mid-thirties. She had lived with a couple who kept her in a tiny cage in their backyard. They had not been able to handle her by the time she had turned about eight years old, so Denyse lived alone in her cage for nearly thirty years. Denyse came to us addicted to beer, cigarettes, and sugar. After the woman passed away, Denyse had lived with her human father, a man then in his eighties, who loved her but had a rather old-fashioned way of viewing a chimp as a pet. He fed her marshmallows, pizza, soda, and canned pie filling—a far cry from the balanced diet of fresh produce her body needed, so we had a tough time getting her to eat the food served at the sanctuary. He thought it was funny when Denyse smoked cigarettes and drank beer with him. We had to give her beer when she first arrived because we didn't want her to go through withdrawal. It took weeks to cut her consumption down until we were finally able to remove beer from her diet completely. Denyse became a healthy eater who loved natural fruit juices and water. Sadly, in March 2015, she passed away at age forty-six from kidney disease.

MARCO

Our eldest ape, Marco, came to the sanctuary in 2005 at age forty-six. Wild-caught in Africa in 1960, he had surely witnessed his mother and other family members being shot and killed when he was poached for the exotic pet trade. By the time he was two, Marco had been sent to a dealer in New York, who then sold him to a circus trainer.

I understood from his records that Marco was very tiny, had rickets, and had performed in a circus for about ten years, which is a long time to work a male chimpanzee. When the circus trainers decided to retire, they sold the other chimpanzees in their act but kept Marco because he was the youngest and the smallest. For the next thirty-five years he lived alone in a tiny cage in their South Carolina backyard and garage. Marco, like Denyse, had not seen another chimpanzee in decades.

Marco's owner had brought him from South Carolina to our Florida sanctuary in the back of an open pickup truck, inside his tiny cage, which was covered with plywood and hidden under a blue plastic tarp. When they arrived, I thought the box could certainly not contain an adult male chimpanzee because it was so small. But then out walked a pint-sized guy two feet tall and weighing only 79 pounds, the smallest adult male chimpanzee I had ever seen. (Most of our adult males weigh between 140 and 180 pounds.) With his silver back and square-shaped hips, he looked more like a miniature gorilla.

"

By the time he was two, Marco had been sent to a dealer in New York, who then sold him to a circus trainer.

Figure 27. Marco

We first introduced Marco to a few of the chimpanzees at the sanctuary, but he was afraid of them because they were so big. Then we introduced Marco to Butch, a chimpanzee about ten years younger who had also been captured in Africa. Butch had performed in the Ringling Brothers Circus for more than a decade, had later spent two years in biomedical research at the Coulston Foundation, and then was moved around to several Florida roadside zoos for the next thirteen years before being retired to our sanctuary. When introduced for the first time, Marco and Butch briefly hugged but then kept apart from each other for the next two weeks though in the same habitat. Every day one of them would stay at the top of the domed enclosure and the other at the bottom. I began to think this combination was not going to work.

Then one day a group of neighborhood ladies in their seventies and eighties came for a brief tour of the sanctuary. As we walked them around a corner toward Marco and Butch's area, both boys let out loud yells and alarm barks. Suddenly, Butch scooted down the ladder from the top of the forty-two-foot dome, and they ran into each other's arms, hugging and comforting each other. Immediately, they began to groom each other's eyes, noses, teeth, arms, feet, and bottoms. Since that day over ten years ago, Marco and Butch have been inseparable. Whatever it was that had frightened them—perhaps the white hair on so many ladies—had the immediate effect of bringing them together. As best friends, they go outside together in the morning and come back in together at night, often waiting until the other one is ready. Marco, now in his late fifties, will hopefully live at least another decade. It's wonderful to see this once solitary chimpanzee enjoying companionship with his friend Butch.

GRUB

Grub, the first chimpanzee to come to the sanctuary, was a wonderful artist. He not only painted but also made masks, which he loved to see others wear. When Grub was about two years old, he lived in a tourist attraction that allowed children in costumes to come in for free during Halloween weekend. The masks and costumes frightened Grub, so the caregivers had the children take off their masks when they came into his area so he could see that they were people. Subsequently, Grub became very interested in masks.

One of the volunteers at the sanctuary brought him a few animal masks, which he liked but didn't wear, indicating that he wanted the volunteers to wear them instead.

Figure 28. Grub making one of his famous masks

Then one day someone brought a paper plate and showed Grub how to tear out eyes and a mouth so he could make his own mask. That was a turning point for Grub, who then started making masks. When he saw a new visitor, he loved to tear out eyes and a mouth from any piece of paper or cardboard box and give the mask to the visitor. At times, Grub's masks were elaborate with many holes, but usually there were two eyes and a mouth or nose hole. Grub never put a mask on himself but did sometimes make a mask to hold over the eyes of Knuckles, a young chimpanzee whom Grub played with occasionally. Nearly always he offered his creations to staff and volunteers. If he wanted to give someone the gift of a mask but didn't have any paper, he would find leaves in his environment and make a mask out of the foliage. Grub crafted a beautiful mask for Jane Goodall out of a red cereal box. I have never heard of another chimpanzee doing this and believe it was quite unique to Grub.

One day a caregiver showed Grub how to roll up a piece of paper and toot a sound through the homemade horn. From that day on, when not making masks Grub would roll any paper that he had and invite people to come hear him make raspberry sounds through it. Grub would then put his ear up to the mesh to hear others do the same. Tragically, our precious Grub died suddenly in 2011 from cancer, at age twenty, breaking our hearts.

KNUCKLES

Knuckles had been born in an entertainment compound in Los Angeles. Early on, realizing that something was wrong with him his trainers had taken him for a medical evaluation at UCLA, where it was determined that Knuckles had cerebral palsy. His trainers then worked with him for two years trying to help him gain some muscle control and motor ability, but Knuckles needed intensive round-the-clock care and frequent physical therapy. In 2002, we agreed to accept two-year-old Knuckles for care at the sanctuary. At the time, I wasn't aware of how disabled he was or what this commitment really entailed, what his needs would be, or even how long he would live. All I knew was that it was going to be a very emotional (and expensive) commitment.

Figure 29. Baby Knuckles receiving reassurance from Grub

When Knuckles arrived, he could sit up and take a few steps, having learned to walk a few months earlier. But his walking was unsteady and lopsided, and he fell over frequently. Knuckles didn't have the use of his left hand (and still doesn't) and was not able to feed himself, even with his right hand. When we sat Knuckles down, he would remain still for twenty minutes or more, unlike a normal two-year-old chimpanzee, who is already running, climbing, and swinging from tree branches. Knuckles's behavior and challenges were very much like those of a human affected with cerebral palsy. Physical therapists, as well as occupational therapists, from Miami, Tampa, Pensacola, and our neighboring towns of Wauchula and Sebring volunteered to help work with Knuckles, initially making great progress. Today, at age nineteen, Knuckles can feed himself and function to an extent. And, although he is able to walk where he wants to go, he moves very slowly and does not run or climb.

When Knuckles was a baby, we decided to introduce him to the chimpanzees in Grub's group—Grub, Noelle, Kenya, and Toddy. Grub, an even-tempered and gentle eleven-year-old at the time, was the dominant male in his group of females. His group was the best choice for Knuckles.

The first introduction was made with Knuckles outside Grub's habitat, where the others eagerly touched, tickled, kissed, and groomed this infant through the mesh. The next step was to take Knuckles inside the habitat to meet the chimpanzees individually, starting with Noelle, the youngest. Knuckles was so excited to meet them that he leapt, twirled, and tried to "play-bite" the older, bigger chimps. Chimpanzees normally play-bite, but Knuckles didn't know how to moderate his biting. I remember Noelle looking at me while trying to push Knuckles's head away from her because his play-bite was too hard. She didn't give up on Knuckles, but instead figured out how to jump all around him to keep him from biting her, and how to safely tickle and hold him.

When it was Grub's turn, we were a little apprehensive because he was so much bigger and stronger than Knuckles. We did their introduction inside the night house, thinking that if it proved to be too much for Knuckles there would be three doors to open and get him out quickly. There were also all kinds of treats on hand to encourage Grub to exit the room if he became too rough for Knuckles. As it turned out, because Knuckles was a baby, Grub was very sweet and gentle with his new friend. But with all Knuckles's exuberant play-biting, Grub was the first to want to leave the room and actually knocked on the door for the caregiver to open it.

Knuckles and Grub had many supervised interactions and play sessions over the years. One day, when Knuckles was about six years old and Grub fourteen, they were playing through the cage mesh when Grub put his finger inside Knuckles's mouth. Knuckles bit down hard on Grub's finger, breaking the skin. Knuckles wasn't being aggressive but likely thought chomping on Grub's finger was part of playing. Had it been any of the other chimps, Grub would have retaliated by chasing them around, screaming, and maybe even biting back. But when Knuckles bit him, Grub ran screaming to the other end of the habitat to show the caregiver his bleeding finger. We were going to remove Knuckles from Grub's area in case Grub decided to retaliate with a bite, but before we could get to him Grub ran back and started grooming Knuckles with total forgiveness.

The other chimpanzees in Grub's group were also gentle with Knuckles, treating him with special care. They seemed to be aware of his limitations and didn't roughhouse or treat him like they did each other. It's known that chimpanzees express empathy to other chimpanzees, and Grub's group clearly knew that Knuckles was different and special.

It surprises me when people ask why we've spent so much time with this handicapped ape. The answer is that our work is about animal welfare and care. While the sanctuary cannot save the whole species, we can work to make individual lives better. Knuckles has the right to live his life with dignity, and he is given as much care and love as the others.

TODDY

Toddy had been captured in Africa in the early 1970s the same way that Chipper, Marco, Butch, and, in fact, all great apes have been captured in the wild—by shooting the mother and other adults in the group since no mother would ever allow her infant to be taken from her. As an orphaned infant, Toddy was shipped out of Africa to be sold in the exotic pet trade for only three hundred dollars to a family in Naples, Florida. There she was raised as a human family member, sleeping in a crib and eating at the table.

At about age two, Toddy started having seizures, at which point the family who owned her drove her to be examined at the Auburn University Veterinary School in Georgia. X-rays showed that Toddy had bullet fragments in her head, which had almost certainly occurred when her mother was shot during her capture. The veterinarians at

Auburn surgically removed some of the lead fragments but had to leave others that they couldn't reach.

Toddy lived with her family for about seven years. But as she had grown older and begun to tear up things in the house, as would any active juvenile chimpanzee, her owners realized they could no longer keep Toddy as a pet. Upon giving her to a man who said he would keep her forever, they were sure they had found her a good home—but the man sold her right away. Toddy then had a succession of owners as she was sent first to a monkey attraction in Miami, next to a horse farm in Ocala, and then back to Miami to a private breeder/dealer of exotic animals.

There Toddy had several babies, who were all pulled from her and sold as pets or entertainers. She then gave birth to male twins, but because she didn't know how to properly care for them both babies rolled out of the enclosure and died on their first night. Later she became pregnant again; that baby was pulled from her right away and kept at a tourist attraction. Toddy had been so ill during the pregnancy that her owner and his veterinarian decided she needed a hysterectomy to avoid becoming pregnant again. After Toddy had the surgery, the other chimpanzees became more aggressive toward her, so Toddy was then separated and kept alone for several years in a small cage at the breeder's compound.

When Toddy arrived at the Center for Great Apes, she was in her late twenties. She came carrying a little stuffed gorilla, which was her constant companion. Toddy was introduced to our first three chimpanzees at the center—Grub (age seven), Kenya (age five), and Noelle (age three). Kenya was actually the last of Toddy's babies who had been taken from her, so I was especially eager to reunite mother and daughter, who had not seen each other since Kenya was only one day old.

We found Toddy to be a sweet and gentle chimpanzee but compromised physically. She wobbled and staggered a bit when walking, probably from arthritis as well as from nerve or brain damage due to the bullet fragments in her head. When Toddy groomed someone, she made a lip-smacking sound as chimpanzees normally do when grooming, but she drooled quite a bit and even accidentally spit on those she "talked" to.

After Toddy had been at the sanctuary for a few years, I received a phone call from a man who said, "I think you have my daughter." It was her first owner from Naples, Larry. He had lost track of Toddy but, by coincidence, had heard from one of his friends who had recently visited the sanctuary that there was a chimpanzee living here

Figure 30. Toddy

with bullet fragments in her head. Larry was teary as he told me about his life with Toddy. He had never wanted to let her go as Toddy was a part of his family, but because she had been so destructive in their house he had had to find her a new home. Larry reminisced about taking Toddy down to the corner Dairy Queen on his motorcycle three or four nights a week when she was young. He shared many stories about Toddy, and I was fascinated because I hadn't known much about Toddy's history with him.

Not long after his phone call Larry came to visit Toddy. We weren't sure if she would remember him because it had been more than twenty years since he had last seen her. When Larry arrived, at first Toddy just sat and stared at him. Then Larry moved closer to the mesh and said, "Toddy, it's Dad," and she jumped up and started to pant-hoot excitedly and clap her hands, so happy to see her old friend. She certainly remembered Larry and seemed ecstatic to see him again.

That day Larry spent a few hours with Toddy. We allowed him to groom with her and her with him—through the mesh. He asked her to make a funny face, and she did immediately, something he had taught her over twenty years before, which she remembered. He ran around the outside of the enclosure playing chase with Toddy, and she pant-hooted and happily drooled the entire time. Then Larry said, "Hey, Toddy, do you want to get a Dairy Queen?" Toddy stopped in her tracks and started food-barking. On his later visits, I would not let him say "Dairy Queen" unless we had some kind of iced treat for her.

I was touched when Larry gave a three-hundred-dollar donation to the sanctuary. It was the same amount he had paid for Toddy when he had bought her as an infant. He came to visit Toddy often during the first few years after their reunion, and he still visits to this day. Without fail, every time Larry walks across the bridge and says, "Hey, Toddy, it's Dad," she starts pant-hooting, excited to see him.

CLYDE

One of the center's most heart-wrenching rescues was that of Clyde, a wild-caught chimpanzee who had been captured in Africa in 1967 for the exotic pet trade. Clyde had been sold to a man who kept him for forty-five years in a tiny cage in his garage. During the first years when Clyde was young, his owner let him sit at the table to eat with him and his wife. He said that Clyde had even known how to set the table. The owner told us many stories about how he would dress Clyde up and take him out to nightclubs to

Figure 31.
Clyde in his garage
cage before rescue

surprise the patrons. Clyde would sit at a table and have a drink, often getting drunk. But as he aged and became more difficult to handle, he ended up in the garage.

When Clyde arrived at the sanctuary, we were shocked. A forty-five-year-old male chimp would normally have the dark face of an adult chimpanzee, but Clyde was still pale white all over his face and body—more like an infant chimp. Lacking exposure to sunlight, his skin had never turned a normal color. Clyde was also emaciated and covered with bed sores on every joint. Atrophied from sitting for decades in a tiny cage with no exercise, Clyde could barely walk and could not vertically climb. We had to install wooden staircases going up to the shelves so he could easily gain access. While holding food in his hand, he shook so much that it was difficult for him to eat.

Clyde spent the first two months at the sanctuary curled up, sleeping in the sunshine most of the day. When we opened the elevated aerial chutes for him to walk out and explore the forested sanctuary grounds, he was terrified at the open door and barked at it for two weeks. When Clyde finally ventured out onto the aerial trails, he walked unsteadily for about thirty feet then came back to his area to lie down and rest. Each week he ventured slightly farther until one day he crossed over the creek, but when he realized there was water underneath him he didn't want to cross over it again, so he sat down and alarm-barked at the creek.

In the first two years following Clyde's arrival at the Center for Great Apes, he gained weight, his skin darkened to a normal color, and his overall health improved, as did his social life. His first encounters with chimpanzees since being a baby in Africa were tentative. After slowly introducing Clyde to a few of the young females here, we noticed that he seemed uninterested as they were livelier and rowdier than he could cope with. Then we had the idea to introduce him to Toddy. Even though Toddy was now in a group with Kenya, Noelle, and two males named Brooks and Mowgli, she seemed to miss Grub a great deal after his passing and also was having difficulty keeping up with the youngsters and their energetic play. So a chimpanzee "date" was planned for Clyde and Toddy.

Their first meeting was traumatic. Toddy was friendly and eager to meet the new fellow, but Clyde was frightened and nervous around her, screaming continually in her face and aggressively attempting to grab her feet. I was disappointed because, of all the chimpanzees at the center, Toddy was the most socially experienced and gentle. We decided to give it one more try. The next day when we opened the doors between them, Clyde ran over to Toddy, touched her, and chimp-laughed. In fact, that day he couldn't keep his hands off her, touching her head, back, and arm and holding her hands.

Figure 32. Clyde grooming Toddy, his first chimpanzee companion since being taken from his mother in Africa

For the next few years, Clyde and Toddy were the "it" couple at the sanctuary. They played chase at a slow and careful pace and, after the exertion, would lie down together to nap. They spent their days sitting together with Toddy grooming Clyde, who became very protective of her. Watching these two elderly wild-caught chimpanzees who had withstood so much in their lives find peace and companionship with each other was like witnessing a miracle.

Regrettably, Clyde passed away in November 2015 at age fifty, after a struggle with both liver and kidney disease. Toddy was with Clyde on the day he died and kissed him gently on the face while saying her goodbye. Toddy passed away a year and a half later, at age forty-five, from congestive heart failure. We take great comfort in knowing that Clyde and Toddy enjoyed their final years at the center to the fullest.

Chimpanzees like Denyse, Marco, Grub, Knuckles, Toddy, and Clyde, each with their own history and challenges, have required individualized care at the sanctuary. Even thirty-six-year-old Bubbles, who once lived with the famous pop musician Michael Jackson until Bubbles, at age six, became too big to handle, has required special care to adjust to living a more natural life as a chimpanzee. And today, as the dominant male in his group of seven chimpanzees, he has made that adjustment.

Thirty years ago it was acceptable to think of chimpanzees as funny little clowns in show business or as surrogate babies in families where they were kept as pets. Today, though, it's known that being raised by humans does not give chimpanzees the skills they need to live successfully with other chimpanzees, even in captivity. It's also known that the chimpanzees seen in movies and advertising are infants and juveniles with only a short time to work but with decades ahead as large, strong adults who cannot live with, or work around, humans.

Although the chimpanzee sanctuary movement is relatively new, it's a hopeful development for captive chimpanzees, providing permanent care and refuge for great apes once used in entertainment, research, or kept as pets. At sanctuaries, chimpanzees who once endured dire conditions have the opportunity to live with respect and dignity. Small miracles happen every day at the Center for Great Apes.

The Goma Five

John Debenham, PhD, DVM

DECEMBER 4, 2006

The roar of the military aircraft seems unable to budge the butterflies nestled into the wall of my stomach. It is my nineteenth birthday today as I fly alone into the Democratic Republic of the Congo (DRC). Aboard the United Nations aircraft destined for Goma are a few soldiers and UN officials. I am the only one not in uniform. The humidity hangs like a hot stench, gluing my new khaki shirt to my chest. It is surreal to think about what has happened over the past twelve months. I finished high school, started university, deferred university, backpacked around Europe, and now I am on my way into the heart of Africa. It's amazing what can result from a childhood dream, a few optimistic e-mails, and a moment of spontaneity. For the next three months I will be a volunteer working at a chimpanzee halfway house in Goma supported by the Jane Goodall Institute, the Centre de Rehabilitation des Primates de Lwiro (CRPL), and the Pole Pole Foundation, a local NGO. The halfway house was set up as a temporary solution to accommodate five orphaned chimpanzees and provide the essential love, shelter, and nutrition they need. My imagination has run wild for five months trying to imagine what the halfway house, Goma, the people, and the chimpanzees will be like.

Flying at a low altitude enables me to see the dense blanket of green forest covering the mountainous terrain, with scattered towns connected by long stretches of red earth road. Goma sits sandwiched between the northern shore of Lake Kivu and the Varunga jungle. Built on a bed of volcanic rock with the active Mount Nyiragongo just ten kilometers north, the city is a place of great contrasts. Grand buildings remain untouched since the Belgian rule; high-rise towers cluster together as proof of the city's recent growth; and, stranger yet, newly constructed UN airfields and barracks sit like islands in a sea of sprawling shantytowns. Surrounding Goma is the Varunga jungle, home to one of the most biodiverse rainforest ecosystems in the world, and the Interahamwe Militia, a Hutu paramilitary organization that was a prominent force in the 1994 Rwandan genocide. In just one hundred days, the Hutus massacred over half a million Rwandan Tutsis. Their plainclothes "uniforms" made it impossible to identify, let alone persecute, them. They were allowed entry into many of the refugee camps in the neighboring countries of Tanzania and what was then Zaire, now the DRC. Other militia subsets of the Interahamwe filtered into the surrounding forests from where they still raid local villages.

I do not speak Swahili or Lingala, the two major local languages, but due to the history of French and Belgian rule most Congolese speak French. Armed with a book on how to teach yourself French, I'm sure this will be the easiest language for me to learn. Luckily, the two volunteers with whom I will be living—Tessa Wiggins, from the UK, and Nicole Geller, from Germany—speak English, as do the workers, who speak very basic English.

JANUARY 1, 2007

My work here is not just a part of my life; it *is* my life. The halfway house is a small three-bedroom cottage with a white perimeter wall topped with some old barbed wire. Apart from five hairy chimpanzees and three tired, committed volunteers, the house looks no different from our neighbors' homes, where well-off Congolese or people working for other NGOs reside. Nicole, Tessa, and I, with the aid of local workers, are caring for all five chimpanzees.

JANUARY 6, 2007

At 6:00 a.m., a fine mist is rolling off the lake and the sun has begun to touch the treetops. The chimpanzees are already awake and begin to pant-hoot as I approach them. Shege, our oldest chimpanzee, around six or seven years old, is always the first out the door in the morning, hitting the ground running with grunts of excitement, clearly celebrating the end of the night's confinement. Shege has a greater love of food than any person I have ever met. She sits and watches, almost in a trance, as the morning food is prepared.

I love watching Shege grow increasingly excited, her mind unable to control her limbs, when she realizes the food preparation is almost complete. She often shakes her hand impatiently while making a lip noise similar to a trumpet player. Early on I learned that in the chimp world that translates into "I want what you have." When the breakfast preparation is complete, Shege snatches her share of the food in all four hands and awkwardly climbs the nearest tree, eating and grunting with sheer delight.

For our three-year-old Etaito, a thuggish wimp of a male, morning means a chance to run around stomping his little frame. In his mind, he is asserting his authority and displaying his role as alpha male, though in reality a simple stern word can make him cry and want to be hugged and comforted—not the behavior of a typical alpha male. Etaito's dominance display makes me want to pick him up and cuddle him rather than run with fear.

Figure 33. Little Etaito waiting to be picked up for a cuddle

"

Sadly, we know little of the chimpanzees' histories. Many of the files were "lost" during the chimpanzees' journey to the halfway house.

Figure 34. Above: Kanabiro
Figure 35. Left: Yonguesa

Figure 36. Gari taking a play break

Three-year-old Kanabiro, the sweetheart of the group, hates the separation from the caregivers that night brings. Morning means that she can be held and comforted again. I love to hug Kanabiro because she squeezes my body with her little arms, showing me that she, too, enjoys a little cuddle.

Yonguesa, also three years old, at times wants to be embraced by a caregiver but often she seeks solitude. I try to comfort her during these times, but she moves away. I always wonder what she is feeling and whether she remembers her past life in the wild, her mother, or her capture.

For Gari, our youngest chimpanzee at age two, whose little potbelly and carefree approach to life has earned him the nickname "little Buddha," tickles and play are always first and foremost in his morning routine.

Sadly, we know little of the chimpanzees' histories. Many of the files were "lost" during the chimpanzees' journey to the halfway house. I do know that Shege got her name from the Swahili word *shege,* which means "street child." She was found caged on the side of a street, most likely waiting to be sold into the illegal pet trade. Gari received his name from his rescue location, crammed as he was inside a tiny cage in the boot of a car; *gari* means "car" in Swahili. All five chimps are victims of the commercial bushmeat and exotic pet trades.

What upsets me most about the commercial bushmeat and exotic pet trades are the monstrous violations to animals and the tragic waste of so many lives. Following an explosion in logging and mining across central Africa, large-scale commercial poaching is now threatening the last pockets of undisturbed primate populations living deep within the jungles. Poachers, heavily armed with modern weaponry and a strong commercial drive, have no concern for ecological balance or sustainability, making this practice a far cry from traditional subsistence hunting. For instance, to bring one baby chimpanzee to sale at the market many adult chimpanzees from the baby's family are killed. The infant is caged—sometimes next to the dead mother, who is to be sold for bushmeat—and fed bananas while the poacher attempts to locate a buyer, though baby chimpanzees do not eat bananas. Separation leaves the baby chimp in shock because chimps that young need twenty-four-hour physical contact with their mothers. If a buyer is not found, or the authorities do not confiscate the infant in a timely manner, the chimp will starve to death. If the baby chimp survives this entire ordeal—lucky enough to be confiscated and transferred to a sanctuary with trained personnel to receive proper veterinary treatment—the psychological trauma is difficult to treat and can leave scars into adulthood.

Chimpanzees are intelligent, conscious beings who feel emotions as intensely as we do. They are capable of complex problem-solving and abstract thinking. They are able to remember large amounts of information as they interact in their world. How can humans let these magnificent animals come to such a miserable end? I have formed bonds with chimpanzees that are similar to those I've formed with humans—relationships filled with mutual care, fun, humor, adventure, and conflict. How can we treat individuals so like us with such drastic double standards?

JANUARY 19, 2007

I spend each day lost in play, with more time in the treetops than on the ground. My body is covered with cuts and bruises, small sacrifices for the opportunity to experience the chimp world. The more I am involved in their world, the more I experience how similar the chimpanzee world is to ours: on the surface it seems very different, but, in reality, it closely resembles ours. Playing with the chimps reminds me of childhood times when friends and I used our imaginations to invent games comprehensible only to us, such as variations of hide-and-seek, tag, and tug-of-war—some of the games I play with Shege. In one game we love, we both hold on to a low-lying branch of a tree with two hands and then use our feet to try to pull the other from the tree. We wrap our legs around the other's waist and transfer our weight onto each other, still making sure we have hold of the tree. My strength certainly is no competition for Shege's incredible

Figure 37. Shege waiting for another game high in the tree

strength. I guess life in the trees gives you an iron grasp. As expected, Shege is usually the victor. Although I do occasionally have an odd win, I wonder if these results have more to do with sympathy than skill.

During such everyday interactions, I marvel at the so-called human characteristics displayed by the five Goma chimps. Lying in the fork of a tree one day with little Kanabiro sitting in my lap, I noticed her looking at a recent cut on my leg, still red and sore. The manner in which she gently positioned her body to ensure she did not bump it, and the way she softly touched around it with her fingers, making soft grooming noises, was considerate and sympathetic. In such moments, I recognize that the relationship I have with each individual chimp mirrors what I share with my human friends.

JANUARY 28, 2007

Etaito is beginning to get sick. He is displaying unusual behaviors, especially not wanting to leave the side of Balume, his favorite local caregiver, who has spent the longest time with the chimps. Behavioral changes are also noticeable in the other four chimps, who do not know what's wrong with Etaito and are very inquisitive about why he is behaving so bizarrely. Etaito is no longer climbing the trees; he is just sitting back and watching as the rest of the group tumbles in the sand. No longer humoring us with his attempted displays of authority, he is seeking solace from the caregivers and does not interact with his young chimp friends anymore. In the eyes of Nicole, Tessa, and I, the chimps are like adopted children, and we are all beginning to worry about Etaito's health.

JANUARY 29, 2007

Over the last twenty-four hours, Etaito's condition has worsened. All movement and signs of hunger have ceased. Any slight knock to his neck causes him intense pain. Sitting with Etaito in my lap, I listen to his whimpers. Watching his facial expressions and his body hunched in distress makes me feel sick to my stomach.

I have not been able to do anything for Etaito, but the veterinarians from the Mountain Gorilla Veterinary Project (MGVP) probably can. By chance, they are close to Goma on their journey to Congo Brazzaville, where an Ebola outbreak had been reported in a population of wild western lowland gorillas. Connections with the Dian Fossey Foundation enabled us to contact them and recruit their expertise.

Figure 38. Left: Etaito seeking solace from a caregiver
Figure 39. Right: John and Etaito waiting for the Mountain Gorilla veterinarians

Using my bed as an operating table, they anesthetize Etaito and begin a hurried examination, taking blood, recording body temperature, listening to his heart, and monitoring his breathing. Nicole and Tessa exchange worried glances with me as our beloved Etaito is transformed into a patient. The veterinarians suspect he has meningitis, an inflammation of the membranes that cover the brain and spinal cord. Since it's commonly lethal and potentially contagious, quarantine is the only option while we await confirmation from the lab, which, we are told, will take several days. My limited experience in Africa has taught me that a few days could mean any length of time—a few hours to several weeks.

In the meantime, Etaito is given a general antibiotic, which could be effective if the inflammation has been caused by a bacteria. Etaito needs to be with people he loves, so isolation is not an option. Nicole, Tessa, the three local workers, and I have not received a meningitis vaccination. The veterinarians say a meningitis vaccination is similar to the meningococcal vaccine I received in Australia, which would provide me with enough protection. It is decided that I will be quarantined with Etaito.

Without delay, my room is transformed from a place of rest to an isolation cell complete with a bleach footbath at the door—an attempt to keep the other chimps from becoming contaminated. Adding to the sense of imprisonment are the heavy metal bars covering all the glass windows, an unfortunate security necessity in Goma. Etaito and I are now living in a tiny room with a double bed, a small bedside table I made out of wire and sticks, and an attached en suite bathroom.

Etaito stirs from his sleep and gazes around the room with a bewildered expression on his face, still clouded by the analgesic. Looking up at me, he winces from pain then raises his arms, a gesture for me to pick him up. I feel his small limbs tighten around my torso. It is comforting to feel the life energy that had been drained from his body return. I embrace him and slowly lower myself onto the bed, but such slight movements cause Etaito a great deal of pain. His little body resting on mine, I begin to fear the worst. Through the night, he drifts in and out of sleep, clenching my chest with a vicelike grip whenever he moves because the pain is so intense.

Three times a day Nicole or Tessa slide food, drink, and medicine through a slit in the door, opening it just enough to get their hands through and let me grasp these small necessities—fruit and milk for Etaito, rice and vegetables for me. I struggle to convince Etaito to take his medication, mixing it with honey, sugar, anything to ensure that it goes down.

Soon the room has an acrid odor of urine. The bed is wet with Etaito's excretions, an environment forcing us to seek comfort in each other. What a surreal feeling I have when I think about my situation—nineteen years old, just out of a private Sydney school, and isolated with a baby chimpanzee in the DRC—not your usual out-of-school experience.

JANUARY 30, 2007

As the sun's rays filter through the window on our second morning together, they bring with them bad news. Etaito has worsened during the night and is now hardly able to move his body. Needing to use the bathroom, I try to gently roll him off my chest. Awakening from his sleep, Etaito thinks that I am leaving him alone and gives me a look of both shock and fear that freezes me in my tracks. As I continue to rise, he screams in pain and throws himself back into my arms. I hug him so closely that tears well in my eyes. How could he know I only intended to walk a short five meters to the bathroom? He trusts me, and from his perspective I have tried to betray this trust. I promise myself I will never again make such a foolish mistake. I vow, unashamed, that I will take Etaito to the toilet with me on subsequent visits, as normal social pleasantries seem irrelevant given the situation.

For the remainder of the day, we lie in bed together, exhaustion allowing Etaito moments of sleep. As Etaito straddles the edge between life and death, the prospect of losing him brings home how much he actually means to me. Unable to understand what is happening in his little body, I feel trapped because there is nothing I can do to alter the progression of his illness. Like most people feel when watching someone they love suffer, I am worried, and at times in despair, as this innocent little chimpanzee seems to be fading away.

JANUARY 31, 2007

Much to everyone's relief, especially mine, Etaito appears to have slightly improved; though there aren't huge changes in his behavior, there are subtle changes in his face that give us hope. We had all noticed at the start of Etaito's illness that he had a dull, blank, pale look on his face, which reminded me of my grandpa's face as he lay in the hospital after having a stroke that ended up taking his life. Now Etaito's color and his usual expressions are returning.

As Etaito's recovery progresses, we enter into the second phase of our time together. Etaito is beginning to spend less time in my arms or lying on the bed, and more time sitting up or looking out the window at chimps playing. The first two days I had struggled to convince him to eat thin slivers of mangoes and pineapple, his favorite foods; now he eats more and no longer needs to be coaxed to take his medicine. As a result, the gloom that has been hanging over the halfway house starts to lift.

FEBRUARY 15, 2007

The chimpanzees are being moved. Recently, Nicole got word from GOAL, a UK-based humanitarian NGO, that it would support us in moving the chimpanzees south to the Centre de Rehabilitation des Primates de Lwiro (CRPL), at the site of an old Belgian research facility that still has twenty-three chimpanzees once used as research animals. The organization has room on its plane for five chimpanzees in their cages, as well as for Carmen Vidal, the manager and veterinarian from Lwiro, and Balume, the head caregiver. Nicole, Tessa, and I will fly on a UN helicopter and meet them in Lwiro.

Entrusted to the NGOs that established the halfway house, the facility at Lwiro is to become a fully equipped chimpanzee sanctuary. This project has much potential because the land borders Kahuzi-Biega National Park, making future release of chimpanzees possible. I wonder if Etaito, Gari, Yonguesa, Kanabiro, and Shege could really be wild one day and if they could join the troop already at Lwiro and learn how to be real chimps again. For their sakes, I hope so.

Despite this hopeful outlook for the chimpanzees, they are in for a scary and challenging period as their entire world changes. To make this transition as easy for them as possible, they will be kept together and gradually introduced to the existing infant group at Lwiro. While I know they are heading toward a better life, with more trees to climb and fellow chimps to play with, I can't help but feel anxious about how it will all play out, a bit like a parent sending a child off to school for the first time. For now, there's still a room full of food and a few more days to play together up in the trees.

※ ※ ※

SEPTEMBER 2015

Since my time as a volunteer at the halfway house in Goma, life has gone on for me and the Goma chimps. They arrived safely at the Centre de Rehabilitation des Primates de Lwiro in 2007. Sadly, a few weeks after I left Africa Etaito's meningitis came back, and this time he was not able to recover. The news of his death brought back the emotions I had felt the night we lay together when he faced death's door with me at his side. I will always remember little Etaito's displays each morning and how he tried to use boldness and aggression to mask his fear.

As for the other Goma chimps, Shege was too old to stay with the infants and so was initially moved to a group of similarly aged juveniles, where her gentle and playful nature made it easy for her to fit in; the rest were kept together as the Goma Group. Yonguesa grew rapidly and soon became the most dominant of them; Gari developed a reputation for being extremely intelligent and cheeky; Kanabiro, with her gentle heart, became good friends with a chimp named Muhungu, and they still remain close today.

Similarly aged chimps were gradually added to the Goma Group, and now there are sixteen members.

Thanks to the incredible efforts of the Lwiro team and its international support, these unique individuals now live in a large society of infant, juvenile, and adult chimps. They spend their days playing in the trees, in the enclosed forest they call home. Living in circumstances that closely resemble the life of a wild chimpanzee society, the Goma chimps are free from harm, as they deserve to be.

The Centre de Rehabilitation des Primates de Lwiro currently cares for sixty chimpanzees and seventy-five monkeys. It is the only wildlife sanctuary in the region, and, due to its location just outside UNESCO's Kahuzi-Biega National Park, it is the ideal venue for great ape health, law enforcement, and conservation programs. Over the past eight years, many new enclosures have been built for the chimpanzees and monkeys, and some large fenced-in forested areas have greatly improved the welfare of the animals. In addition, education initiatives, such as Roots & Shoots, have been working closely with local schools and community groups to teach people about the environment and wildlife conservation.

It was Etaito who had shown me the amazing relationship that can form between a human and a chimpanzee. If someone had tried to explain to me before I went to the DRC just how close humans and chimps are, I would not have believed them. It's one thing to learn how we share 98 percent of our DNA with chimpanzees or how our species, *Homo sapiens,* is grouped taxonomically with other great apes. However, it's another thing to have personal experience open your eyes to just how similar we are. During the five days Etaito and I were quarantined together, the boundaries separating our species began to blur—he and I seemed to no longer be chimpanzee and caregiver but two beings sharing an experience. The manner in which I interacted with Etaito is the same manner in which we interact with humans: being responsive to mood and paying close attention to body language, facial expressions, vocalizations, and actions.

I will never forget the hours of play in the sun with my five Goma friends. I experienced a genuine heart connection with each of them that will forever be imprinted on my soul. I have no doubt that my path will lead me back to Lwiro and the Goma chimpanzees. My only thought is, will they remember me?

A THIN LINE: FADING BOUNDARIES BETWEEN APES AND HUMANS

Rosa Garriga, PhD, DVM

As a veterinarian, I have always had a great interest in wildlife health and working with wild animals in their countries of origin. After finishing my master's degree studies in London, I explored opportunities to work in the field. I accepted a six-month volunteer position through the Orangutan Foundation UK, run by Mrs. Ashley Leiman, at the Orangutan Foundation International's rehabilitation center for orangutans in Kalimantan, Indonesia. The Orangutan Care Center and Quarantine (OCCQ), located in Pasir Panjang near Pangkalan Bun in central Kalimantan, was established in 1998 by Dr. Biruté Galdikas, founder and president of the Orangutan Foundation International. When I arrived at the OCCQ in 1999, there were about 140 orphaned orangutans, and when I left in 2004 there were close to 300. The situation is much more serious now—the number of orphaned orangutans has more than doubled.

Because I was working with over a hundred staff members and only the manager and one biologist spoke English at that time, I had to learn Bahasa Indonesian, the country language. I trained Indonesian veterinarians, veterinary nurses, and laboratory technicians, and together we set up a medical facility that included a quarantine area, an operating room, a laboratory to run samples, and a space for medical procedures. I found the work to be challenging but wonderfully rewarding. Six months turned into almost five years. Working with the Dayaks, the indigenous people of Kalimantan, I learned to be more humble, have more patience, and be cheerful in spite of misfortune. It was an amazing period of my life.

It did not take me long to realize how exceptional orangutans are. They're quiet, resilient, very patient, and free of the anxiety that chimpanzees exhibit. They learn fast and wait for the right time to show their smarts. Orangutans are famous in the zoo world for their subtle and precise escapism techniques. I remember one day when Kristin, a female orangutan, used a branch she had previously brought back from the nursery forest to fish for a bunch of keys that were hanging on the opposite wall. She not only found the key for her own cage door but also opened two more cages. She and her pals were found in the morning roaming the premises, and with some persuasion were brought back to their cages.

When it was time to move on in 2004, I reluctantly returned to my hometown of Barcelona. Shortly thereafter I traveled across Central America for several months and did volunteer work at a wildlife rescue center in Guatemala. During that time a friend told me about a six-month volunteer opportunity for a veterinarian to work with chimpanzees at the Tacugama Chimpanzee Sanctuary in Sierra Leone. Sierra Leone was home to the western chimpanzee (*Pan troglodytes verus*), who faced a number of serious threats, including habitat loss, hunting, and retaliation as a result of resource competition with humans. I thought it would be more useful to spend my time helping these chimpanzees than to wait in Barcelona for the perfect wildlife veterinarian paid job. And, as one of my childhood dreams was to go to Africa I decided to take the position. This time six months turned into fourteen years. I lived at the sanctuary in Sierra Leone for five years and, since then, have been traveling back and forth between Europe and Africa, working at the sanctuary for months at a time.

Tacugama Chimpanzee Sanctuary is the only national organization working actively, and persistently, to conserve wild chimpanzees across the country. Located on forty hectares of government-allotted land in the Western Area Peninsular National Park, half an hour from Freetown, the capital of Sierra Leone, the sanctuary was started, and is still run, by Bala Amarasekaran, a former accountant who opened it in 1995 with seven chimpanzees. Presently there are about eighty chimpanzees living at Tacugama.

Ninety percent of them came to the sanctuary at a very young age, between one and three years old. They are all orphans, the result of the bushmeat trade—their mothers having been hunted for meat and they themselves sold or kept as pets. When chimpanzees arrive at the sanctuary, they are quarantined for three months to make sure they are healthy before being introduced to other chimpanzees. They spend the quarantine period in individual cages to make sure they are not carrying human pathogens, like tuberculosis, that could later be transmitted to the rest of the chimpanzee population, causing an epidemic. When the quarantine period is over, they are introduced into small social groups, which gain members as new chimps arrive at the sanctuary. As the chimpanzees grow older and the groups get bigger, the chimps are moved to larger forested enclosures, where they spend the day, returning to their dormitories in the evening through connecting tunnels.

Our policy is to avoid human contact as much as possible to decrease habituation to humans and promote the chimps' natural behavior. The seven large forest enclosures, ranging from two to five acres, provide a natural environment where the chimpanzees can learn all the skills needed to survive in the wild. However, the enclosures are not big enough to sustain them, so we provide supplementary food like seasonal fruits and vegetables several times a day. We have been struggling for many years to build additional enclosures to accommodate all the chimpanzees joining the sanctuary family and finally secured the funding in 2013 to build two additional large enclosures. Tacugama is working toward finding secure and adequate habitats to hopefully reintroduce rehabilitated chimpanzees back into the wild.

During my years at Tacugama, I have worked not only as a veterinarian but also as a manager and keeper because we were understaffed. I was stunned when I first began to work with the chimps. Orangutans are quiet, sweet, easy to handle, and are very good patients when sick. Most of the time I could do medical procedures like drawing blood, injecting medication, and cleaning wounds without the use of anesthetics. It was quite a different experience attending medically to the chimpanzees. Early on I had to sedate Marcel, a three-year-old chimp, and asked the staff to hold him so I could hand inject him and avoid the stress of darting. The staff did not say anything, but their faces reflected astonishment as they struggled to hold him still. Marcel continued to fight back, but I was able to quickly inject the drug. Immediately afterward Marcel started fiercely barking at me and tried to bite me. I realized in that moment how strong and determined chimps are at a very early age. From that day on, I used a blowpipe to dart the drugs at a safe distance for the sake of the staff, the chimps, and myself.

Many chimpanzees arrive at Tacugama wounded or sick, though all the chimpanzees arrive emotionally traumatized and in a state of shock, having seen their mothers and other family members killed before being taken away from their families and natural habitats to a usually hostile human environment, tied to ropes and chains, and badly fed. It's heartbreaking to witness their profound suffering. We help them recover, both physically and emotionally, with the assistance of our caring staff. Mama Posseh, the head of quarantine, gives the chimps a lot of daily love, treating them as if they were her own children. She feeds them, washes them, plays with them, and keeps a close eye on them constantly. All the new chimpanzees end up loving her, and because of that love they gain self-confidence and eventually recover from their traumatic pasts. The medical room is next to the quarantine section, and it's always wonderful to hear Mama Posseh softly singing songs while cleaning cages, which has a relaxing effect on the chimps and on me.

Chimpanzees are exceptionally passionate—screaming, playing, crying, stealing, hitting, fighting—and talk a lot. You can communicate with them if you learn their language, gestures, and signs. Many chimpanzees understand English words because they were raised by expatriates, and the boundaries between us and them are generally blurred. Although chimpanzees are their own species, they are like humans in many ways. I have learned a great deal about desirable and effective human behavior by watching chimpanzees educate their offspring—take loving care of their children, solve problems, use politics in their groups, and show empathy.

Female chimpanzees play an important role in the dynamics of a group. Male alpha leaders know that keeping a good relationship with the females will help them stay on top of the social scale. In the wild, each individual in a group has a family role; just as important as the mother figures are the sisters, brothers, aunties, and uncles. It is wonderful to see chimpanzees adopt such roles in their groups, where all members are orphans with no blood ties. Some of our females adopt young orphan infants as their own children, caring for and protecting them; and females of lesser rank also take turns caring for the new infants. Males play with and tease youngsters and often carry them on their backs. Some adult males even adopt youngsters as their protégées. The group ties grow as strong as they would in a wild chimpanzee family.

All the chimpanzees love and admire Bala, who understands them well. They unquestionably know that he is the leader. In the beginning, I thought it was because he raised and cared for the chimps and so they adored and respected him as one of them. But with every new arrival, and therefore no previous contact with Bala, I watch their enthusiastic pant-hoot reactions to him. I have never seen this initial response to any of the other staff at the sanctuary.

I had already been living at Tacugama for a while when I read *Next of Kin* by Roger Fouts, a book that describes the relationships between a young scientist and captive chimpanzees, especially one named Washoe. My understanding of, and relationship with, the chimpanzees was significantly changed by reading this remarkable book. Roger Fouts, one of the first people to pioneer communication with chimpanzees through the use of American Sign Language (ASL), discovered that chimpanzees think, feel, and have a lot to say. The book made me realize that I had not really understood chimpanzees and had been arrogant for thinking I was smarter than them. Subsequently, I began to look at chimpanzees differently. I talked to them more. I genuinely paid attention to what they were doing and communicating. When they stoned me or barked and screamed at me, I knew I was doing something wrong.

Now not a single day goes by when I am not surprised by the expressiveness and intelligence of these sentient beings. One such experience happened with Julie, the second chimpanzee Bala had rescued more than twenty years ago, leading to the establishment of the sanctuary a few years later. I have to anesthetize most of the chimpanzees to do their health screenings and vaccinations, and Julie is one of the hardest chimpanzees to anesthetize because she is aware of what is going to happen and she lets us know. Chimpanzees are always in groups, and when it is time to anesthetize one we have to separate them, which the chimps do not like. The first time I isolated Julie, she was extremely stressed and tried to figure out a way to avoid the procedure, including begging me not to dart her. She looked me straight in the eye and extended her hand toward me with her palm up and a telling expression on her face that, without a doubt, was saying, "Don't do it. Don't do it."

Figure 40. Julie

The second time I had to anaesthetize her, before even showing Julie the blowpipe I explained how much less stressful it would be if she'd let me inject her quickly this one time without having to chase her around with a blowpipe. I had a syringe with the anesthetics in my hand. (I can trick some chimps and hand inject really fast before they realize what has happened.) Julie sat very still listening to me talk, then amazingly she turned around and presented her bum to me, keeping that position until I injected her. She completely understood that the hand injection was far easier than being chased with a blowpipe.

Unfortunately, in 2013 Julie got sick, and despite all the efforts undertaken to cure her she died. I was not there at the time, but I cried when I heard the news. Before passing away, she was in a comatose state for several days. Bala spent endless hours by her side, caring for her and talking to her. He told me that even though Julie was unconscious he felt she could hear him because she would emit a soft hoot each time he left her side. Julie's death deeply impacted all of us.

❧ ❧ ❧

Sierra Leone went through a civil war that lasted more than ten years, ending in 2001. The country is peaceful now but still one of the poorest in the world. Although the Sierra Leone government passed a law in 1972 prohibiting the killing, selling, keeping, and eating of chimpanzees, most people living in the provinces are not aware of this law and continue to hunt and trade them.

The hunting of bushmeat, which includes chimpanzees, is an enormous problem in Sierra Leone and other African countries. Besides being an important part of the indigenous diet as a protein source, bushmeat holds powerful medicinal properties according to the traditional beliefs of many tribes. For instance, it is believed that if a woman eats chimpanzee meat while pregnant her baby will be strong. Nowadays people hunt bushmeat not only to eat but also to sell to private consumers and restaurants in Africa and elsewhere around the world.

Such a demand for bushmeat poses huge problems for the future of wildlife. Because chimpanzee babies are too small to be eaten, they are sold as pets—after having watched their mothers and other family members being killed, leaving them severely traumatized. Some people keep the babies, tying them to a small rope and treating them as they would a chicken or a cow, while others take them to Freetown to sell. It usually doesn't take long before the staff at Tacugama is notified because we are well known and respected in Freetown. Once the call comes in, we either send the police or go ourselves to talk to the sellers, who are told that it is illegal to sell chimpanzees and they will be fined or go to prison. Most often they hand over the chimp, but sometimes we need the police to convince them. We always invite the sellers or owners of pet chimps to visit the sanctuary so we can sensitize them to the plight of chimpanzees and their need to survive. Usually such visits have a positive impact on sellers and owners, which then helps spread the word to their families and friends.

Sometimes expatriates come across a baby chimp for sale and are tricked into buying the baby because they are told this will prevent the baby from being killed. But people should never buy chimpanzees or any other wild animals as it just promotes further hunting and trading.

When I was at Tacugama in February 2012, a three-year-old chimpanzee who had been caught by poachers was discovered. According to an eyewitness, a person was carrying a big bag through a village, and there was a lot of noise and movement coming from the bag. Someone saw the moving bag and contacted the police, who found a young chimpanzee stuffed inside. A South African miner who witnessed the exchange between the police and the person with the bag told them about our sanctuary and that chimpanzees are protected by law. They phoned us, and shortly thereafter the miner delivered the baby to us.

We named the baby Nico. He was very wild, covered with wounds from machete blades, and his right arm was cut to the bone, the flesh barely holding on. He had probably received the wounds when his mother was killed. Nico was so terrified that it was only possible to touch him when he was under anesthesia. I had to anesthetize him almost every day for several weeks to treat him. It was heartbreaking for me because Nico was scared of humans and I had to continually dart him so he could get well. If

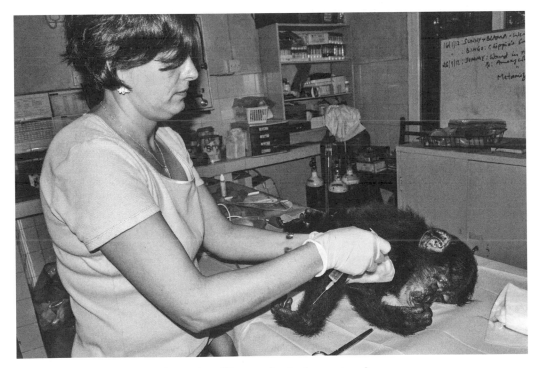

Figure 41. Rosa treating the lacerations Nico sustained when captured

Figure 42. Nico recovering after the surgery to fix his broken arm

I had not done this, he would have lost his arm or died from the infected wounds. We wanted to avoid that and do everything possible so Nico could climb trees again.

Our hope was that as he grew, the bone would restructure itself, but it never did, despite the fact that he was able to use his arm as if it were not broken. He needed surgery to fix the bone with plates and screws. The Sierra Leone medical infrastructure is very basic, with no access to modern equipment or specialized doctors, so we sent an appeal to Tacugama supporters and friends to see if we could secure enough funding to bring an orthopedic veterinary surgeon to Sierra Leone to operate on Nico. Finally, in the early months of 2014, Nico received the long-awaited surgery on his arm. He recovered well and, soon after, joined his chimpanzee group.

⁂ ⁂ ⁂

People often ask me if chimpanzees have empathy and feel compassion. After working with them, I definitely believe that chimps can be altruistic and caring. Generally, chimps mind their own business; if they don't have something to gain, they don't help others. But one day at the sanctuary I witnessed an extraordinary incident in which a chimpanzee assisted fellow chimps. I was in the office when I heard the chimps shouting, and ran out to see what was happening. We had put some provisional electric wire in a small area within their enclosure to keep them away from a space where we were working. The staff had left the wire longer than needed, and the newly grown grass on that spot had become irresistible to the chimps. Kouze, our handy inventor chimp who is always thinking of things to do that no other chimp would and is very good at using any resource as a tool, took action. Kouze had discovered that wooden sticks could be used to touch the electric fence without getting a shock, and had used them to pull the wires down and cross into the small grassy spot. Other chimps in his group had learned this from him and were then able to cross into this area on their own. But when it was time to go back to the other side they got scared and screamed for help. Kouze came down from the trees to rescue them. He not only found a suitable piece of wood to pull the wires down so the chimps could cross but held the hands of the chimpanzees to help them. Kouze did not have to do this because he was not a dominant male, and in fact the alpha chimp, who did not venture to the other side, was throwing stones at him, but he nevertheless continued to help the other chimpanzees in need. Did Kouze's actions reflect empathy? I would definitely say yes.

On another occasion, I experienced a chimpanzee empathizing with me. When I was leaving Tacugama for Europe and saying goodbye to Mama Lucy, one of the most exceptional chimpanzees living in the sanctuary, I suddenly felt very sad at the thought of leaving and started to cry softly. Mama Lucy drew me toward the bars, gave me a tight hug, and patted my back, as if telling me it was fine, which made me cry even more. Then Mama Lucy took my hand and put it on top of her infant's head, letting me caress him, something she had previously prevented me from doing. Mama Lucy's eyes were fixed on mine as she watched me touch her son. There seemed to

Figure 43. Kouze figuring out what to do with a lock he had absconded with

Figure 44. Mama Lucy and her son Duncan looking out from their Tacugama enclosure

be nothing separating us at that moment. I felt Mama Lucy was showing me great kindness, empathizing with me because I was feeling sad.

Despite such moving responses from chimpanzees, they can also be mean and spiteful toward their own kind, as well as to humans. Naturally, wild chimpanzees will avoid humans, but captive chimpanzees have lost this fear and, with their enormous physical strength—four times that of adult humans—they are very dangerous. There have been many incidents around the world involving captive chimpanzees attacking and sometimes killing people, even one at Tacugama. In 2006, a group of thirty-one chimpanzees escaped from one of the enclosures, and, sadly, one person was killed and another badly injured. Adult chimpanzees have their own way of understanding and dealing with right and wrong. Humans keep them as pets or laboratory subjects, and then when accidents happen chimpanzees are blamed. Chimpanzees are wild animals and should not be kept as pets. Chimpanzees belong to the forest, where they have their own set of laws, their own culture.

Over the years, Tacugama has expanded its core work of law enforcement and rehabilitation of confiscated chimpanzees to include other important dimensions of chimpanzee conservation, including nationwide field surveys/assessments of wild chimpanzee populations, local environmental education, habitat conservation, and community outreach activities. Besides caring for the chimpanzee residents, the sanctuary runs an education and resource center that offers tours guided by our staff, so visitors, including local schoolchildren, can learn about the importance of protecting chimpanzees and the forests. Families rely on forests, where they gather wood, plants, and fruits; forests are also important for preventing landslides and maintaining water reserves that serve the local communities. It's important as well to educate children so they understand and appreciate the value of protecting chimpanzees.

We raised funds in 2009 to find out how many chimpanzees were left in Sierra Leone and precisely where they lived so we could implement strategies to protect the country's wild chimpanzee population. Results of the census revealed that approximately 5,500 wild chimpanzees still live in Sierra Leone, establishing it as one of West Africa's most important countries for chimpanzees. The census also showed that half of the chimpanzees live outside protected areas. Because their forest habitats are vanishing due to deforestation, charcoal production, and large-scale mining, chimpanzees are left in isolated forest pockets. To survive, the chimps have adapted to living close to farmlands and villages. We found some populated areas in Sierra Leone where human-chimpanzee conflicts need urgent attention because there the chimps are considered pests and retaliatory actions against them are common.

Armed with this knowledge, in 2011 Tacugama started a community outreach program. Since we could not work with the entire country, we began with areas where the conflicts between humans and chimpanzees were most pungent. We talked to farmers in the villages to find out what the wild chimpanzees were doing to their crops and how to achieve peaceful coexistence between the two parties. We set up cameras to document evidence of the animals present and used the opportunity to sensitize the farmers to the need for chimpanzee conservation. We have found that chimpanzees seem to have adapted well to living in human-modified environments and that they are not the main cause of crop losses; instead, other animals, like cane rats, are the main culprits.

Many of these poor communities are so remote that very few NGOs have reached them to help. So far we have been able to assist a few of the communities. We set up latrines so they would not contaminate the forest with fecal agents, which from a hygiene standpoint is not good for them or for the animals. We suggested cultivating alternative crops that chimps would not damage, such as rice—a staple food in Africa—instead of pineapple, and provided them with special rice seeds that could survive in the worst conditions, along with appropriate tools to farm it. We also gifted several pairs of goats to each village and brought in experts to explain how to raise them. In addition, we helped them set up goat farms with all the necessary materials to build goat shelters and create tree nurseries for reforestation. Of course, we also were able to offer preventative veterinary care. At the same time, we set up environmental workshops to teach each community how to protect its remaining forests and its animals, including chimpanzees. Finally, we showed educational films like *Forest of Hope,* filmed at Tacugama, and explained the similarities between chimpanzees and humans.

As a result of these efforts, we have seen a change of attitude toward chimpanzees in local communities. Recently, when one of the communities we worked with encountered a group of chimpanzees raiding their crops, community members shooed them away. One of the young chimpanzees got left behind and was captured, but instead of killing him, as they normally would have done, they built him a wooden cage, called to tell us they had captured a chimp, and asked us to come get him. It was wonderful that they didn't kill him, but we wanted them to understand that this youngster belonged in the forest with his wild chimpanzee family. They couldn't quite grasp that concept, so our field team went to their village to assist in taking this chimp to the area where he had been caught and release him back into the forest. We were happy to find out that the villagers had taken good care of this young chimpanzee. It showed us that educating and empowering local people in outlying communities works.

Currently, I am devoting my time and effort to protecting chimpanzees in their natural habitats because I want to prevent orphan chimpanzees from arriving at the sanctuary in the first place. When I am old, I would like to look back and feel that my life had purpose, that I pursued a life worth living. One person cannot change the world, but small gestures from many people can go a long way. I am fortunate because I am actually doing what I have always dreamed of doing: working with wildlife and helping, even if just a little, to protect endangered species from extinction.

A FAMILY OF STRANGERS

Nancy Megna

The moment my daughter was born I understood what other mothers have described—an instant love of the deepest nature, unconditional adoration, wonder, and a fierce sense of protectiveness. But what if I had been anesthetized then awakened to find my baby gone after a year of motherly love and vigilance, losing the infant despite my maternal devotion? What if I had seven babies taken from me in such a manner? How could I go on? Shockingly, such appalling exploitation is the cruel reality for many captive chimpanzee mothers, including Ursula.

I met Ursula at New York University's Laboratory for Experimental Medicine & Surgery in Primates (LEMSIP) in Sterling Forest, New York, long before I had my daughter. Born in the wild, Ursula had witnessed her mother and other family members being killed before she had been captured for enslavement in the biomedical research industry in the United States. Used primarily for breeding, Ursula had given birth to seven children—three sons and four daughters—over a period of twelve years. In the wild, where chimpanzee mothers spend an average of five years caring for each baby, investment in seven children would span thirty-five years. It was considered better to be a breeder chimp than a research chimp, who typically endured decades of invasive protocols. But as a mother myself I don't know which is the lesser evil. Unfortunately, Ursula had had to bear both, having been injected with hepatitis C so that she would become a carrier of the disease.

At LEMSIP breeders were allowed to keep their babies for the first year unless they or their babies had a health issue or they didn't know how to properly care for their babies. The mothers didn't live in natural family groups where they could observe and learn mothering skills from their immediate and extended family members; yet many of the LEMSIP mothers' maternal instincts helped them become great mothers, resulting in attachments that made it even more painful to have their infants taken away.

The babies were routinely taken away from their mothers about five times during their first year for at least half a day so the health of both mothers and babies could be closely monitored. None of the mothers gave up their infants willingly or tolerated examination of their babies, so the mothers had to be knocked down (anesthetized). When the little ones were passed back to them through a box attached to the cage door, the mothers would scream with relief. Once they had their babies in their arms, some mothers would scold the caregivers for having taken their babies away. When the infants were finally removed for good, their mothers would look in hopeful anticipation whenever their unit doors opened but otherwise remain depressed for long periods of time.

Figure 45. Newborn in the LEMSIP nursery for a medical checkup

The babies, once removed, were devastated. They didn't eat, play, or sleep much in the beginning. It took about two months before they "adjusted" to nursery life without their mothers. They were separated early because of protocol—the lab needed the young chimps to get accustomed to human handling and interaction because they would be dependent on humans for the rest of their lives in research.

Described by her caregivers as easygoing and never aggressive, Ursula had gotten along well with the other chimps at LEMSIP. She tended to have her babies after her due date, which inspired their names: Tardy, Late, Dali, Timely, Post, O'Soy, and Pozna—also known as Ch-445, Ch-569, Ch-572, Ch-586, Ch-687, Ch-618, and Ch-626. Ursula had raised her first five babies for one year before they were taken to the chimp nursery. She refused to mother her last two newborns—by then she knew the deal.

In spite of my strong opposition to biomedical research, I received encouragement from Jane Goodall, who had visited LEMSIP and recognized the need for extra helping hands and caring hearts. So for a year I volunteered with nurturing and nursery duties before taking a permanent position in the chimp nursery, where I worked as a mother figure for five years. During that time, I had the privilege of caring for five of Ursula's children, including her last two from birth.

There were only a few caregivers and a handful of volunteers to nurture thirty to forty-five young chimpanzees ranging in age from newborn to seven. Due to the limitations of the lab, we couldn't provide the one-on-one round-the-clock care that chimpanzee mothers in the wild give their babies for the first five years and thus could meet only a fraction of their needs. Much as we loved each of them, we were only human replacements, not their chimp mommies.

Up until my last two years at LEMSIP, it was thought that the offspring of hepatitis C–carrying chimps would themselves become carriers, so they were segregated from the rest of the babies in the nursery and given a separate kitchen but no playroom. As caregivers, we had to wear lab coats over our uniforms when working with them, and if they used a regular playroom it had to be hand-scrubbed with bleach afterward. Given the caregivers' tremendous workloads and time constraints, those young chimps didn't get out of their cages much once they outgrew a playpen or blankets on the floor in their kitchen. To offset their limited contact, I used to open their cage doors and give them hugs. I wore a vest with faux fur that enabled the babies to cling and have physical contact while I cleaned. About a year after Ursula's fifth baby came to the nursery,

Figure 46. Chimps cramped in a tiny 32" monkey cage, a size occasionally used in Junior Africa

researchers figured out that the offspring of hepatitis C–carrying mothers were not born carrying the disease, so those babies could finally play with the others.

As each of Ursula's children matured sufficiently to leave the nursery, at about age six they were moved to Junior Africa, the intermediate part of the adult chimp side of the compound, built of cinder block and concrete, windowless, and with stark white plastic walls and inhumanely small cages. The cages in Junior Africa were smaller than the adult cages, many of which were themselves smaller than required by law. Chimps usually remained in Junior Africa for several years.

The babies at LEMSIP, unlike those at many other labs, were exempt from most experiments but went to work as soon as they were transferred to Junior Africa, which meant regular knockdowns and physically invasive procedures. It was an incredibly stressful time for these young chimpanzees, who had no preparation for their ensuing life sentence of biomedical research. They were anesthetized in the nursery and moved—often without their cagemates—only to wake up to the shocking screams and other noises of Junior Africa, with male caregivers in place of their mommy figures. I often wondered if Ursula recognized the screams of any of her children as they were being subjected to knockdowns on the adult side, or if family members knew they were under the same roof, separated by classification, age, and experimental protocol. My experiences with Ursula's children forever changed my perspective on human-chimpanzee relationships, as expressed in the following anecdotes.

TARDY

Although I didn't have the privilege of knowing Tardy personally because he had already been moved to the adult side by the time I started work at the LEMSIP nursery, he was reportedly charming and well-liked by his caregivers. I remember seeing a decorative Christmas stocking in the nursery with his name on it, yet I knew that "Christmas" was over for him.

LATE

Volunteers weren't supposed to go into the nursery rooms of chimps carrying hepatitis, but one day when I was distributing treats in the regular nursery Late, a striking gorilla-like chimp, caught my eye. Knowing from the chimps' calls of excitement that I had delicacies, he begged to be included. As it was impossible to ignore him, I put on a lab coat and gave Late and his roommates Kool-Aid ice cubes. He was very happy to receive them, and me. I remember feeling awful about this big guy stuffed into a 32" monkey cage.

While working overtime one evening soon after being hired, I had to check on Late, who was by then in Junior Africa working alone on a hepatitis research experiment. He had had a liver biopsy that afternoon, and he kept scratching his shaved abdomen. I suppressed my shock at the contrast between Late's normally long velvety hair and his bald itchy abdomen. I wasn't accustomed to sticking my fingers in cages with big chimps who didn't know me, but I wanted to help him. Pressing his belly to the cage bars, Late let me apply lotion, while he made soft vocalizations, as if in appreciation. Overwhelmed with emotion, I held back tears and stayed in that moment of connection for some time.

Over a year later and still in hepatitis research in Junior Africa, Late was involved in a protocol that required him to be anesthetized for seventeen consecutive days. After the first week, the technician didn't need to dart Late with anesthesia anymore, as he

> "
>
> *The technician
> didn't need to dart
> Late with anesthesia
> anymore, as he
> simply surrendered
> his arm.*

*Figure 47.
Late in his adult
unit cage*

simply surrendered his arm, a behavior some adult chimps learned to avoid being shot a minimum of three times, the number usually required to administer enough anesthetic. The technician was overwhelmed with guilt and tears when Late showed such resignation, and as Late was going under, the technician opened the cage and caressed him.

Chimpanzees were scheduled for research, veterinary procedures, and cage changes daily, which meant technicians had to anesthetize them frequently. Sometimes a chimp would get hit in the wrong place with a dart, such as in the face or genital area, a traumatic experience for all the chimpanzees in the room, as well as for those who could hear the fearful screams from other buildings. The chimps being darted would have nowhere to hide and would be terrified, often losing bladder and bowel control. Once the anesthetic took effect, they would fall to the bottoms of their cages and be removed on a cart for the procedure. When they were put back in their cages still anaesthetized, their neighbors watched them flail around, often hallucinating and screaming. Chimps could easily get hurt from falling during such knockdowns, or from banging around in their cages during the recovery process. After being subjected to years of this, a veteran chimp could predict who was going to get knocked down on any day, based on whose food and water had been withheld in the morning. Tragically, during the hot summer months some of the chimps with no air conditioning in their units died as a result of heatstroke.

DALI

Dali and her best friend and cagemate O'Dell were crammed in a 32" monkey cage in the segregated area of the nursery and had already stopped coming out to play by the time I became a caregiver. They were always happy to receive whatever attention I gave them, whether it was tickling or a game of chase. Both three years old, Dali was petite compared to O'Dell and would cling to her whenever she got anxious. They helped each other survive. One day, while intermittently giving them kisses, playing, and mopping, I saw O'Dell's arms wrapped around Dali from behind as they stood rocking side to side—a stereotypical behavior that develops from the traumatic effects of institutionalization. In that moment, the brutal reality of their limited lives consumed me. I wanted to run out of the nursery screaming on their behalf, but I swallowed the scream and retained my happy facade so as not to abandon them.

Inevitably, the day came when Dali and O'Dell had to move over to the adult side. They were darted and given some strain of hepatitis. Dali woke up without O'Dell to hug and rock with. She had a peer in the next cage, but the hepatitis experiment didn't allow for the chimps to be housed together or to touch, so I went to comfort them as often as I could. Fragile to begin with, Dali was now so deeply traumatized that she didn't play or look at me for one year, although she did groom my uniform. I had been her mother figure for five years, and, in essence, I had abandoned her. Fortunately, about a year later she was happily reunited with O'Dell, and our relationship was mended.

TIMELY

Timely, a sweet, lovable, and fun chimpanzee, was much more outgoing and had more confidence than her siblings, thanks to the protection of her cagemate Mocha. Mocha and her siblings were feisty like their mother, Pudding. The similarity of family traits among related chimps, despite being separated, amazed me. As adolescence approached, Timely learned from Mocha how to spit water at us, a behavior common among chimps in captivity, and she was thrilled as her aim improved. Mocha and Timely, still segregated as the offspring of hepatitis C carriers, had limited playtime outside their cage, but it ended prematurely when Mocha started biting the staff. The chimps could continue to come out as long as they were "manageable," but once they started biting or refused to go back into their cages it was over. Though Mocha was exhibiting a perfectly natural response, we dreaded the unnatural consequences of her behavior. Despite the fact that Timely did not bite, we couldn't take her out of the cage without Mocha; as bonded nursery pairs, it was almost impossible for them to be physically separated while awake because they would scream inconsolably for

Figure 48. Timely in her Junior Africa cage

each other until they were reunited. As Mocha and Timely grew, so did their pent-up frustration at having to live in their illegally small cages.

The nursery just wasn't equipped to accommodate the chimps' expanding needs. We would group them in fours in the bigger (relatively speaking) nursery cages so they could be with each other, but with no personal space spats ensued, a reminder that these chimps lived in horribly unnatural conditions—worse than those of human prisoners, although they had committed no crime. I wondered how humans could expect them to be happy with nothing and keep their sanity. I would certainly lose mine if I were jammed into an equivalent space, such as a tiny bathroom stall, with nothing to do for decades. I was frustrated and angry because I was one of the people they counted on to help them, yet I was powerless to change anything and felt like a negligent foster parent. All I could do was be there, love them, and try to ease their misery.

When Timely began relentlessly spitting due to being bored and frustrated, it was clear that she had outgrown the nursery. I didn't want her to leave, but the choice was not mine. Every time I visited Timely on the adult side, she reverted to her toddlerhood behaviors, screaming hello with her belly pressed to the bars for hugs. She never spit at me again. It felt like her message was: "Please, if you take me back home I will be a good girl." The guilt I felt on a daily basis for a thousand reasons was insurmountable.

POST

Post was a beautiful baby with an angelic fair face and onyx eyes. He had been taken from Ursula when he was one, the same day Connor had been taken from his mother. They were put together in the nursery. Connor was the boss and Post the shy little boy. No longer labeled hepatitis carriers, Post and Connor were permitted to mingle with peers in the playrooms. Even while playing, Post was tender.

Our veterinarian, Dr. Mahoney, tried to wean babies in pairs so they would have each other as cagemates during the traumatic experience of losing their mothers. Though the baby chimps bonded with us, they became completely dependent upon, and inseparable from, their cagemates. To fill the void they had created, the researchers were essentially forcing babies to raise babies. But whenever I held Post, even after several years in the nursery, his imploring eyes and little fingers desperately clenching my uniform for reassurance told me that he needed a mother not a brother.

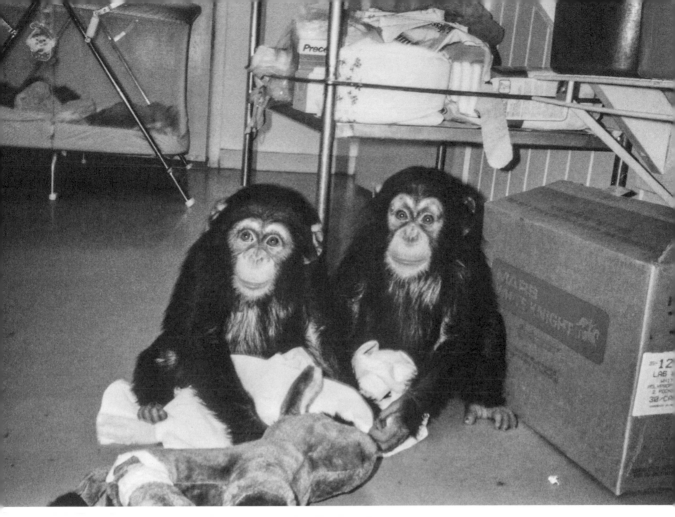

Figure 49. Post (left) and Connor (right) on the kitchen floor in the nursery

Babies who had no peer to be weaned with had even more emotional difficulty until being integrated into an existing peer group. That wasn't easy since new chimps always seemed to get picked on. Nursery babies had to be at least six months old before they could be introduced to peers. By that age, they would be able to move fast enough to avoid accidentally getting crushed or smothered by other young chimps. Being raised in the nursery from birth posed another set of challenges because newborn chimpanzees need to be kept warm and fed often. Dr. Mahoney let us take them home most nights to provide more of the love, care, and one-to-one contact so critical to their development. We didn't take the babies home for our own personal gain, knowing that chimpanzees are not domestic pets and should not live in people's homes.

O'SOY AND POZNA

We had to raise O'Soy and Pozna, Ursula's last two babies, from birth because Ursula refused to love and then lose her babies again. Looking at O'Soy's pleading eyes and irresistible face, we couldn't bear leaving her alone overnight in an incubator or playpen, so my co-worker Jenn and I alternated taking her home during much of her babyhood. Even though I was a primary caregiver and loved O'Soy beyond words, she really became Jenn's, because she was the first baby Jenn was permitted to take home; the first was always very special. O'Soy loved exploring our houses and pestering the pets before falling asleep in our beds, as all the babies did when they were at our homes.

As time went on, we noticed that O'Soy did not see herself as a chimp and didn't want much to do with them either. She did not want to give up her favorite

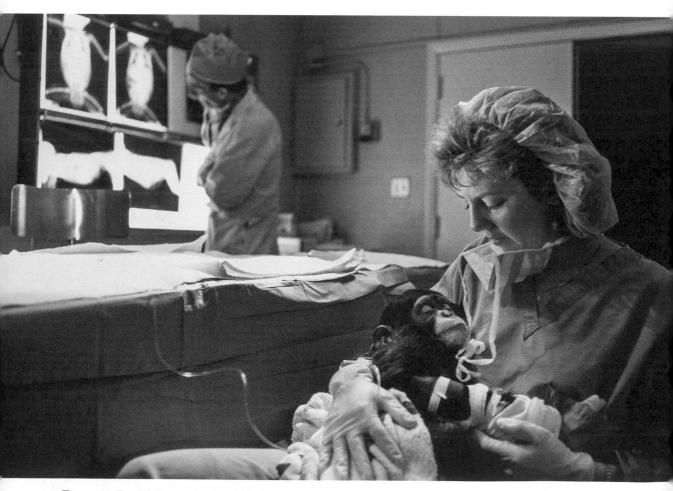

Figure 50. Dr. Mahoney viewing O'Soy's X-rays while Nancy cradles her

food—lo mein—riding on our backs, and the comfort of our beds for a boisterous peer, primate chow, and a steel cage. When caged at work, O'Soy would stand in the front corner staring at us, ignoring her peers and clinging to a stuffed animal while anxiously rocking. In the playroom, she would play a little, but her species identity confusion made it difficult for her to develop the social skills needed to build relationships with her playmates.

To make matters worse, O'Soy didn't tolerate anesthesia or the required fasting. When anesthetized for a health check at eighteen months of age, she nearly died because an area of her intestines became tangled. For two days, Dr. Mahoney and I stayed at her side. Once Dr. Mahoney made the diagnosis, he felt torn between having O'Soy risk surgery in her condition and letting her wait for the condition to resolve on its own, which it finally did.

Pozna's babyhood was a bit brighter. Although we raised her from birth and took her home with us regularly, we made sure that Pozna interacted with the nursery chimps more, and sooner, than O'Soy had so Pozna would know she was a chimp. Pretty as a princess, she carried on the family trait of kindheartedness. Playful and well-rounded, Pozna was able to relate well to both the chimps and humans in her environment.

◈ ◈ ◈

As laws were passed establishing stricter requirements for keeping research animals, New York University (NYU) decided to abandon the lab rather than spend money correcting violations in cage size requirements, so NYU gave the Coulston Foundation facility in Alamogordo, New Mexico, the country's worst primate lab—which already owned more than six hundred chimpanzees—the option of taking it over. Already disturbed by the mistreatment of chimpanzees here, I viewed the idea of working for the kingpin of cruelty as a deal breaker. For eighteen months, we lived under the threat of NYU turning LEMSIP over to Coulston or closing down.

Dr. Mahoney was determined to get the baby chimps to sanctuaries rather than allow them to be subjected to the Coulston Foundation's shop of horrors. Consequently, he went into full swing to find sanctuaries for as many LEMSIP chimps and monkeys as he could. Soon he had arranged for over one hundred chimps, including Timely, Post, O'Soy, and Pozna, to be sneaked out to sanctuaries across North America. I was elated to know that most of the nursery babies I had helped raise would be making it to safe havens and never again subjected to research.

Despite these efforts, at the end of 1996 Frederick Coulston, director of the Coulston Foundation laboratory, secured ownership of approximately one hundred LEMSIP chimpanzees to be transferred to his facility by truck, ten at a time. When Coulston reviewed the chimpanzees on his transfer list, he noted that there were no young ones then called Dr. Mahoney and railed, "You're wasting valuable green animals and sending me the shit," referring to the older chimps who had been on hepatitis and HIV research protocols and already exposed to diseases. At that point, four of our former nursery kids engaged in hepatitis research had already been scheduled for transfer to the Fauna Foundation sanctuary in Canada upon completing the protocol, and so were spared a transport to Coulston. But the thirty-three nursery babies being scheduled to join the chimps already sent to the Wildlife Waystation in California and the three being scheduled to join the five transferred to the Primate Rescue Center in Kentucky were not. Afraid that he might make a stink with NYU to take some, or all, of these youngsters, we decided to get them out via an immediate undercover transfer.

Not knowing how to say goodbye to the babies, I stayed with them much of the night, encircling each sleeping chimp with light and love. LEMSIP employees worked for hours modifying the truck for the comfortable transport of thirty-two young chimpanzees to California. In the afternoon, we loaded the chimps, including Timely and Post, into the truck and, with tears of sadness and joy, waved them off on their journey. Two hours later the truck was stopped by the US Fish and Wildlife Department, which had received an erroneous tip from a disgruntled maintenance worker that chimpanzees were being illegally transported and sold. After being detained for five hours, the transport resumed since everything was legitimate. The chimps had come close to losing their freedom; had NYU officials been called, the youngsters would have probably been given to the Coulston Foundation.

There were still four young chimps in the nursery. Three of them, including Pozna, were slated to join O'Soy and friends at the Primate Rescue Center; the youngest baby, once he was a few weeks older, was to be flown to the Wildlife Waystation with Dr. Mahoney. We felt that their freedom was at risk, so Dr. Mahoney and the administrator agreed that Jenn and I should take them to my house for the night. The catch was that we would have to take full responsibility for the "unauthorized removal" of chimps that were NYU's "property." Did we care? Hell no!

April Truitt, founder of the Primate Rescue Center, magically arranged for a friend to rent a van, pick Jenn and the three babies up from my house the next morning, and take them to her sanctuary. At 1:00 a.m. my husband, Tom, drove his truck to LEMSIP to pick up the required cage for the van to make the transport legal, even though the babies would be wrapped around Jenn for the entire trip. The three of us drove to the house feeling like Robin Hood. Draped with the babies, I barely slept. During my last night with them, I clung tighter than they did. The van arrived early the next morning, and off they went. When the staff arrived at LEMSIP a few hours later, they found the nursery empty. For two weeks, Dr. Mahoney and I jockeyed the remaining little boy between our homes until he was escorted to freedom. We never told anyone our secret until the lab closed.

Coulston continued receiving citations for violations of the Animal Welfare Act, and eventually the government took ownership of the 287 chimps he had housed on Holloman Air Force Base, near his lab in Alamogordo. By 2002, Coulston, who was then eighty-eight years old, was bankrupt. He sold his lab to Save the Chimps, which had already rescued 21 retired US Air Force chimps used in the space program, so the remaining 266 chimps at the Coulston Foundation were rescued, making Save the Chimps the largest chimp sanctuary in the world.

᯼ ᯼ ᯼

Ursula and her children experienced another degree of separation when they were scattered across the country, the lucky ones taken to sanctuaries but the others condemned to doing more time in biomedical research labs. Timely and Post went to the Wildlife Waystation, where they could be outside and supervised by two familiar caregivers from LEMSIP—Darlene Kuhn and Asami Kabasawa. Sadly, Post, who was not yet proficient at climbing high, fell and died less than two years after his arrival. Timely is thriving with Mocha by her side in a group of LEMSIP chimps. O'Soy and Pozna were reunited at the Primate Rescue Center. Ursula and two sons, Tardy and Late, along with twelve other chimps (mostly breeders), were sent to another lab—New Iberia Research Center in Louisiana—so that LEMSIP's founder, Dr. Moor-Jankowski, and Dr. Mahoney would have a breeding base if they decided to start their own lab. Given

Dr. Mahoney's gallant efforts to retire so many chimps from LEMSIP, this seemed odd, but Dr. Mahoney stipulated that the chimpanzees were to be retired to sanctuaries if he and Dr. Moor-Jankowski didn't start their own lab, which thankfully was the case.

The remaining LEMSIP chimps, including Dali and O'Dell, were transferred to the Coulston Foundation facility in New Mexico. There, after having spent most of their nine years together, Dali and O'Dell were separated and never saw each other again. Dali was housed in an indoor/outdoor run with several other LEMSIP chimps. O'Dell was eventually retired to Save the Chimps.

🔶 🔶 🔶

Jenn followed O'Soy, Pozna, and the rest of the LEMSIP chimpanzees to the Primate Rescue Center. It was wonderful for the youngsters, especially O'Soy, to have one of their human mothers there helping them flourish in their new lives. However, even with Jenn there O'Soy struggled socially. Martina, a chimp several years older than the babies, was sent as a big sister figure to help them grow as chimps, but no adult chimps were there to teach and socially challenge them, or to keep Martina in check. Despite Martina's charm, she was suddenly the boss and able to take advantage of the babies. As the second oldest, O'Soy became an easy target given her sensitive, peaceful nature and social limitations with chimps. O'Soy watched Martina nurture Pozna, sometimes even carrying Pozna on her back. The caregivers tried to balance human intervention with opportunities for them to work things out, but O'Soy became anxious. Eventually, she was put in a smaller group of chimps and finally able to have fun foraging for treats and grooming with the others. Sadly, O'Soy became ill just a few months after arriving at the sanctuary, possibly related to the intestinal adhesions from her near-death experience at LEMSIP. Unable to determine what was wreaking havoc on her insides, April and her husband, Clay Miller, drove O'Soy and Jenn back to LEMSIP for medical help. For several days we all took shifts cradling and loving O'Soy in the motorhome situated in the LEMSIP parking lot while Dr. Mahoney tried to save her. One day I had just arrived with lo mein for O'Soy when I was told she had passed. I was devastated, my only consolation being that O'Soy had died in human arms, where she probably felt most comfortable. I treasure the photo I have of O'Soy walking freely in the Kentucky grass.

O'Soy's story reinforced for me the fact that chimps need to know they are chimps. If chimps are raised by humans and have little to no contact with other chimps, they identify with humans. In raising O'Soy, we had decided between the lesser of two evils—letting O'Soy sit alone in a playpen through her infancy or giving her the companionship we could offer.

Pozna, who recently passed away, was the youngest in the group of chimps at the Primate Rescue Center but had adult chimps as mentors. She often sought human attention. We cannot reverse her history of having been raised by humans in a lab nursery, but I am thankful that she had a life surrounded by chimps and humans who loved her for who she was, and that she got to spend a brief time with O'Soy, her real sister.

Unfortunately, Dali was not in the rescued groups; the Coulston Foundation eventually sent her to New Iberia Research Center, where she was subjected to further research and physically and psychologically abused by a technician. Dali died at New Iberia, which, as a private lab, did not have to provide information to the public, so the exact cause of her death is unknown.

After nearly three years at New Iberia Research Center, Ursula, Tardy, Late, and the remaining eleven LEMSIP chimps were finally retired to the Wild Animal Orphanage (WAO) sanctuary in Texas. During attempts to socialize these challenged chimps into groups, petite Tardy was attacked and eventually died from injuries he sustained. And so, sadly, five of Ursula's seven children have perished.

In 2010, WAO closed after the founder's daughter took over and depleted its funds. Save the Chimps rescued Ursula, Late, and nine other chimps from WAO,

Figure 51. Ursula (center) with Emily (left) and Rebel (right), her new family at Save the Chimps

and today they schmooze and roam on acres of velvet grass with lazy palm trees. They can count on their group and human staff to provide them with the best care and motherly protection possible. Though loyal to his group, Late was initially leery of his new caregivers, which is understandable given his long history with humans. But he has learned to trust again; he loves to have his toes tickled and smiles from ear to ear. Ursula remains a gentle and sweet lady.

⚏ ⚏ ⚏

It's amazing how forgiving most chimps are after humans have inflicted pain, isolation, and disease on them. In removing them from their mothers, siblings, and friends, and taking away fresh air, sunshine, and their freedom, humans have robbed them of everything vital for social, emotional, and mental stability. With practically no space to live in and so little choice, control, stimulation, and social support, the captive chimps hang on by a thread day after day, reaching out to human caregivers for kindness and help, and showing affection to humans even when irreparable damage has been done to their bodies, minds, and souls. We can never replace what we have robbed from them.

Chimpanzees' minds, and much of their physiology, are so similar to those of humans that it is difficult to understand why the biomedical community discounted the intellectual and emotional complexity of chimpanzees to justify their use in medical research. All chimpanzees in research become affected in body, mind, and spirit; all become depressed; and many develop anxiety, psychoses, and obsessions they cannot manage without hurting themselves, typically by pulling their nails and hair out; picking, pinching, and biting themselves; attacking their own limbs, from which they have dissociated (floating limb syndrome); and rocking, head rolling, pacing, and eye poking. Extreme boredom and frustration often leads to behaviors not typically demonstrated in the wild like smearing, eating, or throwing feces and spitting water. Sadly, some technicians lack tolerance for these types of behavior and retaliate, or even withhold food and water, as punishment.

The quality of care and degree of compassion chimpanzees receive from caretakers in labs vary, depending on the caliber of the technicians, the number of staff members, and the attitude of the place. Some great people with whom I have worked in labs have walked away burned out and too traumatized to continue helping from either inside or outside the lab. But I know they can't forget. As one of my friends says: "It was my Vietnam."

Fortunately, biomedical research on chimpanzees in the United States has now come to a halt. New Iberia Research Center has agreed to retire its chimps to the Project Chimps sanctuary in Morganton, Georgia. Over the next few years the remaining chimpanzees in labs are supposed to be retired—though for many, a day late and a dollar short. But as long as labs remain open, caring people are needed on the inside to give these precious souls kindness and companionship.

Prompted by hundreds of traumatic memories, I want the unknowing public, whose tax dollars have funded decades of biomedical research, to know that the treatment of chimpanzees has been reprehensible and that the primate-based experiments that claimed to focus on hepatitis, HIV, and other diseases could have instead utilized viable alternative methods. The small differences in the makeup of humans and chimps contribute to big differences in the way their bodies react to diseases. And the ethical issue is irrefutable: torturing other beings should not be an option.

To anyone who thinks it's okay to do biomedical research on chimps, or any other animals, I say, "Imagine putting chimpanzees in tiny boxes marked 'Misery and Violation' then telling them they will never leave their boxes awake or touch another chimp again and that they can count on two extreme conditions almost daily: total boredom and, when they get darted, complete terror. Further imagine removing bits of their livers during biopsies—perhaps more than 350 times over a ten-year period. Then imagine watching them lose their minds and all hope while aware that you are the gatekeeper standing on the outside of the cage bars, holding the keys to their prisons."

For decades, I have had to sleep with the sounds of their screams and horrific images of them that have been tattooed in my psyche. My motto—"Their pain is greater than my need"—keeps me fighting for them. The kind spirits of families like Ursula's remind me to act from the heart on their behalf rather than simply rage about their plight.

Ursula will never know how her children grew up or how they broke down. They were separated by science and tormented for years in the name of the oxymoron called "humane research," yet their scars do not mar the inherent benevolence, humility, and compassion of this chimp family. Whether stuck in a lab or soaking up sun in a sanctuary, they lead by example with their selflessness, forgiveness, sacrifice, and love toward both chimps and humans. Unfortunately, Ursula, Tardy, Late, Dali, Timely, Post, O'Soy, and Pozna did not have the luxury of knowing they were a family, but we can give this family their due respect by sharing their stories and acting lovingly toward all living beings.

Apollo

Sarah Baeckler Davis

The hardest time of my life was in July 2006 when I learned of the death of a young chimpanzee named Apollo. I had said goodbye to Apollo three years earlier but had secretly hoped I would see him again someday. I have been fortunate to know and love many chimps throughout my career thus far, and all of them have touched my heart. But I felt a special connection to Apollo, who touched me in a way no other chimp had before—or since.

I was working for Chimpanzee Collaboratory, an alliance of several nonprofit organizations, including Save the Chimps, the Animal Legal Defense Fund, and the Jane Goodall Institute, which had been established to pool resources for use on chimpanzee issues. At the time, the organization was looking at problems chimpanzees faced in the United States, and one of the key issues it singled out was the use of chimpanzees in the entertainment industry.

There had been many stories over the years about chimps being mistreated on Hollywood sets, but without concrete evidence to support the claims. There was also a great deal of rhetoric in the industry about how bad training had been in the old days of Hollywood and how nice it was now for the chimps because trainers were using more positive reinforcement. The big question for the Chimpanzee Collaboratory's group of experts was: Has the industry really changed so that chimpanzees are treated well or are abusive methods still being used behind closed doors? This is where I came in. I had just gotten my master's degree in primatology and had had some success during my master's research at getting people to tell me stories that weren't necessarily public information. Dr. Roger Fouts, who was part of the Chimpanzee Collaboratory, had been my mentor during graduate school and remembered that I had this skill. So I was hired to research methods trainers used with great ape "actors" in Hollywood to observe what was going on at training compounds and report back to the Chimpanzee Collaboratory whether conditions had, in fact, improved for chimpanzees.

To prepare, I enrolled in the exotic animal training program at Moorpark College in Southern California. Through connections I made there, I was led to Sid Yost, the owner of Amazing Animal Actors and the trainer I ended up investigating. Yost trained chimpanzees and other exotic animals to be used on TV and in movies; he had been responsible for chimpanzee appearances on *That '70s Show, Scrubs,* and *Meet My Folks.* I called him and told him I was a student at Moorpark College looking for volunteer opportunities, and he welcomed me to the team. That was really all it took. I was forthcoming about my full name and my previous experience working with chimps.

Yost's training compound, located in the Malibu Hills above the Pacific Ocean, was a ranch for farm animals as well, so in addition to cages for the lion, tiger, chimpanzees, and hawk there were horse corrals and a big barn. There was also a makeshift kitchen and garage/office area at the top of a big hill, from which I had to walk down a steep dusty path to get to the chimps' cages. That's where I met Apollo, who lived at the compound with four other chimpanzees: Angel, Cody, Sable, and Téa.

On my first day there, I saw signs of psychological stress in all five chimps, who were rocking back and forth, anxious and fearful. They were babies, ranging in age from eighteen months to three years. At this tender age, the young chimps should have been with their mothers; instead, they were on their own.

I worked at Yost's compound for thirteen months, from June 2002 until July 2003, observing the training methods used to get chimpanzees to be docile and obedient so they could perform on cue. During that time, I witnessed the five young chimpanzees regularly receiving brutal beatings. I saw Yost kick and punch the babies in the face, hit them with sticks and metal objects, and subject them to mental and psychological abuse. The trainers routinely screamed at the babies, terrifying them into submission. But the trainers' violent behavior went beyond the training sessions. I watched the chimps receive punishment for such "crimes" as not paying attention or behaving territorially when trainers entered their cages. Sometimes the trainers would strike out of the blue, just to create a controlling dynamic so the chimps would have to pay attention to them at all times. All five young chimps lived in a constant state of terror. Again and again I heard their high-pitched screams as they were beaten into submission. Yost, however, later denied he had done any of the things I saw him and his trainers repeatedly do.

Watching all this happen on a daily basis was unspeakably hard. Every night I logged detailed notes on what I had seen that day. I tried to erase the images from my mind, but they never went away. I forced myself to focus on the happy ending I hoped I could help create by keeping silent and maintaining my position at the ranch.

I felt highly protective of all the chimps, but I fell hard for Apollo at first sight. Sweet and smart, but misunderstood and mistreated, he was the troublemaker of the group, and those boys are always my favorites. I wanted to get to know him better; however, since he was regarded as the bad boy my interactions with him were limited by the trainers. I remember one special day when I was sitting on the lawn grooming Apollo. He head-bobbed at me, a fun, happy gesture that means: "Hello! Play with me!" Before I could stop myself, I accepted by head-bobbing back. Apollo's trainer grabbed me and shouted, "Don't do that! It means he's about to attack!" He had no idea what the gesture meant.

"

I felt highly protective of all the chimps, but I fell hard for Apollo at first sight.

Figure 52. Apollo at the training compound where he spent most of his short life.

Curious and mischievous, Apollo always wanted to look up people's shirts, especially women's. He loved to play and wrestle. He was smart and constantly tested his limits. But he bit people, a natural impulse of juvenile male chimpanzees in the wild though unacceptable at a training compound. As a result, he received the most brutal beatings I saw during my time undercover. Once when he bit a trainer, he suffered greatly. Though I didn't witness this particular beating, I saw the trainers heading down to his cage with a heavy wooden cane, and I saw Apollo's swollen face afterward. When we were alone, I whispered, "Are you okay?" There was heartbreaking acceptance in his puffy eyes. That was his life, and he knew it. Apollo was only four years old at the time.

When I met Apollo, they weren't using him for many production jobs anymore because his mischief had been hard to manage. Since chimpanzees eventually become too strong to control, they can be used as performers only until about age seven. During the subsequent forty or fifty years of "retirement," they are usually stuck in substandard facilities or zoos, where they are condemned to a lonely, brutal existence trapped in tiny cages.

Like many captive chimps, Apollo had had a tumultuous life, even before ending up at Yost's compound. He had been born at the notorious and now-defunct Coulston Foundation, a New Mexico–based research facility well-known for its violations of federal animal welfare laws. He had probably been taken from his mother within hours of birth, thrown in with a group of other babies, and raised with limited maternal influence. At around eighteen months of age, Apollo had been used as a bartering chip—given to Yost in exchange for a rosy documentary about Apollo's not-so-rosy birthplace. It was the first of many exchanges in which Apollo would play an unwitting role. Had he not been a part of that exchange, he would probably have remained at the Coulston Foundation and been used in invasive experiments, so his new trainer was "saving" him from a life in research. Apollo died when he was just seven years old, a few years after I'd left him at Yost's training compound. I had hoped that the information I'd collected from my observations would help free Apollo from a life of abuse. I had been sure I'd see him again.

A few months after I left Yost's compound we went public with the information I had recorded, which drew positive media attention. However, we were faced with legal challenges. Before my investigative information had been released to the public, we had gone to the county prosecutor to seek animal cruelty charges against Yost but had been unsuccessful: without a good explanation, the prosecutor had decided that the beatings and abuse suffered by Apollo and his cagemates did not amount to illegal animal cruelty. This was a huge blow.

Subsequently, we shifted gears and pursued a civil case against Yost, suing him in federal court for animal cruelty, lying to the public about the manner in which the chimpanzees were treated, and violations of the Endangered Species Act. It was a compelling and creative case. After four years of litigation, a week before settling the case my colleagues and I were negotiating an agreement designed to rescue Apollo and his chimpanzee friends and send them to sanctuaries when, during a mediation session in a stuffy office building in Southern California, I was told that Apollo had been bitten by a rattlesnake and died. I stifled my reaction, but inside I quietly fell apart. As soon as I got on the plane to head home, I started crying. By the time I got to my house, I had so completely disintegrated that my boyfriend assumed my mother or father had died. It was days before I could speak out loud about what I was experiencing and months before I could come to terms with the loss. While very proud of the work I did, I will probably always be haunted by the fact that I was unable to save Apollo.

Despite this crushing loss, the settlement had two positive outcomes: Yost agreed never to work with great apes again, and Angel, Cody, Sable, and Téa were moved out of Yost's training compound and into sanctuaries. These were major victories, yet I couldn't help but dwell on the thought that Apollo should have gone with the others after so many years of suffering.

Fortunately, the tides are turning for chimps in Hollywood. Socially conscious writers and directors in the entertainment industry began making different choices after learning what goes on behind the scenes for great ape actors. More and more film directors are opting to use computer-generated imagery (CGI) in movies instead of live animals. With a little education about the practices involved in training great apes, most people are eager to do the right thing. The movement to end the use of great apes in film and television has tremendous momentum right now, and only a handful of great ape trainers are left. Even so, there are still many Apollos out there in labs, training compounds, and backyards. We must help them before it's too late.

RESCUING CHIMPANZEES: A JOURNEY OF LOVE AND AWAKENING

Lesley Day

I am living my dream, but it took me some time to get here. Growing up in Portland, Oregon, around horses, dogs, cats, and a couple of pet ducks, I have always recognized the vital importance of building relationships with living creatures. My parents instilled a sense of responsibility in me at a very young age to care for all animals—before I could eat, I had to make sure my animals were fed and watered. This environment shaped my philosophy about animals and life: if you do not have a relationship with other living beings, it is easy to lose your relationship to humanity.

During the 1980s, I fancied the idea of having a pet monkey, so I purchased a baby spider monkey. Oscar arrived at the Portland Airport in a small crate after a long plane trip from Florida. I was shocked to find a scared, sick monkey covered in lice. I remember thinking to myself, "What a poor, pathetic little guy. I need to get you cleaned up and healthy, and find out what kind of person would sell a monkey in this shape. They should not be in business."

I did the usual pet owner thing with Oscar, dressing him up in clothing and allowing him to eat at the dinner table during mealtimes. He quickly became a member of our family, and we were devastated when he unexpectedly died at the age of four. After mourning Oscar's loss, I began researching where I could buy a baby chimpanzee. I contacted various chimpanzee breeders and professionals; yet the more people I spoke with the more ridicule I received. When I finally contacted Roger Fouts, codirector of the Chimpanzee and Human Communication Institute at Central Washington University, he told me, in no uncertain terms, that I could never take care of a chimpanzee the way the chimp deserved. I remember hanging up the phone wondering why I couldn't provide the same care that he was giving his chimps.

Fouts's critique did not deter me. In fall 1993, I flew to Upstate New York to talk with Dave Sabo, a chimpanzee breeder, trainer, and longtime promoter of chimpanzees in the pet trade and entertainment world. His chimps had performed in many well-known movies and programs, including *Project X, Saturday Night Live,* and *Johnny Carson.*

Upon arriving at his place, I was dumbfounded to find eleven chimpanzees living in a dilapidated windowless trailer with no access to fresh air or sunshine—a hellhole. Sabo believed that if you kept chimpanzees in dark, cramped cages they would regard you as their savior when you took them out to perform. Thunderous chimpanzee hoots and screams echoed throughout the area. As we entered the trailer, the chimpanzees were spitting and displaying, behaviors chimpanzees exhibit to assert dominance or aggression. Glancing into one of the cages, I saw Topo, an adult male chimpanzee whose eyes locked onto mine. His quiet disposition and gentle eyes seemed to make time stop. In that moment, my desire for a baby chimp dissolved. And my true calling became clear: I was to rescue captive chimpanzees in dire need of refuge and provide them with permanent sanctuary.

I realized that I had been so blinded by my love for animals and my ignorance of the realities of chimpanzees in the pet trade that I had inadvertently promoted the pet trade. Only now could I understand the accuracy of Roger Fouts's message—I was the problem. His words led to the first step in my awakening.

⧉ ⧉ ⧉

Upon arriving home in Oregon, I shared the revelation of my mission with my husband, who understood my deep love for animals and was supportive of this new undertaking. There are no college classes in Building a Sanctuary 101, so I had to figure things out as I went along. I picked up useful tips and ideas here and there by visiting several chimp facilities and reaching out to multiple zoos and sanctuaries. We decided to use our four-car heated garage as the first chimpanzee enclosure. Coincidently, Central Washington University was rebuilding its chimpanzee center and auctioning off its caging materials. Over the phone, I purchased four cages for three hundred dollars and then called a girlfriend to tell her we were going on a road trip.

After we arrived in Ellensburg, Washington, we loaded the disassembled cages, which lay in a big pile of galvanized steel, onto our flatbed truck and, with only an inch of clearance on the wheel well, drove home. A friend offered to assemble the cages for two thousand dollars, not realizing what a huge undertaking it would be without instructions. After the tunnels were attached, we built a spacious outdoor enclosure incorporating plenty of ropes and platforms to encourage natural chimpanzee behavior.

However, it turned out that building the enclosure was the easy part; rescuing Topo was another story. I spent two difficult years trying to free Topo from his static existence in Dave Sabo's windowless dwelling, finding it unbearable to think of Topo spending one more minute in such appalling conditions. I stayed in contact with Sabo and traveled east to visit Topo a second time, feeling that the more I kept in touch with him the sooner I would be able to bring Topo home.

From the little we learned from Sabo, apparently the first part of Topo's life had been spent in a family-run roadside zoo, where he had been exhibited as a gorilla and forced to perform or have his picture taken with people. Sabo would not give me any information about his previous owners or any records of his past. According to Sabo, he "rescued" Topo from euthanasia after Topo ripped off the arm of a teenager who had drunkenly punched him on a dare. Sabo said he took Topo from police custody and proved his gentle nature in court. I had legal volunteers look through old court cases but was never able to find documentation supporting Sabo's story.

Once we finally had the authority to move Topo, a wonderful man named Bruce took on the challenge of transporting him, unsedated, across the country, a trip that took four days. Bruce stayed in touch with me throughout, advising me about Topo's well-being. Meanwhile, I felt nervous, wondering if everything was set up correctly, if I would know what to do upon Topo's arrival, and whether he would like the new home we had prepared for him. Even though I understood that no matter how wonderful an environment he had, his life would always be behind bars, I was positive that I could at least give Topo a life of dignity in a safe and stimulating environment where he could enjoy living the rest of his days as freely as possible.

Topo arrived at his new home—soon to be named Chimps Inc.—in October 1995. We immediately sedated him to do a physical exam since Sabo had not provided any medical records. I made sure to not let Topo see me while assistants sedated him, because I didn't want our reunion to have negative associations. When Topo came out of the anesthesia, I was right next to him, and, although I had only seen him twice over the previous two years, Topo recognized me immediately.

The next morning we all gathered around as Topo cautiously stepped outside to explore his new surroundings. He had been with Sabo for three or four years, without once, I believe, leaving his cage. Feeling the earth under his feet and the sun on his skin was something he had not experienced in a long, long time, if ever. Topo began to run laps around the enclosure, letting out ecstatic cries. He ran over to Bruce, giving him huge pant-hoots, as if thanking him for all he had done. Seeing this beginning to Topo's new life was an unforgettable moment.

What started as a small dream to make a difference for one chimpanzee has since blossomed into a sanctuary for many chimpanzees. We have rescued nine chimps— Topo, Patti, Herbie, Kimie, Thiele, Maggie, Jackson, Emma, and CJ. We started with a few cages and an adjoining outdoor habitat and now have two indoor buildings, one of which is a 2,200-square-foot bilevel structure with huge windows, an expansive vaulted ceiling, and heated floors. We also have three outdoor enclosures, the largest of which measures nearly an acre, and aerial tunnels that connect all the buildings and enclosures, allowing the chimps to move from one area to another. All the habitats are specifically designed to meet the physical and behavioral needs of chimpanzees, offering high nesting areas, multilevel platforms and towers, hammocks, and durable ropes and fire hoses from which to swing. The chimpanzees live in two different groups because Topo and Herbie, our two adult males, do not get along. We make a daily effort to move the other chimpanzees back and forth between the groups so their interactions and environments stay novel and stimulating.

Each of our chimpanzees arrived bearing the scars of severe trauma, neglect, or abuse, both physical and psychological. Although their recoveries have been life-changing, there is no such thing as a full recovery following the types of atrocities they have experienced.

Topo, now in his mid to late forties, has held on to his alpha status throughout the years. His youthful spirit is evident in his energetic play sessions with Thiele and games of chase with Jackson. He is extremely patient and gentle but assumes his role as alpha male without hesitation when the need arises. The other chimps respect Topo's authority and look to him for reassurance and instruction in times of excitement or stress. Topo, our peacemaker and soul of the sanctuary, visibly appreciates everything we give him and do for him.

Figure 53. Topo

Patti, who arrived nine months after Topo, is our matriarch. We acquired Patti when two trainers at Marine World/Africa USA, whom I had visited for years, called to tell me that Marine World was getting rid of its chimp show and Patti desperately needed a home. I had known Patti since she was eight years old, visiting her at the theme park throughout her childhood, so I didn't hesitate to take her. To get Marine World to release Patti to us, we had to sign a contract stating that they would get Patti's firstborn. Luckily for Patti, sanctuaries don't breed their animals so we never had to follow through on that promise.

Patti was born in the Marine World theme park in Vallejo, California, in September 1982. Her mother, not knowing how to raise a baby because she had been taken from her own mother at birth, put newborn Patti on the ground and walked away. Consequently, Patti was raised by the caregivers at Marine World, who had taken her home every night in an attempt to simulate the 24/7 contact she would have received if she were being raised by her mother. Patti spent the first two years of her life being reared by human caregivers and was able to spend her days at the park with her chimp family and friends. One day a former trainer, having decided it was time for Patti to start staying at the park at night, put her in a cage by herself in a dark trailer. Because of those isolated and frightening nights, Patti developed a fear of being locked in after dark. When she arrived at the sanctuary, we decided to build her an outdoor heated condo because she refused to come inside at night.

Like so many other entertainment chimps, Patti had been dressed up in clothing and forced to perform for crowds of screaming children day after day. As part of her act, she would swing out on a rope over the crowd, cartwheel, and shoot a basketball through a hoop. Typically, chimpanzees stop performing when they are around seven years old because they become too strong and unpredictable to work in front of an audience. But Patti, being such a sweet chimpanzee, was exploited twice as long—for fourteen years.

Patti has been with us for twenty-two years, and she still gets nervous when caregivers have to lock her inside, regardless of how much space she has. However, she communicates her needs with us and can choose whether to spend the night inside or, if she needs more space, in the outdoor heated condo. She does allow us to close her in at night during the cold winter months. Although Patti still carries the emotional scars of her early experiences, which manifest as anxiety, claustrophobia, and self-injurious behaviors, she has made enormous progress since her arrival. The fact that she will let us lock her inside is a huge step forward. Also, her self-injurious behaviors have significantly decreased in frequency and severity. However, the most important aspect of her recovery is the trust she has in her caregivers and the way she communicates her anxiety to us so that we can help her.

Herbie and Kimie arrived at the sanctuary in 1998 after April Truitt, the founder of Primate Rescue Center in Kentucky, told me about two adolescent chimpanzees who had been discovered in the backyard of a home in Lebanon, Oregon. The chimpanzees were listed as assets in a bankruptcy case and therefore needed a permanent home immediately. With the help of the bankruptcy trustees, Herbie and Kimie were relocated to Chimps Inc. soon thereafter. When found, Herbie and Kimie had been living in a small, squalid, rundown shack made of wood scraps, chicken wire, and tattered tarps. We don't know how long they had been there, but it was clear that their lives had been lonely and turbulent, like those of most exotic pets once they outgrow their childhood cuteness. I didn't have space for them at the time, but an immediate rescue was essential since Kimie was emaciated and terrified, with a hematoma on her head and sores covering her body. So we first moved Herbie and Kimie into two of our four cages then immediately began building them a larger enclosure. In three weeks, we had constructed a tunnel from their cages to an outdoor habitat so they could be outside.

Kimie, born in a breeding compound in 1988, was an infant when she had been taken from her mother and sold to a private owner in Federal Way's Enchantment Parks. Kimie spent the first four years of her life performing at birthday parties and corporate functions; we don't know what happened to her over the next six years. She lived at our sanctuary for thirteen years before suddenly passing away in 2011 from unexpected complications related to heart disease, the number-one cause of premature death in captive apes. It breaks my heart that nearly half of Kimie's short time on this planet was rife with trauma, fear, and neglect, but I am grateful that the second half was spent in a place of refuge.

Born at a breeding facility in 1986, Herbie had been pulled from his mother's arms and sold to a human family when only a few months old. Part of his childhood had been spent performing with Kimie. At some point, Herbie was dropped off at a mechanic's shop whose owner had agreed to take care of him for a couple weeks while the trainer took Kimie away to perform. Herbie had lived in a small holding cage in the mechanic's garage for two years until the trainer had finally come back to get him.

Figure 54. Herbie

Though Herbie did not require the same type of physical recovery as Kimie, he had great difficulty adjusting to sanctuary life. He was bigger and stronger than Topo, but because he had been raised by humans he had no idea that he could be the alpha male. The other chimps frightened him, and he struggled to understand their language and social rules. Since then, Herbie has improved tremendously and developed wonderful friendships with a few of the chimps. A perfect example of what happens to a wild animal when humans intervene, Herbie is still learning how to be a chimpanzee.

Thiele, Patti's biological sister, and Maggie, their foster sister, were next to arrive at Chimps Inc., in 2005. They were both entertainers from Marine World who were retired when they had grown too strong and dangerous to perform. Thiele had been born at the park in July 1986 and Maggie at Goin' Ape, a breeding and entertainment facility in Auburn, California, in September 1990. Unlike most chimps in the pet and entertainment industries, Maggie spent an entire year with her mother before being torn from her arms and sold to Marine World. Patti and Thiele, along with their caregivers, had helped raise Maggie.

Like Patti, Maggie and Thiele had been forced to perform unnatural tricks throughout their childhoods for the amusement of crowds of screaming people. They would swing out on ropes over audiences; ride tricycles; and perform acrobatics while dressed in costumes. Thiele even rode on the back of a llama as part of her act. Marine World accepted many donations toward the construction of a retirement home for their performing animals, but the home was never built. All the chimps except Patti, Maggie, and Thiele went to a private zoo in Virginia, where Patti's dad died the first week when he fell into a moat. Thiele stopped performing after only a few years because she had become too aggressive, but she had been kept at the park as a companion for Maggie. When Maggie was retired at age eight, they were both given to the Auburn facility where Maggie had been born.

Figure 55.
Maggie working
at Marine World

Nine years later, when the facility had run into financial difficulties because of decreasing revenues in the movie industry and commercial world, the staff contacted me to see if I could take them. I had met Thiele and Maggie on multiple occasions during my many visits to Marine World, so reuniting these long-lost sisters seemed the least I could do. After nine years of separation, Thiele, Maggie, and Patti, against all odds, were brought together again. Chimpanzees have long-term memories, so it was no surprise that the sisters instantly recognized one another, sharing elated pant-hoots and gentle embraces. From then on, the three of them were inseparable, and when Maggie passed away unexpectedly in October 2013, Patti and Thiele were at her side.

Our sanctuary grew again in March 2007 with the arrival of Jackson and Emma, rescued from an animal facility in Texas that no longer had funds to care for their animals. Jackson and Emma, our youngest adolescents, born at a breeding facility in Festus, Missouri, in 2001 and 2002, respectively, had been taken away from their mothers at birth and sold to different families, who raised them.

"

Chimpanzees have long-term memories, so it was no surprise that the sisters instantly recognized each other.

Figure 56. Left to right: Sisters Thiele and Patti

Jackson had been with his human family for less than two years before he became too unmanageable for them and was given to the Texas facility before his second birthday. That day Jackson's world was turned upside down—one moment he was a child in a warm home, and the next an animal in a cage. At some point during his childhood, Jackson had been castrated—a barbaric and ineffective management tactic performed in an attempt to lower hormone levels and make animals less aggressive and easier to control. Because of this, Jackson will never reach the size or gain the muscle mass of a normal adult male chimpanzee, most likely eliminating his chances of ever climbing the social hierarchy to become an alpha male.

Emma had been raised by the owner of the Texas facility, and though we do not have detailed records about her past it is clear that she suffered some sort of trauma. Emma's body shows signs of her psychological scars: the majority of her inner arms, legs, and chest are bald from plucking out her hair, a type of self-injurious behavior common among captive primates. Since arriving at Chimps Inc., Emma has made

Figure 57. Above:
Emma at a Texas
facility before rescue

Figure 58. Right:
Emma sitting outside
at Chimps Inc.

remarkable progress, both socially and psychologically, but she still struggles with inner demons that we will never comprehend. Yet to see Emma grooming with the other chimps, something she would have never done when she first arrived, makes all the challenges of running a sanctuary worthwhile.

CJ is our most recent resident. Born at a breeding facility in Texas in May 1999, CJ had been purchased for $60,000 and kept as a pet in a backyard enclosure in Las Vegas, Nevada, with a chimp named Buddy. Raised as human children, CJ and Buddy had been used as an entertainment attraction at a local flea market, where visitors had paid to have their photos taken with them. In August 2012, both chimpanzees had made national headlines when they escaped their enclosure. Buddy had been shot and killed by local authorities, but fortunately CJ had been anesthetized and returned to her enclosure unharmed. When CJ had escaped again a few weeks later, it had become apparent that she needed to be placed in a sanctuary. Considering that CJ arrived traumatized, both by having seen her companion gunned down and by having been darted three times in one month, her adjustment to sanctuary life and her ability to learn chimpanzee behavior has been extraordinary. Having spent the first part of her life treated as a human child, with only one chimpanzee friend, who had been treated in the same manner, CJ had no experience being a chimpanzee. But through careful observation she figured out the proper behaviors faster than any other chimpanzee at the sanctuary.

⸎ ⸎ ⸎

Perhaps the most remarkable part of this journey has been discovering how forgiving chimpanzees are. After everything they have been through and all that humans have done to them, they still love, trust, and forgive people. The relationships they have formed with their human caregivers show their great capacity for compassion and empathy. It is this, above all else, that has made sanctuary work so rewarding for me.

To stop the exploitation of our closest living relatives, we must stand up for these magnificent creatures. We can begin by educating people about how chimpanzees are treated in captivity. Chimpanzees used in the pet and entertainment industries are separated from their mothers during infancy, often immediately after birth; this not only traumatizes mother and baby but also deprives them of the crucial mother-child

Figure 59.
Left to right: Maggie,
Herbie, CJ, Jackson,
and Emma

bond and the opportunity for the baby to learn how to be a chimpanzee. Though sweet and cuddly while young, they quickly grow up to be unpredictable and dangerous wild animals, so, in an attempt to control them, trainers and owners often subject them to social isolation, food deprivation, and physical and emotional abuse. Though some improvement has been made since I first went to see Dave Sabo twenty-four years ago, sadly there is still a long way to go in raising public awareness about the plight of captive chimpanzees and improving conditions for them. Today, the methods used to train chimpanzees to perform unnatural behaviors are, to quote Jane Goodall, "harsh at best and absolutely cruel at worst." And the trauma to which they are subjected leaves them permanently scarred, as it would humans.

Once wild animals are deprived of their intrinsic right to be wild, we forever condemn them to a life behind bars. Chimpanzees like Topo, Patti, Herbie, Thiele, Jackson, Emma, and CJ are stuck with us because the life they deserve was taken away from them and they had nowhere else to go. These chimpanzees are simply too human to live in the wild and too much animal to be with humans. The bottom line is that no sanctuary, regardless of how beautiful, enriching, or full of loving caregivers it is, will ever be good enough.

ONE VOICE

Eileen Dallaire

The first time I drove down the steep driveway leading to the lush, green, thirty-acre valley in central Kentucky that nearly fifty primates consider home, I knew I was about to experience something special. I had just arrived at the Primate Rescue Center (PRC), a nonprofit sanctuary, when I heard the chimpanzees hooting to alert one another to my intrusion. When I finally saw them up close, they immediately captured my heart. After the novelty of my visit wore off, the chimpanzees' excitement changed to curiosity, as each of them approached the window to examine me, with only a thick pane of glass separating us. That was the moment I knew I wanted to be a part of their lives. I was about to finish college and wanted to work with animals but had never dreamed that I would have the opportunity to take care of chimpanzees.

In fall 2003, I applied for the Short-Term Internship Program at the PRC—a twelve-week training program that allows students to shadow caregivers and learn about the care of primates. My program focused on primate behavior, rehabilitation, enrichment, and general care management. I was eager to learn each of the chimpanzees' and monkeys' names and to make them enrichment and meals they would accept with excitement. It was satisfying to know I could make a difference in their lives. After my internship ended in mid-December, I applied for a caregiver position and continued to volunteer at the sanctuary. Then on January 4, 2004, I became a full-time caregiver. Over the years, I served as animal care and staff supervisor, sanctuary manager, and assistant director. Upon the retirement of our cofounder, April Truitt, in fall 2017, I began serving as the executive director.

The PRC currently cares for nine chimpanzees, ranging from young to mature adults, and nearly forty monkeys from a variety of undesirable situations. The sanctuary focuses on eliminating primate suffering wherever it occurs, whether this involves helping surrendered or confiscated pets or laboratory primates, or assisting laboratory researchers and zoo personnel across the United States seeking to place primates in appropriate facilities. When educating individuals about the suffering of primates in the exotic pet trade, the PRC strives to end the breeder-dealer-buyer cycle, as well as promote regulations and laws at all levels of government that will prohibit private primate ownership.

The captive primates lucky enough to consider the PRC home live in enclosures designed to encourage species-specific behaviors. The chimpanzee enclosure offers towers with platforms for the chimpanzees to sleep on and fire hose "vines" for them to climb and swing down to forage for nuts on the ground. The PRC is not open to the public; therefore, the primates are able to spend their days in peace with the backdrop sounds of Jessamine Creek.

It is difficult to uncover our chimpanzees' histories due to the secrecy of the animal trade business. Chimps in entertainment and those privately owned often exchange hands many times as they grow older. This is especially true of those who are young, less dangerous, and relatively easy to handle. Older chimps are often sold to breeders or roadside zoos because they are too strong and dangerous to handle. Only from hearsay do we know the personal histories of our older chimpanzees before they came to the sanctuary. Many had survived lives devoid of any type of enrichment, companionship, or comfort. A few had endured barbaric "training" methods, including electric shocks and beatings. Most had suffered loneliness, depression, malnourishment, and confinement in small cages after becoming too strong to handle. All of the chimpanzees had been pulled from their mothers' arms at birth to be sold to biomedical labs, the entertainment world, or as house pets. All had suffered emotionally and physically from this separation—and would for the rest of their lives.

THE DAHLONEGA FIVE

Five adult chimps—Donald, Hazel, Victoria, Zulu, and Debbie, known as the Dahlonega Five—were rescued by the Primate Rescue Center in 1998, when the owner suffered a heart attack and agreed to give custody of them to the center. The owner had brought the five chimps to Dahlonega, Georgia, in 1977, early enough

Figure 60. Hazel

to be grandfathered in when the state enacted its Exotic Animal Law barring the private possession of certain types of primates. For more than a decade, these five chimps had been forced to live in a filthy, windowless 10' × 10' concrete bunker, with no regular access to food or water. The chimps had pushed the decaying debris, including newspapers, food containers, and excrement, against the front walls of their tiny cells in a vain attempt to make room so they could move around. First, the owner refused to give up the chimps and only allowed the PRC to clean and repair the caging. But the PRC rescue team didn't give up until the chimpanzees were physically removed from the deplorable conditions. Limited space and lack of regular food and water had caused conflict and hostility among the group.

According to rumors, before coming to the PRC Donald, the alpha male of the troop, had lived in a pet store, in a crate above a tiger. Hazel, the alpha female, had been in the circus, bearing the nickname "Lump Lump" because she would not perform tricks. We have an old newspaper photograph of Victoria wearing a dress and roller skates. Her feet are still deformed from being crammed into those skates day after day as she was forced to perform despite the pain and irreversible physical damage it was causing. Zulu, an abnormally petite chimp, had rickets, a disease that affects bone development, probably caused by poor nutrition during her time as a pet. Unfortunately, we don't know anything about Debbie's early history, only that she was purchased as a pet. Victoria, Zulu, and Debbie were purchased as babies, and Donald and Hazel were purchased when they were a bit older.

The Dahlonega chimps were all victims of the exotic pet trade, callously pulled from their mothers' arms days after birth to become novelty pets and commodities for human entertainment. Surely, it was not long before each of them quickly outgrew the diaper and bottle-feeding stage, and the lure of these helpless babies faded. Then they experienced yet another cruel abandonment when they became too strong, too curious, too unpredictable, and too dangerous to continue being "part of the family" and were recycled back into the breeder-dealer system or left to languish in small cages with inadequate care in meager living conditions. Unfortunately, their stories are far too common.

While working to build an enclosure to house these chimpanzees at the sanctuary and eventually move them, the PRC was fortunate to have the cooperation and support of Dr. Sarah (Sally) Boysen with the Chimp Cognition Lab at Ohio State University; Dr. George Rabb, Dr. Tom Meehan, and Vince Sodaro of the Brookfield Zoo; and Yerkes Regional Primate Research Center, which made the rescue and transport to Kentucky possible. On July 6, 1999, the Dahlonega Five walked through the new tunnel system into their outdoor enclosure at the sanctuary and felt the sunshine on their faces for the first time in decades. Having escaped their dungeon of distress, they now had space to climb, swing, display, groom, and play. They also had access to water twenty-four hours a day, and even wasted some by filling their mouths and spitting it at the occasional visitor or new volunteer.

Sadly, soon after her rescue Debbie passed away. Her years spent in the dank, dark, and bacteria-infested cell had compromised her health so dramatically that she had succumbed to complications of a pneumonia infection. We remember Debbie's long delicate fingers as a symbol for the many chimpanzees reaching out for help. Fortunately, we were able to improve conditions for the four other chimpanzees before they suffered the same consequences, although they still bear physical scars from their imprisonment, along with emotional scars from abandonment, neglect, and cruelty. Now that the pressures and stress of their pasts have been eased, they can relax and behave more like normal chimpanzees. For instance, I always smile when I see Donald taking advantage of a beautiful spring morning by basking in the sunshine on a platform high above the ground after having spent the night under the stars like alpha males in the wild, who sometimes sleep away from their troop as a sign of confidence and leadership.

Donald is an extraordinary chimpanzee and a very distinguished alpha male, much older and larger than the other males. When living in Dahlonega, he lacked the ability to provide for or protect his group. He must have felt helpless to stop the fights they had and provide the females the reassurance they needed due to the dearth of space and resources. Like humans, some alpha leaders are diplomatic and strategic while others rule more like dictators, with fear and strength. Donald, who does not usually have to use his size advantage to maintain order in the group, takes a diplomatic approach, asserting his authority with tolerance and understanding. He could easily gather all the choice food items for himself, but he shares his food with the females in exchange for a relaxing grooming session. The only times I have witnessed Donald take advantage of his alpha-male status—insisting on first choice of food items during mealtimes—are when his favorite frozen juice treats are in the forage mix, and even then he leaves enough for the rest of the troop to enjoy. He is greatly respected by every member of the troop, and rightly so.

While Donald spends time maintaining his alpha-male status through occasional displays of strength (throwing barrels or pounding the ground) and settling disputes, he also takes time to relax and enjoy himself. He likes to stomp around the enclosure as I follow him, also stomping. Donald sometimes plays with the young chimps, pulling on their feet and tickling them. He does not make play faces like the younger chimps, but it is evident that he is enjoying himself when he grunts and shakes his head from side to side. Although the young males have now reached an age at which they are beginning to challenge Donald's status as alpha male, for now Donald need not be concerned with this. Eventually, a new alpha male will assume the throne, but I anticipate this transition will occur rather smoothly because of Donald's kindness. He has already stepped back a bit and let Ike, the oldest and strongest of the young males, referee some of the minor disputes among the group.

Figure 61. Donald, the alpha male of his group

Despite the emotional and physical pain he has endured at the hands of humans for most of his life, Donald shows understanding, thoughtfulness, and trust toward his caregivers. He understands that I am different from humans he has encountered in the past, that I am here to ensure that his needs are met, abate his fears, and encourage his rehabilitation. He also comprehends that I will not surprise or trick him. When I clean his enclosure with a water hose, he knows I will not spray him; he sits a few feet away as I spray one section and trusts that I will warn him before spraying in his direction. Whenever I need to close one of the hydraulic doors that he is near, I let him know; Donald always answers by knocking on the door to indicate when he is ready for me to close it. It is amazing how we communicate with each other.

In the spring, summer, and fall, the mornings are usually warm enough for the chimps to nap or play outside. At such times, I have seen Donald digging in the yard with a stick where we filled a hole with new dirt. I love moments like this, when the chimps do something similar to what they would do if their lives had not been dominated by humans. The more choices we allow them to make and the more control they have over their own lives, the more emotionally fulfilled they seem to be.

❧ ❧ ❧

The other seven chimpanzees in the troop—Noelle, Martina, Jenny, Pozna, Ike, Cory, and Rodney—were rescued in 1996 from the Laboratory for Experimental Medicine & Surgery in Primates (LEMSIP). Now in their early twenties, they arrived at the PRC before the Dahlonega group, when they were babies between the ages of one and five. New York University was preparing to close LEMSIP, and hundreds of chimpanzees were slated to go to other laboratories, mainly the Coulston Foundation facility in Alamogordo, New Mexico. But the Coulston Foundation, notorious for its violations of the Animal Welfare Act, was being scrutinized by many animal welfare groups concerned about its treatment of chimpanzees. As a result, a select few were rescued and sent to sanctuaries for permanent retirement. Our seven youngsters were part of the rescue effort, narrowly escaping the brutality of that laboratory's invasive experiments. However, they did experience the trauma common to most chimpanzees born in laboratories, beginning with being pulled from their mothers' arms at birth. Luckily, their young age provided them with the resilience necessary to recover from the neglect and abuse of their earlier years. Noelle, Martina, Jenny, Pozna, Ike, Rodney, and Cory now live as a family unit with the Dahlonega adult chimps.

Thousands of less fortunate chimpanzees have had to endure the indescribable tortures that come with a life in biomedical research. These intelligent and majestic beings have been robbed of their health, sanity, and freedom in exchange for the "advancement" of human health. Many have been housed alone in concrete jail cells and subjected to daily sedations, countless liver biopsies and body scans, radiation exposure, removal of sections of their brains, and destruction of their teeth and jaws for studies of dental reconstruction. Hundreds of chimpanzees have undergone horrible procedures for the studies of human HIV and AIDS, without scientific evidence indicating that the results translate to human biology. It was grant funding and other monetary gains and pressures from the research community that influenced the decisions to continue such experiments, regardless of the needless suffering they were causing our closest relatives.

After spending so much time with chimpanzees, I find the similarities between humans and chimpanzees undeniable. When chimpanzees get colds, they have runny noses and use the paper towels we hand out to blow and wipe their noses. Zulu cries if Cory won't come play with her. Rodney laughs if you hit your head with a balloon. The chimps protest every injustice, no matter how minor, with screams that inform the rest of the group about what has happened. While the chimps may be a bit more dramatic than humans when expressing their emotions, the similarities between our species are evident.

Because sanctuary settings lack the natural mental stimulation available in the wild such as patrolling territory boundaries, hunting and searching for food, and hiking to the next night's sleeping trees, in our sanctuary it is important for us to provide the chimpanzees with things to keep them stimulated and occupied throughout the day. Thus the chimps have access to a variety of enrichment items to sustain their interest. Though chimpanzees in the wild do not play with toy cars, dolls, soapy water and sponges, or nontoxic finger paint, use of these types of items are important in the sanctuary setting. When such avenues of expression and entertainment are not provided, chimpanzees

Figure 62. Zulu

can develop abnormal and repetitive behaviors, as commonly seen in laboratory and pet chimpanzees who have been kept in small cages without enrichment.

In our sanctuary, I do my best to mimic wild situations and environments for the chimps by providing suitable enrichment items that will allow them, for example, to make nests from straw and paper, or to fish for treats in "termite feeders" as they would for termites in the wild—using sticks to retrieve peanut butter, applesauce, honey, or other treats. The termite feeders are always a big hit. Victoria and Noelle can sit for

> **"**
>
> *Sometimes Noelle puts magazine pages on her back and struts around her enclosure beautifully draped in images and words.*

Figure 63. Noelle viewing images on a handmade card

hours fishing for little drops of honey. Other enrichment items are equally stimulating, as illustrated in the following vignettes about Noelle and Martina.

Noelle entertains herself a lot of the time. She loves magazines and shoes. Each morning when we put these items out, along with frozen treats and other toys, Noelle immediately goes for the magazines and shoes. Wearing shoes makes it harder for her to climb around the enclosure, but she doesn't seem to mind and loves stomping around in them. One time we had a pair of high heels that fit her, and she spent hours clicking around in them on the concrete floor of her playroom. Noelle examines every page of magazines, ripping out those that most interest her, such as photos of shoes, and then putting them in her "pocket"—the groove where her leg meets her stomach—so she can carry them around with her the whole day. Sometimes Noelle also puts magazine pages on her back and struts around her enclosure beautifully draped in images and words.

Martina, a very communicative chimp, usually greets me with pants of excitement when I hand out a piece of fruit to all the chimps first thing in the morning before the main breakfast forage. She often points and gestures to explain herself. She also listens to me carefully, tilting her head and watching my mouth. Martina, who knows many words, is the chimp we ask to get things in the enclosure. She enjoys being helpful, probably because she expects a treat in exchange, but I sense that she also loves the praise and attention her assistance elicits. Martina is known for collecting frogs that wander into her space and bringing them to us. I have seen her play with them by placing them on her head and catching them when they jump off. The frogs get a bit stunned, but she is usually gentle with them. Most of the chimps would just fling them across the enclosure, like they do with other animal intruders.

Not only do I appreciate Martina's intelligence and emotional complexity but I realize that she has captured my soul by the way she looks into my eyes, trying to communicate with and understand me. She pouts or cries when she is sad, laughs and smiles when she is happy, and romps and chases when she is feeling playful. All the chimps exhibit these emotions and behaviors; however, Martina can use them to manipulate and captivate both humans and chimps. Having a bit of a bossy streak, Martina holds a very interesting social position in our chimpanzee troop. She is much younger than our older female chimpanzees, who are in their mid-forties, so she gets more attention from the males. And she is older than the younger chimpanzees, who are in their early twenties, which earns her more respect and authority. She uses these advantages to gain status and wield influence.

Martina's ability to get away with stealing breakfast from higher-ranking chimpanzees reflects the politics of the troop. For instance, she can steal breakfast items, such as mangoes, from Ike and Cory, and sometimes even from alpha male Donald, free of protest. But if Cory tries to steal their mangoes the whole Chimp House erupts in screaming and Cory is chased outside and reprimanded for his blatant disregard for the troop hierarchy.

Gaining Martina's support will be a huge advantage for the young males when the transition to the next alpha male occurs in the future. Martina's influence may also sway the females in the troop toward her choice. The young boys still have a bit of growing up to do before one of them can lead the troop; in the meantime, Martina is enjoying collecting political favors.

Not as silly as some of the younger chimps in the troop, Martina would rather sit and groom than play a rowdy game of chase, but she does have a playful side. When I

Figure 64. Martina

am feeling down, she tries to cheer me up by hanging upside down or engaging me in a game of chase. Intently interested in shoes, Martina will stare and point at mine, then bang on the bars in excitement. If I am wearing a new or different pair of shoes, she will gesture for me to move so she can get a better view. Still, as much as she loves shoes I believe she might be more interested in the toes inside them, as she loves to examine and compare my toes to hers. Martina was not raised in a home where she would have seen shoes, so I feel that her fascination with shoes and toes is more a reflection of her observation skills and ability to notice novelties.

Martina knows what she wants and has no trouble expressing her desires. She brings me to tears when she communicates her deepest desire—pointing to the keys I wear on my belt and then to the locks on her enclosure, knowing I hold the keys that keep her locked up. Martina's confinement is not only for my safety but also for hers, so she is not exposed to objects and environments that would be dangerous. But I cannot explain that to her; I can only work each day to give her the best life possible and hope that she feels my compassion. Even though her situation is a drastic improvement over the fate that awaited her in the lab, she will still live in captivity for the rest of her life—

another forty years or more. As much as I treasure my time with Martina, I would give up seeing her again if it meant she could live free of metal bars.

In addition to providing enrichment materials, I teach the chimps certain behaviors to help us assist in their daily care, such as presenting their body parts for examination and opening their mouths with tongue depressors to allow administration of topical medications. Currently, I'm working on getting the chimpanzees desensitized to needles so that knockdowns for physicals are less stressful for them. Unfortunately, we can't alleviate the pain caused by a needle prick, but we can make that pain more tolerable with a great reward. During the training sessions, I use a blunted dowel to simulate the needle. After a short time, the chimpanzees begin to understand what I am doing. This training also creates a trusting relationship between us. Cory and Noelle are most eager to train with me because they are both reward crazy. They present body parts unprompted, in hopes of getting a Tic Tac. Cory will show his teeth, wrist, belly, then his butt, hoping that one of these behaviors will earn him a treat.

We do not have direct physical interaction with the primates at our sanctuary. I wish I could interact with the chimps without any bars between us, but I am aware of how dangerous that could be since even when chimps aren't being aggressive they are so strong and fast that their play can cause major damage. Instead, I connect with them using objects that allow contact from a safe distance, such as a squeegee handle or piece of water hose, with which to bump and tickle the bottoms of their feet, or feather dusters and scrub brushes for them to rub against. Chimpanzees are ticklish, especially around their necks and sides. It is even more fun to peek through the window and watch two chimps, who don't know I am there, wrestling and playing with each other. They yank on each other's feet and legs, and tickle each other's necks and sides, while grunting and laughing—a companionship they have with each other that I can never replicate. No matter how many activities are provided, sanctuaries can never re-create the freedom and experiences of the wild.

Sadly, our chimpanzees cannot be introduced to the wild because they have no survival skills and would face a new set of problems that threaten wild chimpanzees— deforestation and rapidly shrinking habitats, poaching, bushmeat hunting, disease, and the pet trade. If we cannot find solutions to these problems, the future of the chimpanzee species is sure to be bleak. We must protect their wild homes as well as their right to live and raise their families without the threat of kidnapping and murder.

As wild chimpanzees struggle to survive in Africa's jungles, their captive brothers and sisters continue struggling in laboratories, homes, and entertainment compounds. In the United States, the biomedical research community, animal entertainment industry, and the government should accept responsibility for the continued care of the hundreds of chimpanzees they have exploited for gain.

Fortunately, some efforts are underway. With the advancement of technology and use of superb computer-generated imagery (CGI), there is a trend away from the use of primates in entertainment, so the number of chimpanzees owned by entertainment trainers in the United States is decreasing. Likewise, the National Institutes of Health (NIH) recently decided to retire all the chimpanzees they are holding for medical research.

The final major battle regarding protection of captive chimpanzees, considered the hardest because it is the most secretive, is to address the future of those still owned by private individuals, breeders, and dealers. Without laws prohibiting ownership of these animals, or at least requiring owners to secure permits, we have no way of knowing the true number of chimpanzees hidden in dark basements or confined to small cages in attics. Although the buying and selling of chimpanzees is illegal in some states, regulations and laws vary from state to state, and many contain language that allows primate ownership while banning exotic animal ownership. In addition, most deals are in cash and lack documentation. As a result, it's difficult to determine which states actually ban the buying and selling of chimpanzees, how rigorously those laws are enforced, and the total numbers of such transactions.

Maybe it was fate that brought us together. Maybe the chimpanzees chose me. Whatever it was, the universe sent me on an unexpected life-changing journey that has defined who I am and what I believe. I never imagined the intensity of the bonds I have forged with each of the chimpanzees in my care over these last fifteen years. But I serve as only one voice for one group of chimpanzees. There are thousands of chimpanzees who need help and support. These amazing souls have given us a great deal, and now it is time for us to give back to them. Our obligation is not only to protect them but to ensure that their lives are enriched, peaceful, and gratifying. We need to unite as a voice for change, accountability, and justice.

A MEASURE OF HOPE

Diana Goodrich

I have always had an interest in great apes, especially chimpanzees. When I moved to Portland, Oregon, after college, I realized that I was only a few hours from Washoe, the first chimpanzee to communicate using American Sign Language (ASL). Washoe lived on the campus of Central Washington University (CWU) in Ellensburg, Washington, with four other chimpanzees. She had been raised in a cross-fostering project, immersed in a human culture that included constant communication with her human caregivers using ASL signs. I had first learned about this project while writing a paper for an anthropology class about communication in great apes, and I was fascinated.

I began to hatch a plan to meet Washoe and her family. Working with troubled children in a day treatment program, I thought I could get a master's degree in clinical psychology from CWU, continue to work with kids, and somehow get involved with chimpanzees on the side. However, when I spoke with Dr. Roger Fouts, director of the Chimpanzee and Human Communication Institute (CHCI) at CWU, he told me I had to make a full-time commitment to work with the chimpanzees in addition to being a graduate student. I decided to take a leap of faith and applied for the experimental psychology graduate program so I could learn more about the chimpanzees.

Within my first two weeks of entering the graduate program, my superficial, academic interest in great apes changed. As I began to learn what was happening to chimpanzees in captivity, I came to think of them as individuals and to care more. Meeting Moja, Tatu, Washoe, Loulis, and Dar was a humbling, life-changing experience.

They all communicated using ASL signs, and while I was able to communicate with them a little, they were much smarter than I was.

The chimpanzees had a largely utilitarian use of language. Although they signed to themselves and each other, they most often used ASL to ask for things they wanted from the humans. Moja, who loved the color red, frequently signed RED CLOTHES. Tatu often signed BLACK, not only to identify color but to communicate that she liked something. Washoe signed DIRTY PERSON if her meals weren't served quickly enough, an insult aimed at her caregivers. Washoe also signed HUG to her adoptive son Loulis, and Loulis signed CHASE to Dar when he wanted to play.

While the use of ASL illustrated their intelligence, signing was just one of many communication tools the chimpanzees used in their complex social lives. Chimpanzees, I was to discover, continuously communicate their likes and dislikes to one another and their caregivers through vocalizations and nonverbal behaviors.

As a graduate student at CHCI, I learned how to care for the chimps, making them smoothies in the morning, cleaning their night areas, and developing personal relationships with them. I was impressed by how smart Tatu was when one day she signed PAPER. I went into the enrichment room and brought out paper, paint, and paintbrushes. I slipped the paper under the caging and gave Tatu a little paint on a brush, carefully putting the bottles of paint to the side because I knew that she also enjoyed eating paint. She painted for a little while and then asked me for something else. I was gone for all of sixty seconds to retrieve what she had requested, which was plenty of time for Tatu to locate a tool that fit under the caging, snag the bottles of paint, and run off with them, quite pleased with pulling one over on a foolish graduate student.

I've always loved school, but the most valuable learning I did at CWU was while face-to-face with the chimpanzees. I learned a lot about them, and I learned a lot about humans too. Discovering that so many amazing chimpanzees had been living in captivity their entire lives was, for me, a lesson in human arrogance and disregard toward other species. I realized that Moja, Tatu, Washoe, Loulis, and Dar were lucky chimpanzees compared to the thousands living in squalid roadside zoos, biomedical research laboratories, cages in people's homes, or entertainment training compounds.

After graduate school, I wanted to continue working with chimpanzees. I got a position, along with J.B. Mulcahy, a fellow graduate student and now my partner, at the Fauna Foundation in Quebec, Canada, caring for fifteen chimpanzees who had been rescued from the Laboratory for Experimental Medicine & Surgery in Primates (LEMSIP), a biomedical laboratory in upstate New York. Working directly with the chimpanzees, along with many other species of animals at the sanctuary, was an incredible experience.

The founder of the Fauna Foundation, Gloria Grow, accepted chimpanzees who had been through hell during their years in research. Some of them, like Pablo, had been terrorized by their experience. Pablo, labeled a "hard-core research animal" in the laboratory, fought each time the staff attempted to anesthetize him. He clearly had lingering emotional trauma and was not fond of many humans, but he had very sweet relationships with the other chimpanzees. Thinking of what Pablo and the other chimps had been through was heartbreaking. However, there were many moments with these chimpanzees that would make anyone's heart soar—seeing the special fondness that Donna Rae had for Annie, or sitting with Billy Jo as he did everything he possibly could to make you laugh, or having a quiet interlude with Jeannie as she sipped her tea. It was even fun to be the object of daily target practice for adolescent Binky as he threw apples or oranges from his cart at me. Fauna was a special place, and my experience there led me to want to do more. Consequently, after three years at Fauna I went to Tufts University and earned a second master's degree, this one in Animals in Public Policy.

In 2007, the Texas state attorney general temporarily took control of Primarily Primates (PPI), a sanctuary that had over seventy chimpanzees, as well as hundreds of other animals. A colleague from graduate school, Sarah Baeckler Davis, went to PPI during this time and recruited everyone she knew with chimpanzee experience to help. J.B. and I worked as short-term volunteers. Caring for seventy chimpanzees in contrast to the five at CHCI and the fifteen at the Fauna Foundation was an entirely different experience. We used a wheelbarrow, rather than carefully arranged plates or trolleys, to bring food to the chimp enclosures. There were long days of many brief interactions with the chimpanzees instead of prolonged play sessions with one particular chimp. The experience at PPI made us all realize there was a need for more chimpanzee sanctuaries.

Spearheaded by Sarah, the three of us began to establish our own nonprofit with the goal of building a chimpanzee sanctuary. We formed a board, incorporated, wrote bylaws, and researched real estate in different parts of the country, as well as funding possibilities. Then we spoke with Keith LaChappelle, who was starting Chimpanzee Sanctuary Northwest in Cle Elum, Washington, to rescue chimps in need. PETA found out about his project and told Keith about a group of seven chimpanzees living at Buckshire, a private biomedical laboratory in Pennsylvania. Keith, who was still constructing the indoor part of a facility that would house five to ten chimps, was looking for people with chimpanzee care experience. It seemed meant to be. We merged our organization with Keith's, moved to Washington, and immediately set about putting systems in place to care for the Buckshire chimpanzees.

Buckshire conducted experiments on other animals, but for chimpanzees it was more of a holding compound. In the 1980s, when the number of chimpanzees used in biomedical testing had skyrocketed due to HIV/AIDS research, Buckshire had housed over seventy chimps, leasing them to different laboratories or, when the laboratories had a surplus, holding them for a housing fee. Buckshire was one of the first private biomedical facilities to retire chimpanzees, "retiring" them to Primarily Primates. Buckshire had moved most of its chimpanzees by the mid-1990s, largely to other laboratory facilities, and was left with a group of eight chimpanzees languishing in little cages in a dirty, windowless basement.

Sarah, J.B., and I traveled to Pennsylvania in 2007 to meet the Buckshire chimpanzees. We met Annie, Burrito (the only male), Foxie, Jamie, Jody, Missy, and Negra, and found out that the eighth chimpanzee, a male, had died a year or two before our visit. As we opened the door to the basement where they were living, we saw that a blaring television and one hard plastic ball on top of the caging were the only forms of "entertainment" for these individuals, our closest living relatives, whose minds craved mental stimulation. We had been told the chimps were housed in pairs for at least some of their time at Buckshire, but when we visited them they were all living together. We had naïvely thought they were being prepared to live in a group so they could go to a sanctuary, but soon discovered that they were grouped together because otherwise Buckshire would have been out of compliance with the legal minimum space requirements. Nonetheless, living together had given them the welcome opportunity to socialize, develop friendships, and work out their social structure before coming to Chimpanzee Sanctuary Northwest.

It was sad to read the chimpanzees' records. Among other things, they revealed that these chimpanzees had spent a lot of time at the Coulston Foundation, a notoriously dreadful laboratory in Alamogordo, New Mexico. We learned that Jody's life there consisted of a constant rotation of male chimps to impregnate her. Jody had become pregnant eleven times, had two miscarriages, and had given birth nine times. In each instance, her baby had been taken away almost immediately and, within a few weeks, another male was put in her cage to impregnate her again. Jody had been a breeding machine for the Coulston Foundation.

There was nothing in the records indicating that the chimpanzees had unique personalities, individual needs, or any desires. The lab technicians had recorded only the most minimal facts, such as injuries or births, and wrote each one on a single line, with an entire year's record fitting onto a single page or less. This is one reason our focus at Chimpanzee Sanctuary Northwest is to share everything we can about the chimps. For too long they have lived as numbers on paper and in research studies, but now we have the chance to tell the world about their amazing, unique, and charming personalities.

Figure 65. Jody, her breeding days behind her, enjoying a new life at Chimpanzee Sanctuary Northwest

◧◪ ◧◪ ◧◪

The Buckshire Seven chimpanzees, now called the Cle Elum Seven, arrived at Chimpanzee Sanctuary Northwest on June 13, 2008. During their first three weeks at the sanctuary, they were on edge, wary of our every move, and oddly compliant. For example, when we opened the door between one part of the building and another, the chimps would file through very calmly, and we could close the door behind them with no objections—behavior very different from that of the chimpanzees with whom I had previously worked, who would try to hold a door open or loudly bang on it after it closed. In general, the subdued behavior of the seven chimps was in sharp contrast to the way chimpanzees usually behave, as normally they are boisterous, often performing territorial displays meant to intimidate others by making as much noise as possible or spitting water, throwing things, and generally keeping their caregivers "in their place." It took a while for the Cle Elum Seven to get comfortable and realize that we weren't going to do anything nasty to them, and that the blankets and food would keep coming.

Dr. Debra Durham, a primatologist living in Seattle, and her colleague Dr. Hope Ferdowsian, a medical doctor who had studied post-traumatic stress disorder (PTSD) in humans, were working on a method of identifying the signs of PTSD and depression in chimpanzees and asked if we wanted to participate in their study. This was research we could support—an observational, noninvasive study that could benefit captive chimpanzees and perhaps other animals, too. The results of their study indicated that the Cle Elum Seven showed signs of PTSD and depression. I was not surprised. Chimpanzees who have lived in laboratories for decades have been physically and emotionally beaten down. Negra, the oldest chimpanzee in the group, spent most of her time by herself, sleeping. When Jamie had first arrived, she had a huge bald patch on her stomach, having plucked out most of her abdominal hair, which had left scabs covering the area. It's not uncommon for chimps in captivity to engage in this type of behavior, whether from anxiety or from crushing boredom, especially if they, like Jamie—who always needs new things to wonder about—had lacked sufficient mental stimulation for most of their lives. Jaime stopped plucking out her hair as soon as she arrived at the sanctuary, and didn't do it again until a few years ago, though not as badly as before. Unfortunately, it's not unusual for chimpanzees to continue such ingrained behaviors even after their environments have improved.

Figure 66. Jamie showing her bare belly the day she arrived at the sanctuary

When Foxie arrived at the sanctuary, she was wary and suspicious, especially around men, perhaps because most of the people in her life had been male. Her caretaker at Buckshire told us not to trust her and that she would "get you" any time she could. But she warmed up to Sarah and me right away. It took her longer with J.B., and they are now great friends. We recognize that all chimpanzees are strong and potentially dangerous, so we have very strict protocols for interacting with them—we never share their space or put our fingers through the caging. When we play chase with Foxie, we run on our side of the fencing and she runs on hers.

Foxie wasn't always so carefree. The first time we let the chimps into the larger area of the indoor space—the playroom—Foxie stomped around nervously, staying close

to the perimeter, while the other chimps went right in to explore. More nervous than the others, Foxie wouldn't touch any of the blankets we put out, which was a big deal because, as far as we knew, the chimps had never gotten blankets or anything else with which they could make nests at Buckshire or any of the laboratories where they had lived. Foxie also wouldn't touch the toys or enrichment that we put out, pushing the items aside. One day I bought a troll doll at a thrift store in Seattle, thinking some of the other chimps might like it. Unexpectedly, Foxie spotted the doll and immediately hugged it, then put it on her back like chimps do with their young in the wild. Now, ten years later, Foxie still loves troll dolls and has even expanded her interest to Dora the Explorer and Strawberry Shortcake dolls, often carrying at least one doll, and often three or four, at a time. Since Foxie had been used as a breeder and had five babies taken

"

Foxie's mothering instinct may be propelling her love of dolls, although she also recognizes dolls as inanimate objects and plays roughly with them.

Figure 67.
Foxie kissing one of her new troll dolls

away from her right after birth, her mothering instinct may be propelling her love of dolls, although Foxie also recognizes dolls as inanimate objects and plays roughly with them. Either way, there is no doubt that dolls are one of the most important aspects of her life at the sanctuary.

Though she began her stay at the sanctuary very wary and somewhat subdued, Foxie, at age forty-three, is now the youngest at heart and acts like a juvenile chimp. She spins and twirls and passes her troll dolls to caregivers, always enjoying it when we laugh, chimpanzee-style, with her. Good friends with all the chimps, Foxie often intervenes in disputes and plays the role of peacekeeper.

Negra, the oldest chimpanzee in our group at age forty-six, won my heart the first time we visited Buckshire. It was clear that the chimps were not accustomed to having human visitors, especially people familiar with chimpanzee behavior, and most of the chimps were thrilled as we made chimp faces and engaged them in play—all except Negra, who never moved from her small bench in the back corner of the room. When we were about to leave and I went to say goodbye to Negra, she stomped one foot against the wall. It was a big deal to acknowledge me, and I was honored. In that instant, all our thoughts and efforts became focused on her. We needed to get her out of there and into a sanctuary before she died.

Negra had been captured as an infant in Africa. As far as we know, with the exception of her brief months of freedom in her homeland, she had spent her entire life—more than thirty-five years—in the cages of biomedical research laboratories. As a breeder, she, like Foxie and Jody, had had many babies taken away from her. As a biomedical test subject, Negra had spent eighteen months in complete isolation after being incorrectly diagnosed as having a contagious disease. Chimpanzees who were used in breeding programs were often housed in pairs, while chimps on active biomedical studies were kept in individual cages in a room with other singly caged chimps. It must have been incredibly stressful to hear other chimps but not see them, or see other chimps across the way yet not be able to touch them. But to be completely isolated the way Negra had been, in a windowless room with no other chimpanzees around, must have been horrific, like being a prisoner of war kept in isolation, where time has no relevance. Negra must surely have given up hope, or never even experienced it.

Many of the plans and dreams for the chimpanzees' new lives at the sanctuary were about giving back hope to Negra. Because she was the oldest, and not nearly as active as the other chimpanzees, we felt a sense of urgency to provide the best life we could, as quickly as we could, so Negra would be around to enjoy it.

When the chimpanzees first arrived, the building was just being completed, including a small caged outdoor area; however, wanting to give them more outdoor space, in August 2011 we created a two-acre open-air habitat surrounded by a double electric fence. J.B. had built a test fence so the chimpanzees could learn about electric fencing before being released into their new enclosure, which we named Young's Hill after donors Karen and Don Young. Now, for the first time, the chimpanzees had grass underfoot and blue skies overhead.

I couldn't wait to see Negra outside for the first time. Though the other chimps were one-trial learners—with Missy learning just by watching others—Negra was not.

During her first day out on Young's Hill, Negra was nervous and unfortunately touched the electric fence more than once, which was hard for all of us to watch. We worried that the experience might prevent her from going outside again. But while she didn't spend as much time on the hill as the other chimpanzees, her reluctance to go out was due more often to the weather than to fear. She now spends most of her time on the hill in the spring and early summer, when the grass is green and lush. Negra basking in the sun and peacefully eating grass is the culmination of our years of work and the epitome of what a sanctuary is capable of doing for an individual.

Negra has an interesting role within the group. Jamie is clearly the boss, but we call Negra the queen because she has a revered elder statesman role. She can take food from the other chimps if she wants to, without consequences. During a conflict, Negra always has the last word by letting out a pant-hoot when she thinks the conflict should be over.

Very funny at times, Negra likes to have the other chimps hit her on the head when she's playing. The look of complete joy on Missy's face when she's doing this to Negra

Figure 68. Negra on Young's Hill

is one of my favorite things to witness. She'll look at us with an expression that seems to be saying, "Can you believe what's happening?" and then hit Negra on the head again. They both seem to consider this the greatest game in the world.

Perhaps the most important thing we are able to give Negra at the sanctuary is the opportunity to make choices. Negra can choose to go outside and eat grass for hours, or she can choose to sleep on a bed of blankets in her favorite spot on the catwalk in the playroom. The sanctuary is still captivity and can never compare to the environment the chimpanzees should have been able to experience, but there are elements of freedom woven into every activity.

Annie is the chimpanzee who has changed the most. When she first arrived at the sanctuary, she had tremendous social anxiety and was especially nervous around mealtimes, when we were serving all the chimpanzees. Annie screamed for no reason, sometimes flattening herself on the floor while doing so. It was difficult to witness. Unsure about where she fit in and what was going to happen to her, she attached herself to Missy. Annie is in love with Missy, no question about it. In the first couple of years, when Missy was not with her, Annie would watch what Missy was doing. In the last few years, Annie has come out of her shell, rarely getting anxious anymore, and asserting herself, even to Jamie, which is surprising because Jamie is pretty intimidating. Annie has played with some of the other chimps, too, and is now comfortable going out on the hill by herself. Her emotional transformation has been remarkable—another testament to what a sanctuary can do for a chimpanzee.

⁂

As a caregiver, I am in an awkward position. While I am friends with the chimpanzees, I am also the one who makes sure the locks and the fences are secure so that the chimps remain captive. I turn off the lights and go home at the end of the night, whereas the chimps stay where they are. It's a difficult and complicated relationship on both sides of the cage. I do my best to make their days interesting, but I recognize that sanctuary life is not an optimal situation for chimpanzees, who in the wild live in family groups, travel long distances foraging for food, and have real freedom. Many of us involved with sanctuaries are working toward the day when our jobs will no longer exist.

"

Annie has come out of her shell, rarely getting anxious anymore.

Figure 69. Above: Annie (left) grooming Missy (right)

Figure 70. Right: Annie walking alone on Young's Hill

The chimpanzees at our sanctuary appear to accept that this is their life, though Jamie seems also to understand the unfairness of the situation more than the others. The rest go about their business, finding things to do and spending most of their time with one another. By contrast, Jamie is constantly watching human activity, having spent her first nine years in a human home with a trainer and identifying as a human being rather than a chimpanzee. Most trainers believe that chimpanzees need to be intimidated to perform on demand, so she was likely subjected to physical abuse. After her entertainment days, Jamie was sold for use in the biomedical research industry. After all she's been through, I admire her for not accepting captivity passively. She's very demanding, gesturing for items she sees or things she wants, such as boots or drinks from the hose, and she sometimes gets frustrated if we don't find exactly what she wants right away. But as far as I'm concerned, she can be as demanding as she wants, and we will keep doing our best to make her as happy as possible.

It would be wonderful if we could give Jamie, and all other captive chimpanzees, what we have taken from them—a life in the wild. But we can't send them to Africa, where they belong, because they do not have the skills to live on their own and would never survive. There's also the hard fact that wild chimpanzee populations are facing extinction due to human encroachment.

As humans, we've done wrong by our fellow great apes. Biomedical research, to my mind, is the most obvious wrong. It's hard for me to understand how anybody can look into the eyes of chimpanzees and be okay with experimenting on them. I know many people who believe that everyone involved in using chimpanzees in biomedical research is pure evil. But while I have no doubt that there are terrible people in that business, I think there are many others who simply switch off—avoid seeing the personalities of the chimpanzees they are working with—to protect themselves emotionally. There is usually great distance between the researchers who design the experiments, possibly never seeing the chimps, and the technicians who inject the "animal subjects" with diseases and take notes on their responses. Both parties—the researchers at a distance and the technicians only following orders—are impeded from feeling responsible for the outcomes of their actions.

Some people believe research on chimpanzees is a necessary evil that must be done to help humans, but most experiments do not further the treatment of human disease. I'm not anti-science in any sense; I believe we should be exploring many avenues of medical research. I just don't believe that mistreating animals should be one of them.

Fortunately, the tides have turned for chimpanzees. The National Institutes of Health, the federal entity that controls chimpanzee testing, has announced that the use of chimpanzees in biomedical testing is unnecessary from a scientific standpoint and questionable from an ethical perspective, and they will be retiring all their research chimpanzees. Private laboratories have also ended their use of chimpanzees in experimentation. All these changes are a testament to the many people who have been working diligently on this issue for decades; but there is still a lot of work to be done, especially creating more sanctuary space, which will take a great deal of funding. While it's painful to know there are chimpanzees still suffering in laboratories, entertainment compounds, and small cages in people's homes, there is more hope for chimpanzees in captivity now than ever before. I personally know seven chimpanzees who have embraced their new lives, and every day I have the privilege of watching them increasingly distance themselves from their past experiences.

Figure 71. Jamie hugging one of her favorite boots

FULL CIRCLE

Amy Fultz

My journey with chimpanzees began with my first job as an adult, working with monkeys as a behavioral research assistant at the University of Texas MD Anderson Cancer Center, Veterinary Resources Division, a biomedical research facility that also had chimpanzees. I shared an office with two research assistants who worked in the chimpanzee area, and we spent our lunch hours observing the chimpanzee families. The dynamics, politics, and individual personalities of the chimpanzees drew me in immediately. I was amazed by their loud communicative vocalizations; the way they looked me in the eye and held my gaze; and how they understood gestures, facial expressions, and body language. I decided then and there that I would work with chimpanzees. Four years later I was offered a position as a behavioral research assistant at another research facility in Texas, known at that time as the Southwest Foundation for Biomedical Research, where I worked with 3,000 baboons and 240 chimpanzees. That position changed my life.

During my four years of working with chimpanzees in biomedical research, my job title and duties often changed. As part of training the chimpanzees, I taught them to urinate into a receptacle on command for special treats so we could do pregnancy testing. I also encouraged the chimpanzees to get into a small portable box that would allow us to move them from place to place. Movement of the chimpanzees occurred for many reasons, including research, study protocols, and management of the colony (moving the chimpanzees into all-male or all-female groups to prevent breeding). Some of the chimpanzees enjoyed going for a ride in the transfer box, while others remained frightened of it no matter how appealing I tried to make it with special treats, toys, juice, or ripe fruits.

Captivity is not a natural state for any wild animal, especially chimpanzees, who roam extensive territories and live in large social groups in the wild. Limited space and small to nonexistent social groups, common in labs of the 1970s and 1980s, as well as other places where animals were a means to an end, are not the norm for chimpanzees. This is one reason captive chimpanzees engage in abnormal behaviors, which may be coping mechanisms to deal with the stressors of an unnatural environment. Abnormal behaviors might be mild—such as a chimpanzee sucking his thumb as a result of being taken from his mother when he was just a few days old—or extreme—such as a chimpanzee biting and injuring herself, similar to humans cutting themselves and deriving pleasure and comfort from their pain. The more extreme abnormal behaviors can perhaps be alleviated or reduced by providing additional space, placing chimpanzees in larger groups, or putting singly housed chimps together with companions, but these options are not always feasible.

I observed chimpanzees plucking out their hair, circling and pacing repeatedly, and injuring themselves by biting their own arms or fingers. I tried many approaches over the years—additional attention, food puzzles, toys, positive reinforcement training to provide more choices, and even changes in social groups—to help reduce their boredom and arrest their anxiety, with varying success. It is important that people like me have worked in biomedical research labs to make the animals' lives better, looking out for the psychological welfare of the animals as required by law since the mid-1980s.

An amendment to the 1966 Animal Welfare Act, known as the US Farm Bill, was passed in 1985, mandating that the psychological well-being of primates be taken into consideration. This amendment was intended to provide minimum guidelines that assured satisfactory living space for captive primates, including more complex enclosures that offered multilevel structures and perches, giving the chimpanzees a variety of ways to utilize both horizontal and vertical space. Passage of the amendment resulted in a flurry of activity as those in the field worked toward a definition of "psychological well-being" acceptable to all parties. Defining the term was a challenge as central questions such as the following are still being considered: Should the definition be related to engineering standards such as space? Should it be a matter of individual preference?

What criteria should be used to assess well-being? I believe that some positive changes were made for primates held in laboratories at the time by increasing group size and space and adding vines, ropes, and fire hoses for the chimps to brachiate from or walk across, or hammocks for rest or play. However, the extent of changes varied from one facility to the next and in many cases was minimal. We had just begun to realize how behaviorally complex chimpanzees really are.

One of the best ways to get to know chimpanzees is through quiet observation, which has been a part of my work over the years. During my earliest days in the laboratory, I watched chimpanzees consistently beg for attention from an observer because they had limited social partners, especially chimpanzees who had been raised by humans. The chimpanzees who fascinated me the most, however, were those who did not want human attention—those wild-caught in Africa in the late 1960s and early 1970s now in captivity without their mothers and extended families, who had likely been killed during their capture. These chimpanzees saw humans as tools for the acquisition of food.

In the 1960s and 1970s, chimpanzees were used in medical research for studies on leprosy, kuru, and Creutzfeldt-Jakob disease, as well as language and development studies. And in the late 1970s and early 1980s they were commonly used in infectious virus studies and research on reproduction and malaria. Chimpanzees were also used to study various forms of hepatitis and the effects of monoclonal antibodies. During the 1980s, there was an increase in chimpanzee breeding as scientists and laboratories pushed the government to fund breeding programs, believing that large numbers of chimps would be needed for HIV research. But by the 1990s, scientists realized that chimpanzees were not good subjects for the study of HIV as they did not typically develop full-blown AIDS from the HIV virus, confirming that the disease process was not the same in chimpanzees as it is in humans. Meanwhile, chimpanzees continued to be kept in small groups in limited spaces, waiting for new research projects that didn't materialize, so people began to talk about retiring the "surplus" chimpanzees.

Then in the summer of 1995 at a primatology conference, Dr. Linda Brent, whom I had known because of our mutual interest in chimpanzees, said, "Everyone is talking about the issue of retiring chimpanzees in captivity. But they are just talking. Let's go do something about it!" The sanctuary Chimp Haven began that day. We returned to San Antonio, where we both worked, and through the efforts of Linda and many others, Chimp Haven was incorporated as a nonprofit organization in the fall of 1995.

I left the world of chimpanzees for eight years to start a family of my own, staying in touch with Linda and assisting Chimp Haven in any way I could. In 2000, Chimp Haven received a donation of two hundred acres of forested land in the northwest corner of Louisiana, twenty-two miles from Shreveport. In 2004, when Chimp Haven was making plans to welcome the first chimpanzees, I accepted the position of behaviorist, which involved encouraging species-typical behavior among the chimpanzees. The first two chimpanzees arrived in the spring of 2005. Now more than 380 chimpanzees have been retired to Chimp Haven.

Chimp Haven provides spacious, enriched permanent housing for chimpanzees retired from the pet trade, entertainment industry, and biomedical research labs. Its forests offer naturally enriched environments that encourage behaviors similar to those of wild chimpanzees, such as using tools to fish for ants, eating a variety of foods, climbing trees, swinging, brachiating, foraging, living in large groups, and making nests of vegetation. In addition to naturalistic enclosures, emphasis is placed on encouraging the chimpanzees to be active and social, and giving them choice, a very important determinant of both psychological and physical health, especially for chimps who had few choices in their earlier lives. All the chimpanzees enjoy the freedom that comes with the choice to sleep inside or outside, who to sleep next to, and whether or not to eat natural vegetation from the forests in addition to their balanced diet of fresh fruits and vegetables.

At Chimp Haven, the human caregivers are sensitive to the chimps' many needs and desires. For instance, chimpanzees receive enrichment items every day to stimulate them mentally and physically. And when chimpanzees want to interact the caregivers oblige, yet when chimpanzees want be left to themselves that option is respected. Chimp Haven is open to the public only six days a year for no more than five hours, during which time the chimpanzees have the choice to be social or retreat to their private bedrooms. Chimp Haven's staff lovingly cares for all the chimpanzees, treating them as individuals who deserve the opportunity to live happy lives with friends and family, with every choice possible.

One of my first tasks in encouraging species-typical behavior was to create suitable social groups for the arriving chimpanzees. Much like putting pieces of a puzzle together, it was necessary to combine knowledge about a chimpanzee's history with what I learned from observation and come up with a best-case scenario for that chimp's social partners or family members. As a result, Chimp Haven now has a variety of housing options that address the special needs of our chimpanzees. Several have arthritis and can't climb trees very well, while others need to be more closely observed because they are diabetic. Some new arrivals won't put their feet on the grass at first, so housing has been designed that allows them to gradually become accustomed to the natural environment.

The habitats vary from three to five acres, all roughly pie shaped with concrete walls bordering two sides. There are moats at the larger ends and indoor housing at the narrow ends. The areas that are concrete and steel all have indoor and outdoor access. Indoor rooms in all areas are heated and have bedding, hammocks, perches, and toys. Each group has access to more than one large bedroom, but the chimpanzees frequently congregate near their group mates no matter how much space they have. Most areas are connected by a series of chutes and doors to enable the groups to be moved or rotated as needed, or to provide novel areas for the chimps. There are also round quarter-acre play yards with grass and wooden structures for learning that grass is not something to be feared. As of 2018, we have three multiacre forested habitats available to the chimpanzees, through which the groups are rotated while three more habitats are under construction.

꙰ ꙰ ꙰

As fate would have it, the first chimpanzees to arrive at Chimp Haven were Rita and Teresa, whom I had known well at the laboratory. They had been living in a breeding group at the Southwest Foundation for Biomedical Research. At that time, Rita had a unique hairstyle, with the hair at the back of her head standing straight up. Teresa, who was balding, had a prominent forehead and beautiful amber-colored eyes. They were best friends, having been housed together since the late 1960s. Rita and Teresa had both given birth but had not been allowed to keep their babies for more than a year—a very unnatural situation for both chimpanzee mothers and infants as the infants would otherwise nurse until the age of about four. Now both in their forties, Rita and Teresa were elderly, thin, and, unsure of their new surroundings, very quiet. Many people talked kindly to them, gave them attention and special food, and invited them to play. Having never experienced such spacious living quarters or so many caring people bestowing undivided attention, Rita and Teresa simply needed time to adjust to their new world, which they soon did.

Puddin' was the next to arrive at Chimp Haven. We quickly realized that the information about Puddin' given to us by the laboratory that had retired him didn't match up with our observations. We had been told he was very aggressive, had bitten off the ears of another chimpanzee, and, as a result, had been singly housed and continually medicated for over a decade. Weaned from his medication before making the trip to Chimp Haven, Puddin' arrived overweight, with little muscle tone and dreadfully pale, as chimpanzees often are after spending much of their lives indoors. Contrary to the information given us, we found him to be very sweet toward people and starved for attention. Puddin' liked to groom himself and other things, almost fanatically, possibly because he had not had a grooming partner for such a long time. And when he groomed he had an impressive loud vocalization that sounded like sputtering raspberries.

Merv, another male chimpanzee who arrived during the first days at Chimp Haven, had also been medicated and singly housed for many years due to his "aggressive tendencies." We were told Merv would never be able to live in a large chimpanzee

Figure 72. Merv

social group, but we found Merv to be affectionate and playful. He did, however, tend to confuse play and aggression, and, if overstimulated, would display by loudly hooting, shaking the mesh, and aggressively charging, sometimes even throwing feces—behaviors male chimpanzees often exhibit as territorial displays. In assessing how the chimpanzees' pasts might influence their futures at Chimp Haven, we decided that our focus should always be on giving them a new start and not letting their pasts dictate their futures.

When considering an appropriate social group for Merv, we decided to introduce him first to experienced, sophisticated, and wild-born Rita and Teresa, who, having lived in small social groups in the past, exhibited normal social behaviors. Teresa had always been welcoming toward new chimpanzees, while Rita had been a bit more standoffish; but the two together, we believed, would not put up with any improper behavior from a male. It is challenging to introduce former research chimpanzees to one another in a new environment. Although we predict how they might act, the chimps often surprise us. We might expect male chimpanzees to be aggressive at first to establish their dominance; however, we have often seen male chimpanzees so happy to be with another chimp that they immediately embrace and begin grooming each other.

Merv did well with his new friends, and eleven days later, after Puddin' had repeatedly tried to groom Merv and the girls through the steel mesh squares from the enclosure next door, we allowed Puddin' to join the group. Merv and Puddin' immediately had a long grooming session and began to play. Over the next three months, this group of four was introduced to fourteen other chimpanzees, including Mason, a handsome chimp with a soulful gaze who stole my heart.

Based on the limited information we had from the sending institution, we planned to house Mason with two of our special needs and more handicapped males, Woody and Lyons. But when Mason arrived I knew he did not belong in that group; he was stocky, muscular, and very healthy in contrast to Woody and Lyons. Mason was also playful and mischievous, with a twinkle in his eye. Interestingly, he had a distinct odor about him, just like his mother Gwennie, who had also recently joined us at Chimp Haven. Their body odors were similar to a gorilla's—musky, primal, and very pungent. Mason did well during the introductions to our first group of eighteen, which included Rita, Teresa, Merv, and Puddin'. I particularly enjoyed his sense of humor and antics as he acted like a pesky little brother to the other chimpanzees, although he was

Figure 73. Mason

never malicious. On occasion, Mason liked to tease the people who cared for him, and although he would frustrate some, he always made me laugh with his goofy smiling play face and enthusiastic vocalizations when receiving special treats.

In July 2005, just weeks after they had been introduced, this group was released into a forested five-acre habitat. Watching Rita and Teresa walk into the forest for the first time, looking up at the sky with no bars above them, was an intensely emotional experience for me. After more than forty years in captivity, Rita and Teresa could now climb trees, make nests out of vegetation, and spend their time however they chose with their new family. Mason initially tiptoed through the forest, trying to shake the mud off his feet with each step he took. Puddin' immediately walked outside and explored the perimeter of the forest. He did this regularly and over time began to lose weight and put on muscle. Puddin' and Mason became best friends, spending time sitting near

Figure 74. Rita napping in the forest

the young sweet gum trees while peacefully eating the leaves and grooming each other. Sometimes we found them holding hands or touching as they slept. Merv wasn't as comfortable in the forest as the others, and it took him longer to venture away from the humans he had come to trust. I began to think of Mason and Merv as brothers who would occasionally fight but never intentionally hurt each other. Like brothers, they had each other's backs when the more dominant and aggressive males in the group threatened them. Puddin', Mason, and Merv all became important members of their family, providing support for the alpha male of the group, as well as befriending the females.

Figure 75. Good friends Puddin' (left) and Mason (right)

Teresa stepped out of the woods in 2007 carrying a baby girl—the first infant she would be able to raise and keep forever. A donor, who has agreed to support the baby financially for the rest of her life, named her Tracy. Teresa taught Tracy how to climb trees, use tools, make nests, and behave appropriately in a chimpanzee family, which meant respecting the alpha male and dominant females, grooming those to whom you want to ingratiate yourself, and sticking up for your friends and allies. Teresa was very patient with Tracy, and watching them helped shape my own view of a good mother. Mason became Tracy's "uncle" and was very proud the first day Teresa allowed him to carry Tracy on his back as they traversed the habitat. Mason often slept next to Tracy, curling his body protectively around her.

"

Teresa taught Tracy how to climb trees, use tools, make nests, and behave appropriately in a chimpanzee family.

Figure 76.
Teresa climbing an elm tree
with ten-month-old Tracy

Because chimpanzees often come to Chimp Haven in their later years to retire and live out the rest of their lives, death is a common visitor. I have been present when chimpanzees had their lives ended humanely and when they passed on their own. I have also been in attendance when staff members tried desperately to save their lives, not always succeeding. Chimpanzees, like humans, mourn their dead and may become depressed. Mothers may carry dead infants around for days before being able to say goodbye.

In Teresa and Rita's group, there have been many deaths. Puddin' died of congestive heart failure the day after Christmas about four years after his arrival. He became lethargic and withdrawn, no longer ate normally, and showed signs of swelling in his extremities. The staff, as well as the chimpanzees in his group, knew that his time on earth was nearing an end. Often when chimpanzees become ill their group members treat them differently—sharing food, grooming them more, or leaving them out of group disputes in which they may have previously participated. Puddin's group responded by grooming him and respecting his space, giving him attention when desired, leaving him alone to rest when needed, and keeping minor disagreements to themselves.

Mason did not want to leave Puddin' the day the veterinary staff decided he should suffer no longer. At first refusing to budge when asked to move to a room that would separate him from Puddin', he aggressively displayed at the staff. Recognizing Mason's need to say goodbye, staff members gave Mason and Puddin' additional time together, after which Mason willingly moved to another room. Staff members were then given the chance to say their tearful goodbyes to Puddin', who had become their friend and a favorite of both the chimpanzee and human communities. On the last day of Puddin's life, our veterinary technician approached him with the syringe to sedate him, and Puddin' gently presented his arm to her with a look of peaceful resignation in his eyes. I believe that Puddin' knew it was time to say goodbye.

When grieving the loss of my chimpanzee friends, I often cried during my forty-five-minute drive home. But with the death of Puddin', who had become a beloved friend, my tears came immediately as I watched the life force leave his body.

After Puddin's death, Mason withdrew—eating less, not acting as playful or mischievous as usual—and spent more and more time alone down by the moat where he and Puddin' had often sat eating sweet gum leaves. Staff members gave Mason more attention and also respected the fact that he was grieving the loss of his good friend.

Mason lost three additional group members that winter and went through a grieving period until spring. This was a hard time for all of us at Chimp Haven.

Two years after Puddin's death, I received a call that Teresa was unable to move her legs. Diagnosed with a degenerative spine disease that had paralyzed her lower body, Teresa was placed on soft blankets and cushioned mats, and monitored round the clock. She could have lived with paralysis, but her vital organs, including her liver and kidneys, had stopped working. To keep her more comfortable and allow our veterinary staff to observe her, she was sedated and moved to a special treatment room, where she was housed with her daughter Tracy and oldest friend Rita. Because the paralysis and associated complications occurred so quickly, it was not clear whether Rita and Tracy understood that it was time for us all to say goodbye to Teresa. I accompanied each staff member, many of whom loved her, to the special treatment room so they could say goodbye to her, crying myself as I listened to their heartfelt goodbyes.

A few days later euthanasia was chosen as the most humane option to minimize Teresa's suffering. Afterward, her body was brought back to her group so they, too, could say their goodbyes. The chimpanzees poked and prodded Teresa, as if to say, "Wake up," but when they realized she was dead they became very quiet, touching her body one at a time. I believe that when a chimpanzee is chronically ill group mates usually recognize the situation, while sudden and unexpected deaths seem more difficult for them to accept. At such times, the chimpanzees try to awaken their friends, possibly thinking, due to their past experiences in research, that the chimps are sedated. Recently, a male chimpanzee named Trevor passed away during the night after having a heart attack while asleep in his nest of hay and blankets. For many hours, Sheena, who had been his group mate for nine years, refused to leave his body, even trying to drag him outside.

Like humans, chimpanzees respond to death in their own ways. Some go on with their days as usual; others become depressed, reflecting the strength of their relationship with the deceased; still others, who weren't "friends" with the deceased, grieve because the individual was a member of their group, just as we might grieve the loss of an acquaintance. Grieving not only occurs among chimpanzees in captive settings; both popular and scientific articles describe chimpanzees grieving in the wild as well. And, like humans, chimpanzees, after a period of grieving, go on with their lives.

Teresa died the day before her daughter Tracy turned four years old. Still dependent on her mother, Tracy had been nursing at least ten minutes every hour and counted on her mother to comfort and protect her. Tracy viewed her mother's body from her perch on top of her group mate Suzanna's back. When Tracy was ready, she got down and moved closer to smell and touch her mother's body and then quickly ran into Suzanna's arms for a warm embrace.

Freckle-faced Suzanna, in her early thirties, had never had a baby of her own but immediately took over as Tracy's adoptive mother. Suzanna had been protective and loyal to the younger, or lower-ranking, members of her group, so it made sense for her to step into the role of mother. Tracy's grieving lasted approximately six months. In the month immediately following Teresa's death, she spent most of her time alone, except when sleeping in Suzanna's arms at night. Fortunately, Tracy's group responded to her needs, showering her with the attention and affection she required to get through the grieving process following her mother's death.

Figure 77. Auntie Suzanna and Tracy enjoying time together

Figure 78. Mason

One year later Mason began to have heart issues that put him at risk for a stroke. After that, whenever I was getting ready to go on vacation I would say goodbye to Mason in case I might not see him again. I received the dreaded call that Mason had died early one Saturday morning in January 2012. I drove to work crying, needing to see Mason one last time to say goodbye. That day I experienced a renewed sense of our mission at Chimp Haven after hearing someone say that Mason had been one of the lucky chimpanzees: he got to come to the sanctuary and live in the forest with friends, enjoying a dignified life until the very end.

Through my tears I said goodbye, touching him and holding his hands. I told Mason that in his honor I would continue to work for his species, especially those who had not yet made it to sanctuary. He joined Puddin' and his other group members in a forest far from our earthly experience—at least, that's what I like to believe. Mason will always live in my heart.

In December 2012, Merv passed away due to heart issues. After Merv's death, Tracy, who had often played with him, eventually became more independent and reengaged with other members of her group; she now teaches newly retired chimpanzees about her forest home. Rita, the oldest female, who, for many years had carried herself as the matriarch, watching over her family, passed away in December 2016 of simply old age. We were lucky to have spent the last twelve years of Rita's life with her.

I have experienced captive chimpanzee care at both ends of the spectrum. Many of the chimpanzees I worked with in biomedical research labs lived in sterile environments with limited social opportunities. They were stressed, easily frightened, and reactive. After decades of confinement, the chimpanzees who were living on metal bars and concrete floors now have grass under their feet. Some have even learned to climb trees for the first time. They are relaxed, playful, and happy living with their fellow chimps. This gives me hope for the future of other captive chimpanzees.

The lessons I have learned from chimpanzees I could not have learned from any other species. Chimpanzees have taught me the importance of relationships, the individuality of every being on earth, what it means to be adaptable, that adversity can be overcome, and that it's okay to forgive and move on. As a result of my work with chimpanzees, I came to care deeply about other creatures on the planet, concerned and involved with their happiness and survival. That caring rippled throughout my life, changing my worldview and personal beliefs, as well as my goals. As a result, I have developed a keen interest in conservation, ethics, and people's attitudes toward animals. I have become more cognizant of how my choices and behavior affect the environment and the lives of other species, gaining a broader perspective on the interconnectedness of all life. This has naturally evolved into teaching and mentoring as a way to pass on my knowledge.

Life eventually ends for chimpanzees, just as it does for humans. We created a beautiful memorial garden for the staff and the public to remember the chimpanzees who have lived and died here. It is in a quiet setting, away from the hustle and bustle of Chimp Haven's daily routines. The area smells of loblolly pines and decaying leaves, and breezes sometimes seem to linger there. With a weeping willow tree as the centerpiece, the forest as the backdrop, sounds of chimpanzees in the distance, and a view of them in the woodlands across moats, it is the perfect place to remember all the chimpanzees I have known, reflect on the lessons they have taught me, and dream of those still waiting in laboratories to come to their forever home.

PART II

SIGNING CHIMPS:
USING AMERICAN SIGN LANGUAGE TO
COMMUNICATE WITH US AND EACH OTHER

When the animals come to us, asking for our help, will we know
what they are saying?...Will we be able to wake ourselves, and act?

—GARY LAWLESS, *First Sight of Land*

Figure 79. Bruno behind bars at LEMSIP

KEY OUT: A CHIMPANZEE'S PETITION FOR FREEDOM

Mark Bodamer, PhD

In the fall of 1988, during the second year of my experimental psychology PhD program at the University of Nevada–Reno, Friends of Washoe and the Jane Goodall Institute hired me to spend three months working at the Laboratory for Experimental Medicine & Surgery in Primates (LEMSIP), a large biomedical research facility in upstate New York affiliated with New York University. At that time, LEMSIP had close to one thousand nonhuman primates, three hundred of whom were chimpanzees—approximately two hundred adults and one hundred youngsters. Most of the primates, including vervets, tamarins, marmosets, and gibbons, were being used in a variety of intensive biomedical research, including research associated with HIV; hepatitis B; cervical, liver, and lymph node biopsies; blood transfusions; reproduction; and bone marrow transplants. There was also ongoing research in reproductivity using artificial insemination and electro-ejaculation on the chimps to provide the lab with a steady supply of chimpanzees.

While I was considering the job at LEMSIP, Jane Goodall said to me, "Mark, if they are going to do research, which they are, and we cannot stop it right now, then let's do whatever we can to make the chimpanzees' conditions better." Even though I was personally opposed to the use of primates in biomedical research, I knew that the research was not going to end that day, that month, that year, so I took the job, which entailed identifying safe, inexpensive enrichment activities and developing an enrichment plan so LEMSIP would be in compliance with federal regulations.

Dr. James Mahoney, the head veterinarian at LEMSIP, was eager for me to develop and implement the plan for ten adult male chimpanzees who were part of the HIV vaccine program, requiring them to live alone—indefinitely. The chimps in this HIV unit were Billy Jo, Sparky, Chaz, Robert, Tom, JR, Zippy, JoJo, Magilla, and Doc. If human beings volunteered to participate in an HIV research program, we would regard them as doing something noble for humanity. But these chimpanzees had not volunteered to be part of the experimental projects; not one of them had given their informed consent.

Figure 80. Cages in one of the adult units at LEMSIP

In an atmosphere reminiscent of an army barracks, the ten cages in each building for adult chimpanzees were arranged in two parallel rows of five cages facing each other. About twelve feet of space down the middle of the room separated the front door surfaces of the cages, with three feet on the sides between the cages. The chimpanzees could partially see each other but could not touch. With no room to climb or swing in that tiny, barren, dismal environment, the chimps were clearly suffering. It wasn't as if they were going to put in three years of service and then be free. Every chimpanzee at LEMSIP had to endure circumstances that most humans could not bear without losing their minds.

The doors at each end of these buildings were kept closed and partially barricaded. When the food door at one end was opened, the room typically filled with food grunts and excitement. But when the research door at the other end was opened there was quite a different response. Many chimpanzees became bipedal, swaggered back and forth, and increased their banging and screaming. Others crouched in the backs of their cages, screaming with full fear grins. By chance, I was in the unit a few of the days when research was being conducted. On occasions when the chimpanzees were in absolute fear, I was able to squat and quietly be with them in a way that helped lower their arousal levels. A few of the chimps reached out and patted my shoulder. Once sure that I was safe, I offered reassurance contact with a brush. Such cross-species physical contact calmed the chimpanzees that I touched, as well as other chimpanzees in that unit who had no direct physical contact with me.

One of my goals at LEMSIP was to get every technician as excited about socializing safely with the large adult males as they were with the small, young chimpanzees. It was a goal inspired by something Jane Goodall had emphasized on one of her visits to LEMSIP. She had encouraged the staff to spend more time with the chimpanzees, especially the older ones, saying, "For you are all they have. You truly have a remarkable responsibility for the care of our sibling species."

During my first few days at LEMSIP, I could see and hear the technicians chuckle each time I entered the building that housed the ten HIV-positive adult male chimpanzees, a unit that had some of the largest and least understood chimpanzees, the outcasts. Whenever anyone entered their building, these chimpanzees made such a cacophony of noises that many staff members thought the chimps were possessed by demons, so it seemed unlikely that such staff members would ever visit or interact with the chimpanzees in an enriching way. They had very little in their cages, as did all the

facility's chimpanzees, except maybe a suspended tire to sit on to get their bodies off the metal bar floor, though many tires just lay on the ground.

In a very short time, to the staff's surprise I was able to calm the chimpanzees and reduce the noise level of the unit almost completely, gaining the technicians' respect. Soon the chimpanzees were making new sounds, such as food grunts and laughter, rather than fear faces and fearful screams. The key was to convey from the very first interaction that the chimpanzees were superior and humans were uninvited visitors in their home, as well as to give the chimpanzees the respect they deserved. I explained that at no time should any staff member reach in and touch the chimpanzees or initially allow them to touch the staff. Instead, it was necessary to acknowledge the superiority of each chimpanzee by crouching down, offering a pronated wrist, bobbing the head, and making breathy pants or soft grunts. This was how I approached all chimpanzees.

"

They had very little in their cages except maybe a suspended tire to sit on to get their bodies off the metal bar floor, though many tires just lay on the ground.

Figure 81.
Shirley, a research chimpanzee at
LEMSIP, covering herself with
sheets of paper in her barren cage

After spending time together, depending on individual reactions I allowed a few of the chimpanzees to touch my elbow through the bars of the cage, indulging their interest in removing dry skin. I sometimes used a hairbrush for grooming or as a tool for tickling, the handle making a safe extension of the hand. When such interactions are done properly and safely, a relationship based on play, not fear, can emerge. I repeatedly experienced the pleasure of greeting chimpanzees with a few head bobs and seeing them respond with playful faces and laughter.

One of the worst aspects of the LEMSIP facility was the chimps' daily living conditions. The 5' × 5' × 6' cages were nothing more than tiny closets with bars hung from the ceiling on runners. While I was there, new federal guidelines regarding cage size led to long and heated debates. The new cage size requirements turned out to be an abominable 5' × 5' × 7', and the administration at LEMSIP felt that this minor change would do little for the chimpanzees yet not implementing the change would make every cage there out of compliance. However, there were many loopholes. If the researchers could make a case for the legitimacy of their research protocols, the chimpanzees could live alone in the smaller cages the entire time they were "on study," which might be for the rest of their lives.

There was another reason LEMSIP did not want to change the size of the cages. If they were larger, the cages would not fit into the autoclaves for cleaning. The daily cleaning protocol involved collecting the chimpanzees' urine and excrement that fell through the cage bars onto big plastic sheets on the ground. The sheets were rolled up once a day, put into incinerators, and burned. The staff could walk away from the horrid smell, but the chimpanzees could not; they were exposed to the smell of their building and of the furnace.

Some of the cages were not cleaned the entire time I was there, which was reprehensible. At the very least, the cages should have been sprayed or hosed down every day so the chimpanzees could live in clean and uncontaminated cages. The main reason for the lack of cage cleaning was that Dr. Jan Moor-Jankowski, the director of LEMSIP, was fearful about spreading airborne germs. As a graduate student, he had been responsible for a colony of monkeys and returned one day from a conference to find the monkeys dying from an airborne pathogen; Moor-Jankowski had then vowed to find a way to clean, other than spraying or hosing down the cages, that would eliminate airborne pathogens. He believed he was keeping hundreds of chimpanzees safe, but they were living in toxic putrid squalor.

🝔 🝔 🝔

Since the chimps were going to live out the rest of their lives alone in small cages, relieving their boredom with daily enrichment was especially important. I created three categories of enrichment activities—social, food, and object manipulation—and provided the technicians with examples of each one. The objective was to select one activity from each of the categories so the chimpanzees could receive a variety of enrichment every day. A score sheet was made available for the technicians to monitor the chimps' daily enrichment activities, enabling us to ensure that whatever each chimp liked the most was included on a regular basis. Technicians were also to identify inexpensive and safe activities in which the chimps could engage twice a day or, at a minimum, once a day. It wasn't important how the chimps interacted with the enrichment; the goal was to counteract their boredom with something they enjoyed doing.

The notion of finding an enrichment activity that could be given to all the chimps was naïve, because each individual had unique interests and preferences that often changed. I emphasized the importance of recognizing the intelligence and individual differences of the chimps, as well as the need to be sensitive to those issues in making decisions about enrichment. The chimpanzees were receptive to their enrichment almost immediately.

Social enrichment was the most important one for both the chimpanzees and the staff. The chimps might be given the most extravagant treats or objects with which to interact, but it was individual time with humans that the chimps needed most. Chimps by nature are social beings, so isolation is unquestionably the worst thing for them to endure.

Some chimpanzees were indifferent about interacting with humans, but others, like Billy Jo, were very excited by it. Billy Jo wanted attention so badly he would make noise by rattling his tire, hitting the door, or shaking and banging whatever was in sight, including the metal food box—stopping his banging only when a person came to say hello. A few chimpanzees enjoyed looking at magazines and simply spending time with their technicians. One staff person dressed up like a clown, blew bubbles, and made popcorn that the chimpanzees enjoyed. Once Tom, a remarkable chimp, got to know me he would reach his arm through the bars as far as he could and pat me on the shoulder, as if to say, "Way to go. Good job, buddy." His slap was gentle, though I could feel his enormous strength. With Tom, I always felt like I was being greeted by a very dear old friend. Social interactions, like grooming and play, were especially fun to watch because such activities encouraged humans and chimpanzees to enjoy each other's company.

Object manipulation offered the chimps opportunities to interact with and maneuver items using their hands, feet, or both. Sparky loved to color and spent hours marking on paper with crayons. While Tom and Doc liked to look at themselves in a mirror, others liked playing tug-of-war through the bars with a six-foot piece of plastic tubing.

To replicate a chimpanzee behavior that was common in the wild—using twigs or branches to fish for termites—we stuffed raisins and marshmallows into plastic tubing and gave the chimps willow branches to "fish" out their treats. Some chimpanzees

Figure 82. Sparky coloring

Figure 83. *Above top: Doc observing himself in a mirror*
Figure 84. *Above bottom: Gus playing tug-of-war with a technician*

"fished" for raisins, and others tore open the tube with their teeth. We did not care which they did since the goal was simply to give them something to do. Billy Jo was excellent at fishing with a willow branch. He had no choice. As a young pet, Billy Jo's teeth had been pulled with pliers so he'd be less likely to hurt someone, which put him at a big disadvantage if he were ever to join a group of chimpanzees. Chaz had a clever style of retrieving the raisins. He delicately inserted the willow branch with its leaves into the tube and, instead of just pulling it straight out, held the tube in his right hand and pulled the willow branch up very slowly with his left hand. Not only did Chaz

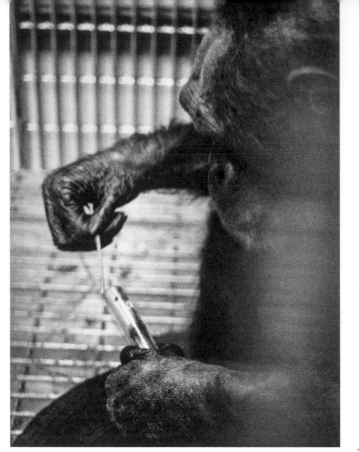

Figure 85.
Chimp fishing
for raisins

bring up all the food, but the leaves were still intact, and he methodically licked them to obtain the sticky treat. We referred to this as the "roto-rooter method" of extraction. Chaz was the only chimp observed to use this technique; it would have been interesting to see if his particular style of "fishing" could have been adopted by others.

The enrichment the chimps enjoyed most was food, undoubtedly because they did not get a variety of food in their usual diet. I wanted the LEMSIP chimps to get a mixture of healthy food in addition to their daily monkey chow. I explained the importance of offering a variety of food types to the chimps, given Goodall's report that chimpanzees in the wild had been observed to eat over 250 types of plants. We also paid attention to how the food was presented to the chimps because presentation could influence how they responded. When the chimps weren't excited about the treats, the technicians gave them little sales pitches in the form of food grunts to indicate that the food treats were special. Of course, when we offered a treat like frozen Kool-Aid pops no extra food grunts were needed.

Initially, the plan was for me to create enrichment only for the ten HIV-vaccinated adult chimpanzees, but after hearing about the chimpanzees' responses many other technicians asked me to introduce the same activities and items into their units. Consequently, Dr. Mahoney and I agreed to provide as much enrichment as we could for the entire facility. It was exciting to see the effect of enrichment on each of the participants—human and nonhuman. The chimpanzees received much-needed stimulation, and the humans gained new perspectives on the chimpanzees under their care.

※ ※ ※

When I considered taking the position at LEMSIP, I knew that four chimpanzees were there from the Institute for Primate Studies (IPS) in Norman, Oklahoma—Bruno, Booee, Cindy, and Thelma—who could communicate using American Sign Language (ASL). I hoped to meet them and learn what was important to them. These four chimpanzees had been subjects of a study by Dr. Roger Fouts that had been published in 1972 in *Science*, a prestigious journal that encourages creative, leading-edge scientific research. The intention of this study had been to see if older chimpanzees could acquire ASL as easily as Washoe, the first chimpanzee to learn it. Even though they were older than Washoe when first exposed to ASL, the Oklahoma chimpanzees had all successfully acquired the same set of signs but with individual variations in the rate of acquisition. The study reinforced the observation that chimpanzees were unique individuals, just like humans.

Dr. Mahoney told me that Bruno, who was hepatitis positive and living in the hepatitis hot unit, often made hand gestures his staff members did not understand, and he wondered if any were ASL signs. Many years before, while working on my master's and PhD degrees, I had learned ASL so was eager to see if Bruno would use it with me and, if so, what he would sign.

Bruno had been born at the Institute for Primate Studies (IPS) and taken away from his mother soon after birth to be a test subject in Dr. Herb Terrace's ape language study in New York—preceding Terrace's highly publicized and eventually controversial language study work with a chimpanzee named Nim. After about a year, Bruno had been returned to IPS and then unsuccessfully placed in a series of human foster homes before ending up back at IPS, where Dr. Roger Fouts taught him most of his signs.

My desire to meet one of the chimpanzees featured in the *Science* article was soon fulfilled. Dr. Mahoney invited me to join him on a walk through the units to do a visual check and say hello to the chimpanzees. Entering the hepatitis hot unit, I noticed Bruno's name on a cage and stopped. While Dr. Mahoney continued down the unit greeting the chimpanzees, I stayed behind to meet Bruno. He was quite a handsome chimpanzee, very large with dark, shiny hair. Approaching him in a submissive posture—crouched, holding out a pronated wrist, bobbing my head, and making a few soft grunts—I conveyed that I knew my position as an inferior uninvited guest in his territory. Bruno crouched and watched me quietly. After a few minutes, I stood up slightly and signed HELLO.

Following a brief pause, during which Bruno continued to gaze at me, I signed the phrase WHAT'S YOUR NAME, eager to see if he would sign his name. Bruno did not sign his name, but he did sign two words. I was not amazed that Bruno signed; I was amazed at *what* he signed. The first sign was difficult to see because he made it near the floor and his body was at an angle to mine. But a few seconds later Bruno repeated the same sign. This time the sign was clear, although it took me a moment to interpret it because it wasn't one that I was used to seeing. Bruno had signed by bending his index finger at the first knuckle, then making contact with his knuckle in the opposite palm, followed by turning his knuckle in his palm. Bruno had signed KEY. He then signed again, pulling one hand out from the grasp of the other—the ASL sign for OUT. I signed NOT UNDERSTAND SIGN AGAIN. Bruno shifted his posture, orienting his body more directly toward me; raised his hands slightly, making it easier to see his signs; then signed again. This time both signs were very clear: OUT KEY OUT. I was spellbound. Bruno began to bob and then crouch by his cage door. He signed OUT OUT, bobbing and crouching even more excitedly. He continued to sign OUT several more times. Of all the phrases Bruno could have signed, he signed KEY OUT. I didn't think his message was by any means random. Bruno wanted out of his tiny cage.

I signed back CAN'T SORRY CAN'T. Bruno's shoulders dropped, and he walked to the back of his cage, crestfallen. I started to cry as an avalanche of sadness hit me in the gut. Bruno had directly asked me to free him, expressing emotions just like any human who had been wrongfully imprisoned, and I had to say no. I couldn't take him out because, as humanized as he had been in his early life, he was still a wild animal

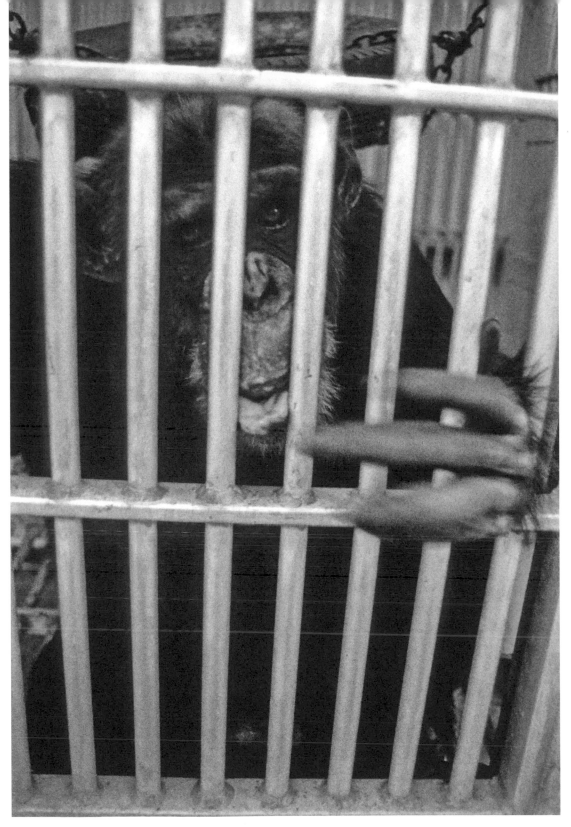

Figure 86. Bruno communicating with Mark

and could easily hurt, or even kill, someone. This communication with Bruno broke my heart and still remains one of the most powerful experiences I have ever had. I wished I could accompany him as he enjoyed fresh air, felt the warm sun, climbed a tree or two, and perhaps played a game of tickle and chase as he had done prior to having been abandoned at LEMSIP.

As the tears streamed down my face, Dr. Mahoney glanced back at me. I quickly wiped my tears away because I didn't want him to see me crying. One of Dr. Mahoney's expressed concerns was that the enrichment person be able to do the work without showing emotion, and I wanted to ensure that I would have access to all the units. But that wasn't the only day I was emotional; the sheer number of chimps at LEMSIP—three hundred of them—was overwhelming for me. I'm sure every chimpanzee at LEMSIP wanted KEY OUT. Sadly Bruno, like so many others, took his last breath inside a horrid cage.

As a result of my encounter with Bruno, I began teaching a basic class in ASL to encourage better communication with the chimpanzees. The technicians and, to my surprise, a few researchers attended the class regularly. We discussed basic grammar and selected signs that would be helpful in the care of the chimpanzees. I taught them the sign HURT, made by touching the ends of extended index fingers, and how the meaning was modulated by putting the index fingers onto the corresponding part of the body that is hurt. I asked the staff to imagine how beneficial it would be if a chimpanzee could tell them where it hurt before a serious ailment manifested, thus allowing them to eliminate discomfort and possibly save a life.

One day sign class was interrupted when a technician abruptly entered the room, his excitement suggesting at first that perhaps a chimpanzee had escaped. But, like a proud father showing a child's picture, he held out a page from a coloring book depicting an image of an octopus and said, "Look, guys, you are never going to believe this." The paper showed that a chimpanzee named Kelly had markings that were not random but rather corresponded with lines in the drawing. Kelly had drawn lines over the tentacles and face of the octopus, as well as filled in all the air bubbles, indicating that she had made sense of the image, using her advanced visual motor coordination to fill in the outlines. The picture was very interesting; however, the most important thing to me was the technician's sense of awe. My hope was that it would influence not only his relationship with the chimpanzees under his care but his view of all chimpanzees.

Roger Payne, founder of the Ocean Alliance and the scientist who discovered the songs of humpback whales, talks about embracing our connection with nature in such a way that we "catch the listening." He believes that bumper stickers saying "Save the Whales" should say "Saved by the Whales" because of the awe these animals inspire in us, motivating us to help them. The technician who experienced Kelly's drawing caught the listening in that moment. Very possibly this technician was "saved by the chimps." I hoped his epiphany would sensitize the entire staff to be more aware of their special moments with these remarkable beings.

※ ※ ※

Late one afternoon Moor-Jankowski called me into his office. He asked me to put together a videotape demonstrating the enrichment activities at LEMSIP for a meeting to be held in upstate New York celebrating the twenty-fifth anniversary of xenographic research, which involves transplanting body parts from one species into another. At first, I wanted nothing to do with this and had an impulse to burst out of the room, interpreting his request as an unacceptable exploitation of my work and of the chimpanzees.

Walking out of the room dejected, I called Jane Goodall, who advised, "Put the film together, Mark. Perhaps some good will come of it." I began work on the film immediately, though still distrustful. After collecting and editing footage to be used in the film, I worked on the script with Dr. Mahoney for several days and nights until it was finished.

Early the next morning I was startled when I heard Moor-Jankowski's booming voice over the facility intercom, saying, "Mark Bodamer, Mark Bodamer, Mark Bodamer, to my office immediately." As I nervously entered his office, he said with a sense of urgency, "I watched your film last night and then had trouble sleeping. Where do you draw the line?" I replied confidently, "I don't believe in a line, I believe in the Darwinian notion of continuity—not just of blood and bone, but the continuity of cognition and emotion across species." Moor-Jankowski answered in a soft, almost apologetic tone, "But I am a Roman Catholic." I fired back quickly and excitedly, "Well, so am I." We then had a discussion about what it really meant to embrace our blood brothers and sisters when you are Catholic. Most Roman Catholics believe that nonhuman animals do not have souls. I told Moor-Jankowski that I didn't believe that and then said, "Why isn't God inside the redwood tree or a rose or a chimpanzee?

Everything is special. Everything is God." Such beliefs embody Albert Schweitzer's philosophy to live with a reverence for all life.

LEMSIP and other biomedical research facilities use chimpanzees for research because they are physiologically similar to humans. The blood of humans and chimpanzees is 99.8 percent identical, and the DNA of humans and chimpanzees is 98.6 percent identical, making chimpanzees the closest living beings to humans.

Most people, including the founders of LEMSIP, embrace the notion of continuity of blood and bone, which is why so many nonhuman animals are used in research and testing with minimal opposition. But our likeness goes much further. Research has found that chimpanzees and humans are alike in terms of emotions, personalities, and intelligence; we equally experience pain, passion, sadness, and grief. We are also similar in what we eat, do, and our ability to feel empathy and be altruistic. Many of the previously believed gaps between humans and chimpanzees have come to be gaps only in knowledge.

Subsequently, I learned that Moor-Jankowski had trouble sleeping because the video had shown the LEMSIP chimpanzees using tools creatively. Seeing both Doc and Tom looking into a mirror and recognizing themselves had stunned Moor-Jankowski. He was excited and asked me to call the *New York Times* to report the behavior. I explained that chimpanzees' use of mirrors had already been documented—actually, this information had been known for almost a hundred years. In that moment, I thought Moor-Jankowski finally recognized that chimpanzees were not passive hairy test tubes but rather our true sibling species, and that Darwinian continuity went beyond just blood and bone.

In the years following his "epiphany" of experiencing Doc and Tom as conscious individuals, and up until the day he left LEMSIP, to my knowledge Moor-Jankowski did not improve conditions for the LEMSIP chimpanzees. Sadly, he did see—and treat—the chimpanzees as hairy test tubes, disregarding their intelligence, emotional aptitude, and sentience.

After leaving LEMSIP, I was haunted by memories of what the chimps there had to endure on a daily basis. I had left the enrichment plan with the LEMSIP technicians so they could continue providing daily enrichment for the chimps. A year later, when I returned for a visit Dr. Mahoney said that this was happening, but some of the technicians told me that enrichment was no longer being encouraged—that the manager of husbandry had thwarted the enrichment project, instructing the staff to move on to other tasks when they were finished feeding and cleaning the chimps' cages. When the technicians had asked for a little more time to give enrichment to the chimps, they had been advised to forget the enrichment. Clearly, caring for the chimps on an emotional and social basis held no value to this manager. Unfortunately, there were no standards for enrichment in the federal guidelines, so LEMSIP could easily get off the hook when inspectors were on the premises by just showing them a plan; they didn't have to actually give chimpanzees enrichment. This really upset me; I felt that if we were going to exploit chimpanzees in the name of biomedical research, enrichment should be a high priority.

My work at LEMSIP made me reflect more intently on the perception people have of chimpanzees, not only in biomedical research but in the larger context of life on earth. People are accustomed to seeing chimpanzees in zoos or in Super Bowl commercials, but most individuals know very little about how chimpanzees are treated in biomedical research, the entertainment industry, and the pet trade. Chimpanzees are usually viewed as hairy clowns or hairy test tubes. However, if people spent time watching chimpanzees engage in social or solitary play, object manipulation, or mother-infant interactions, they would never see chimpanzees in that way again.

In addition, many people feel uncomfortable, or even threatened, by the great similarity between humans and chimpanzees. Watching chimpanzees engage in behavior that is very similar to our own and in contrast to our preconceived notions can be intimidating, forcing viewers to adjust or reinterpret their beliefs, or even deny the reality of the situation. For example, while at a zoo I once heard a woman who was observing a chimpanzee looking at a magazine say, "Oh my God, he's reading a magazine." As she got closer, she said, "Oh, it's upside down," adjusting her interpretation with a sigh of relief. Contradictions between a person's thoughts and perceptions create cognitive dissonance, resulting in a feeling of uneasiness. Using the analogy of a car radio that's emitting static, if we adjust the dial to eliminate the irritating noise, we change that aspect of the input and thus relieve the uneasiness. The woman watching the chimp reading the upside-down magazine breathed a sigh of relief because the chimp's behavior no longer challenged her preconceived belief.

To understand the significance of all animals, we must slow down and experience them. When we move too fast, we miss the connectedness of life. As humans who notoriously separate and categorize, we run into problems when we see ourselves disconnected from other species and life-forms. Having grown up in the Jesuit school system, known for academic excellence and social justice, I remember the expression "God in all things," which I took literally to mean God is in all living things—trees, flowers, rain, rivers, fish, and animals—that we are all connected. Decades later, when I arrived at Gonzaga University to teach, Father Moynihan gave an opening address in which he quoted a short poem by Meister Eckhart, a fourteenth-century Christian mystic, that perfectly expresses my relationship with chimpanzees, nature, and all of creation:

Apprehend God in all things,
for God is in all things.
Every single creature is full of God
and is a book about God.
Every creature is a word of God.
If I spent enough time with the tiniest creature—even a caterpillar—
I would never have to prepare a sermon.
So full of God is every creature.[1]

I encourage my students to be humble, open-minded, and compassionate in relation to animals and the earth. Further, I use a Jane Goodall adage as a beacon in my classes and in my own life: "Only if we understand, can we care. Only if we care, will we help. Only if we help, shall all be saved." Believing that it is important to see and experience God in all things, we need to stop, listen, and be part of the moment so we can embrace our connection with chimpanzees. Then we will actually catch the listening and have a chance to be "saved by the chimps."

CONVERSATIONS WITH CHIMPANZEES: WHAT THEY HAVE TOLD ME

Mary Lee Jensvold, PhD

I have worked with the chimpanzees Washoe, Moja, Tatu, Dar, and Loulis since 1986. These chimpanzees use American Sign Language (ASL) to communicate with humans and each other. Signing is also a way for humans to communicate with chimpanzees using a human language. Knowing how and what these individuals communicate tells us what's important in their world.

I have always been intrigued with communication between species; it's a window into the minds of other beings. I remember, as a high school student, watching a television documentary about the life of Dian Fossey, who studied gorillas in Rwanda, and thinking, "That's what I want to do—work with apes." My goal wasn't just to study apes but specifically to study those who communicated using a human language. This was in the early 1980s, when the various language projects begun in the 1960s and 1970s were well underway.

I prepared during my undergraduate studies at the University of Oregon by taking classes in ASL and primatology, majoring in psychology, and minoring in anthropology. Many of the classes I took in primatology were taught by Dr. Paul Simonds, who had studied macaques in India. A kind professor, he gave me the encouragement I needed to pursue my dreams. After graduating with a bachelor's degree, I applied for a job as a research assistant to work with Koko, a signing gorilla, and secured an interview with Koko's human guardian, Dr. Francine Patterson. I then traveled to Palo Alto, California, for what would be a life-changing experience.

Koko lived in a specially designed building, and I initially met her through a sliding glass door. She invited me inside. I had brought Koko gifts—a hat and a bandana—which she accepted and signed about. I had just had a conversation with a nonhuman, and its impact on me was far more significant than the details of the conversation. It was one thing to read about such interactions in books and newsletters, but quite another to actually be part of one. It transformed my perspective on human-nonhuman relationships.

Prior to this encounter I had, like most people in our culture, assumed there were inherent differences between humans and nonhumans. Otherwise, why would we be allowed to keep them in cages, experiment on them, use them for work, and eat them? But when my conversation with Koko seemed reminiscent of those with children I realized that my perceived boundary between humans and apes was no longer clear and wondered where the boundary was. Then suddenly I realized that there was no absolute boundary but only degrees of relatedness. This was the first glimmer of a much greater understanding about relationships between species that I would gain later.

I didn't get the job with Koko, but I was accepted to Central Washington University (CWU) in Ellensburg as a graduate student in experimental psychology, studying under Roger Fouts. This was the beginning of my lifelong commitment to chimpanzees. Roger and his wife Deborah Fouts, who had directed the project with Washoe, Moja, Tatu, Dar, and Loulis for many years, were exceptionally welcoming.

In class, Roger explained what I'd experienced after meeting Koko—the errors in Cartesian dualism. Cartesian dualism is the perceived separateness between humans and nonhumans, allowing us to objectify nonhumans. This view is an inherent part of Western culture postulated by René Descartes, an influential seventeenth-century French philosopher who thought animals did not possess souls or minds as did humans, saw animals as machines (*automata*), and suggested that since they felt no pain they could be treated like machines. Because of these philosophical underpinnings, we objectify nonhumans in our laboratories, while hunting, at our dinner table, and in forms of entertainment, which allows for disrespect and exploitation of them. But how could I objectify a gorilla who had signed to me about her thoughts, and if my conversation with Koko reminded me of speaking with a child, how could she be that different?

The chimpanzees at CWU lived in what we called the Chimp Lab, which was not a typical laboratory. It was on the third floor of the psychology building, with three hundred square feet of inside space and no access to the outdoors. What the physical space was missing was offset by the social environment. The caregivers were friends with the chimpanzees. There were never more than a dozen students on a project, each one individually trained to interact with the chimpanzees. The routine was to prepare homemade meals, clean enclosures, and provide activities. It had the feel of a home because it *was* a home, the chimpanzees' home. The Foutses had established the nonprofit organization Friends of Washoe to support the chimpanzees, selling T-shirts and buttons to raise money for their food. We gleaned produce from the grocery, and we all gave of our time.

Those early days of learning to care for the chimpanzees were exciting. Experts at reading nonverbal behavior, the chimpanzees instantly knew what type of person someone was and if the person was afraid, arrogant, angry, or sad, often reacting to those feelings. The chimps taught me a great deal about myself, especially about recognition and acceptance of my own emotions and temperament, as well as about the mind of another species.

First Washoe, and later Moja, Tatu, and Dar, had been raised like deaf human children from a very young age under the direction of Allen and Beatrix Gardner at the University of Nevada-Reno. Allen Gardner had been trained in experimental psychology, and Beatrix Gardner had worked under the famous ethologist Niko Tinbergen. They reasoned that if chimpanzees couldn't learn to talk perhaps they could use their hands to communicate gesturally, and thus used only ASL around the chimpanzees. These young cross-fosterlings (chimps raised by humans) acquired signs in patterns that resembled how human children learned language—their vocabularies grew, they combined signs, and they asked and answered questions. They signed to themselves like humans talk to themselves, signed in imaginary play, and signed to each other. Later research showed how chimpanzees skillfully navigate a conversation, initiating interaction, maintaining topics, rectifying misunderstandings, and persisting in the face of them.

Roger Fouts had received his PhD while studying with the Gardners and working as one of Washoe's caregivers. He and Washoe left the University of Nevada-Reno for the University of Oklahoma in 1972. Then the Gardners had begun a second

Once I brought Washoe a five-headed hand puppet and asked her what it was; she signed STUPID.

Figure 87. Washoe

cross-fostering project with Moja, Tatu, Dar, and Pili, a chimpanzee who later died of leukemia at age two.

At the University of Oklahoma in 1978, Washoe, at age fourteen, adopted ten-month-old Loulis. Under the direction of Roger Fouts, humans had not been allowed to sign around Loulis; thus his only sign language input had been from Washoe and the other signing chimpanzees. Little Loulis had begun to sign in seven days, combining signs after five months, and by the end of the five-year signing restriction had acquired over fifty signs. Loulis's sign acquisition was later reported in books and scientific journals by the Foutses and their colleagues. Loulis's first sign had been the name of his human caregiver, George. Another of his early signs had been COME. As his vocabulary grew, Loulis had signed mostly to other chimpanzees, often requesting social activities such as chase and grooming.

The cultural transmission of a gestural language between humans and chimpanzees, and among chimpanzees, had come full circle. Wild chimpanzees who live in communities communicate with each other using gestures, with each community having its own repertoire of gestures. Young chimpanzees learn the gestures of their fellow community members just as the young cross-fosterlings had learned the gestures of their human caregivers. This was how Loulis had learned the gestures of his chimpanzee companions.

During the weekend shifts at CWU, I was alone and had the opportunity to converse with the chimpanzees while preparing and serving meals, cleaning enclosures, and providing activities for the day. While flipping through a magazine, Tatu would sign about pictures. She had favorites, such as cheese, sandwiches, and things that were black. Sometimes she would point to a picture and describe it, such as signing THAT TREE in response to a picture of a Christmas tree. Once I brought Washoe a five-headed hand puppet and asked her what it was; she signed STUPID. At the end of such shifts, I had a wondrous feeling.

Figure 88. Mary Lee and Washoe signing about an image in a magazine

Social relationships are particularly important to chimpanzees, so many conversations were about their relationships. For example, when Dar and I played a game of peekaboo he asked for another game by signing PEEKABOO. I signed I NEED GO WORK. He signed FRIEND, which was a sure way to keep me in the game. My playslaps (playful chimpanzee behaviors) were followed by more signs of FRIEND from Dar. Sometimes the chimpanzees commented on their world or pointed things out to me. For instance, when Tatu and I looked at a picture of a hamburger Tatu signed FOOD. I pretended not to understand her, signing WHAT? She signed THAT FOOD. I continued to feign a lack of comprehension, signing I NOT UNDERSTAND. She clarified, signing THAT SANDWICH.

Many other conversations were about the daily routine. In a typical bedtime conversation, Dar asked me for DRINK. I replied NO. He asked again for DRINK. I responded YOU HAD MANY THINGS—CEREAL, BREAD, AND BANANA. TIME BED. Dar agreed and answered BED. About five minutes later, he began again asking for DRINK. I replied TIME BED. A minute later I asked Dar WHAT TIME? He answered BED.

The chimpanzees included their signs in the interactions they had with each other. For instance Washoe, if ready for a grooming session, would follow Loulis and sign COME HUG, COME PERSON until he gave his mother attention. Washoe, the matriarch of the group, usually settled family squabbles, reassuring everyone and signing HUG. The chimpanzees frequently solicited games of chase, signing to each other CHASE to begin or continue the game. After thirty-one years of conversing with chimpanzees, I am still fascinated with what they have to say and their perspective on things.

My master's thesis explored chimpanzees' imaginary play, and I was able to videotape the chimpanzees signing to stuffed animals and singing songs. Dar had a small stuffed animal he pushed to his side and signed TICKLE. Moja signed to herself RED RED RED CRY CRY CRY FUNNY. In ASL this rhymes; the shape and movement of the signs perseverate through the different signs just as "rat" rhymes with "cat" because "at" perseverates.

During those days in the late 1980s, there was considerable focus on chimpanzee welfare issues, and Roger Fouts was deeply involved in advocating for better care. A federal breeding program throughout the United States at national primate research centers was increasing the number of chimpanzees born in biomedical labs

Figure 89. Dar's hand in the sign for CHASE

at places such as Yerkes Primate Research Center in Georgia, Southwest Biomedical in Texas, and New Iberia Research Center in Louisiana. AIDS and HIV were on everyone's minds, and the industry was pushing the idea that chimpanzees were the answer to finding a vaccine. The Animal Welfare Act in 1985 required us to promote psychological well-being in captive chimpanzees, a new idea that generated much discussion and research.

Roger Fouts's laboratory in Ellensburg was a leader in environmental enrichment—by defining it, implementing it, and quantifying its benefits. Providing a stimulating environment for captive chimpanzees through use of a variety of food puzzles, objects, and activities, we tested which ones the chimpanzees preferred, how they used their enclosure, and ways to make food puzzles last longer. It was a privilege to be a part of these efforts to improve the lives of the chimpanzees in our care, which taught me the importance of doing the right thing for them.

However, since captive chimpanzees were primarily used for human benefit, such as in biomedical research and entertainment, putting chimpanzees' needs first, which was what Fouts advocated, was not a popular position. This was particularly true for the pharmaceutical industry and the National Institutes of Health, which used hundreds of chimpanzees for invasive studies.

❧ ❧ ❧

While approaching another crossroad, wondering if I should pursue a PhD or do something else with my life, I realized that with a PhD I would have a more influential voice in advocating for chimpanzees, so I entered the PhD program at the University of Nevada–Reno to study under Allen and Beatrix Gardner. They no longer had cross-fostered chimpanzees; instead, they had mountains of data. During the cross-fostering project, the Gardners and caregivers had taken detailed notes on the young chimpanzees' behaviors and signing. As a graduate student, I assisted with analysis of these records. I read about the antics of infants Moja, Dar, and Tatu, the chimpanzees I had known as adolescents and young adults living in enclosures, gaining a window into their lives as babies and toddlers. Their developmental milestones had all been recorded: first smile, sitting up, lifting the head, pulling to a stand, and crawling. The cross-fosterlings had sat in high chairs and learned to use spoons. Bathing, moisturizing, dressing, house cleaning, meals, playdates, and naps had all been routine. The youngsters had colored, painted, sorted, stacked, climbed, swung, rode, and camped. Their behaviors indicated the presence of many parallels between chimpanzees and humans. After completing my coursework in Reno, I returned full-time to Ellensburg to begin my dissertation research.

The Foutses had spent many years raising funds for a new building that would allow the chimps access to the outdoors, and in May 1993 we moved to the new facility.

The building had seven thousand square feet of indoor and outdoor space, a thirty-two-foot rise, and climbing structures, making it a much better place for chimpanzees. Prior to the move, we made videotapes of the new facility and showed them to the chimpanzees, explaining that they would be able to go outside. The chimpanzees watched with fascination, and they signed OUT, a sign they hadn't used in years. Moving day began at 2:00 a.m. when, one by one, each chimpanzee was anesthetized, given a physical, and moved to the new facility, which was named the Chimpanzee and Human Communication Institute (CHCI). Deborah Fouts and I sat with each of the chimpanzees in their nighttime enclosures as their anesthesia wore off. Washoe woke up and panted with excitement when she saw the outside area.

We let the chimpanzees settle in for a few days before giving them access to the outside. Then on a warm, sunny spring day the chimpanzees enthusiastically explored outdoors, and the girls got sunburns on their bottoms. The chimpanzees had become atrophied in the small space in the psychology building, and consequently Moja and Tatu had a difficult time climbing up and down the terraces, but they quickly grew healthier and stronger and within a year could easily climb up and down.

The new facility transformed the chimpanzees' lives. They now played more and revived old signs, such as OUT and GRASS. The outside area became a new place for conversations pertinent to my dissertation research, which explored how the chimpanzees responded to a series of misunderstandings. We grew vegetables in the adjacent area we called "the berm." One day while I was on the berm Moja came and signed SHOE. We walked together along the berm, where chives were just starting to grow. Moja signed ONION. I signed YES ONION. She signed PICK THEM. I responded CAN'T TIME EAT LITTLE LATER. Moja chose another topic, signing GROOM. I asked WHO GROOM? She answered GROOM MOJA. I asked WHO ME? She hesitated, and for a moment it looked like she was going to sign the name of another intern, but instead she signed FRIEND. I thanked her and reminded her of the sign for my name. Another day on the berm I was standing by the onions in the garden. Moja again signed ONION. I feigned ignorance, signing HUH? She repeated ONION. I again feigned ignorance, signing WHAT? She repeated ONION. I signed I DON'T UNDERSTAND. She signed LOOK THERE, pointing to the onions by my feet. It was remarkable how Moja kindly navigated my feigned lack of understanding and clarified her communication with me.

During the years it took to complete my PhD, we began many programs at the new facility, which was a university entity that functioned in conjunction with Friends of Washoe to support the chimpanzees. Still, the responsibility of raising funds for chimpanzee care fell on the Foutses, with operations only minimally funded by the university. In the new building, along with the larger chimpanzee living area there were also observation areas for the public, allowing for many different educational programs—Senior Ventures, Elderhostel, Earthwatch, Chimposiums, Advanced Chimposiums, and the Summer Apprentice Program—through which people could learn about the chimpanzees as well as help generate funds to support them. Students at CWU who were in undergraduate and master's programs were involved as well, including some who later established their own chimpanzee sanctuaries. For example, after volunteering in our Earthwatch Program, Gloria Grow founded, and continues to direct, the Fauna Foundation, a chimpanzee sanctuary in Quebec. Apprentice Keith LaChappelle established the Chimpanzee Sanctuary Northwest in Cle Elum, Washington, which later was directed by CWU graduates Sarah Baeckler Davis, Diana Goodrich, and J.B. Mulcahy (Goodrich and Mulcahy continue to direct the sanctuary). Into the wild went CWU graduate Dr. Crickette Sanz, who is now director of the Goualougo Triangle Chimpanzee Project in the Republic of Congo, and CWU graduate Dr. Cleve Hicks, currently the lead scientific director of the Bili Apes Project in the Democratic Republic of the Congo.

My commitment kept me with the chimpanzees in Ellensburg. I married, and my subsequent pregnancy was of great fascination to the chimpanzees. Once, when I chatted about the baby in my tummy, Moja signed MY BABY. I conceded and signed OUR BABY. Dar loved looking at my extended belly and was helpful with blanket cleanup during the morning routine in exchange for a look—I would lift my baggy shirt and let him see my stomach. After our daughter Hannah was born, my husband and I stopped by CHCI on our way home from the hospital so the chimpanzees could meet her. The chimpanzees quietly gathered around to examine the tiny being in my arms, fascinated to see this new life.

Later I often brought Hannah to visit the chimpanzees. Tatu got a kick out of scaring babies and young children, and Hannah was a prime target. As an infant, Hannah was oblivious to Tatu's knocks on the window; but one day when Hannah was three years old Tatu set her up for a scare that had a lasting effect, thereafter making

Figure 90. Tatu signing YOU to Mary Lee and baby Hannah

Hannah wary each time she visited the chimpanzees. With an innocent face, Tatu held her hand by the window, her gesture encouraging Hannah to put her hand to the window. But once Hannah's hand was there Tatu banged against the glass, causing Hannah to cry. The next day, when I visited with Tatu alone, she signed BABY? This is what she called Hannah. I replied YOU SCARE BABY. YOU MAKE BABY CRY. Tatu signed SORRY. I signed I TELL BABY YOUR SIGN SORRY. Tatu signed FRIEND. I replied YOU NICE. Hannah, now a young adult, is no longer afraid of the chimpanzees and even has close relationships with them.

Parenthood has changed my perspective on the chimpanzees; I see them as children who never grow up and move out, a reality that is deeply disturbing to me. I watch Hannah and my second daughter, Addy, grow and change. I enrich and broaden their worlds, taking them on trips and exposing them to different cultures. Meanwhile, the chimpanzees remain in captivity, their exposure limited, day in and day out, by what we bring to them. It breaks my heart that no matter how much I love them I cannot give them what I can give my daughters—freedom and the opportunity to grow, explore, and reach their greatest potential, as would be the case if chimpanzees were where they belong, in Africa. There they would grow up nurtured and enriched by jungle life. Females would be able to travel and maybe move permanently to neighboring communities. Males would patrol their territories, encountering neighbors along the way. They would hunt for meat, a regular part of the diets of free-living chimpanzees. Everyone would learn to use tools to acquire local foods, such as rock hammers to crack nuts or sticks to catch ants. Within and between the communities, dramas would unfold, similar to the stuff of *People* magazine. But none of this can happen in captivity.

⚜ ⚜ ⚜

While on a family vacation on the East Coast in June 2002, I received news from Roger Fouts that Moja had died unexpectedly after a sudden illness. She was only twenty-nine years old. This news shocked me. I'd never lost a friend as close as Moja or experienced grief as a physical pain in my heart. Every day at CHCI in the year after her death, I passed a tree we had planted in Moja's memory and experienced grief with the same intensity as that day. During our last interaction, Moja and I had shared breathy pants about bananas for dinner, a nice memory to have of my dear friend.

Several years later, after being on the East Coast following the death of my grandmother, when I visited Washoe upon my return to CWU she momentarily seemed a little dizzy and unresponsive. Thus began the slow decline of Washoe, which paralleled that of my grandmother—good days punctuated by fewer good days.

Washoe died on the first anniversary of my grandmother's death, October 30, 2007. That evening, I had already made the forty-minute commute home when Deborah called and said I needed to return to CHCI right away as Washoe had taken a turn for the worse. Roger and Deborah were with Washoe when I arrived. Deborah said, "Washoe, Mary Lee is here," and Washoe lifted her arm toward me. I told her how much I loved her, and she took her last breath. We were so glad she had her dearest friends beside her as she passed from this world. She was now free.

Washoe left behind Tatu, Dar, and Loulis, her little prince. When he was younger, Loulis would walk into a room, take a look at whatever human was there, and start to scream, at which point Washoe would come barreling in to defend her son, displaying at the supposed aggressor. Yet if Loulis was displaying and it seemed unwarranted, Washoe would stop him. Washoe was the matriarch of the group, so every time she supported Loulis in a conflict, he gained rank. Now, having lost his greatest advocate, Loulis began spending hours staring into space, an expression of grief that lasted several months.

Throughout the first year after Washoe's death, Loulis's relationship with Tatu and Dar began to change. Before Washoe's death, Dar would back down in conflicts with Loulis, but with Washoe gone he slowly realized the game had changed, that he could engage in conflicts with Loulis virtually unabated. Certainly he showed some restraint since male fights can be fatal, but the conflicts between the two boys lasted longer than before. Loulis also didn't seem to know when to quit. He would grow increasingly angry and was unable to disengage from the conflict even if Dar was backing off— perhaps because Loulis had never had to negotiate a conflict, a role that had been

Figure 91. Loulis

played by Washoe. However, after several years Loulis seemed to develop some control, a lesson learned late in life.

Loulis is a different chimpanzee from the others since he wasn't cross-fostered. Loulis, having lived with Washoe, has known the inside of enclosures for most of his life. To him, humans have varying degrees of importance because they weren't his conversational partners for the first five years of his life. Humans provide him with the necessities of life and many games of chase, but he has sought grooming and reassurance from chimpanzees. When there was an enrichment of pocketbooks filled with treats, Loulis struggled to unbutton the snaps and unzip the zippers, tasks quite easy for chimpanzees who were cross-fostered. Loulis would sometimes indicate that I was more than a plaything to him, which always surprised me. I remember once I'd been out of town, and when I returned and greeted the chimpanzees Loulis wouldn't look at me, squeezing his eyes shut every time I looked at him. It took a couple of days for him to want a little hand holding.

Loulis tempered my work with chimpanzees and taught me valuable lessons. When I first met him, he was eight years old, an age when male chimpanzees can be very challenging as they start to dominate other members of their community, beginning with females and working their way up the hierarchy of males. In captive chimpanzees, this manifests as highly aggressive, quick, and intimidating displays. For Loulis, it included spitting water; many times I had to squeeze the water out of my eyes. But Loulis also taught me the importance of using chimpanzee behaviors in interactions with chimpanzees. He liked to play a game of shoe touching. I'd hold up my shoe, and he'd tickle the end of it. I remember once during such interactions I bobbed my head and gave a breathy pant—friendly chimpanzee behaviors—prompting him to extend our game of shoe touching, enriching the interaction.

⁂ ⁂ ⁂

On June 15, 2011, Roger and Deborah retired and made me the new director of CHCI, which meant I was now the prison warden. It was my job to keep my dearest friends incarcerated, and I struggled daily with the dissonance this created. I didn't support keeping apes in captivity, yet this is what I did. I dealt with this circumstance by doing everything in my power to ensure that each of the chimpanzees' days was the best it could be. The staff provided interesting activities for them, access to the outdoors, a roomy facility, and enjoyable meals. More importantly since chimpanzees, like humans, are so social, I tried to ensure that the caregivers had a positive spirit in their thoughts and actions.

I also endeavored to have all caregivers take the chimpanzees on their own terms—that is, accept them as who they were and not expect them to adjust their behaviors to accommodate humans. When I go to Japan, for example, I take the Japanese on their own terms; I bow in greeting, eat with chopsticks, and speak some Japanese words. Since the CHCI chimpanzees used ASL in addition to their facial expressions, postures, and gestures to communicate, CHCI caregivers used ASL and appropriate chimpanzee facial expressions, postures, and gestures. For instance, when greeting a chimpanzee a caregiver crouched, offered a pronated wrist, and made breathy pants. We did not allow human arrogance; caregivers respected the hierarchy of the chimpanzees and showed submissive behaviors to them all. My research at other facilities shows that these practices are beneficial for all chimpanzees, and that their relationships with caregivers are friendlier and more playful as a result.

Yet while such practices may improve the treatment of chimpanzees in captivity they don't alter the bottom line—that these chimpanzees are deprived of freedom. Although some projects successfully reintroduce apes into the wild, they are rare. These are not home- or cage-reared individuals but rather chimps perhaps confiscated from the pet trade, young and already in Africa. Unfortunately, I cannot send my chimpanzee friends to Africa. They are, in a sense, displaced refugees who can't go back or, like Tatu and Loulis, were born in American laboratories and wouldn't know how to live in Africa; after all, Tatu likes her ice cream and oatmeal, and Loulis doesn't like grass. Chimpanzees learn the ways of the culture in which they are reared, and for lifetime survivors of Western middle-class culture, a safari may not be beneficial. The home-reared signing chimpanzee Lucy was returned to Africa, and after years of being depressed and missing her middle-class comforts of home, her human companions, and signing, ultimately she was poached.

During the thirty-two years I spent in conversation with my chimpanzee friends, I've learned two significant things. First, chimpanzee minds and hearts are very much like ours. They are thinking, feeling, loving, hating, worrying, wanting, joyful, and contemplative beings. Like us, their relationships with family, friends, enemies, and caregivers are immensely important to them. Second, they don't belong in the places we keep them—captivity restricts their capacity to live life to its fullest.

Unfortunately, major developments have led to the closure of CHCI and the transfer of its chimpanzees to another location. As the director of CHCI, I had developed a strategic plan that took into account the age of the chimpanzees, the inevitable future attrition to the family size, and the necessity of bringing in new chimpanzee family members. CWU requested $1.7 million from the Washington State Legislature to fund renovations to the building. Before the request was honored, the university completed the preliminary phase of the project. Then when Dar suddenly died on November 24, 2012, the renovation project became more urgent—I felt it was necessary to bring in new chimpanzees as soon as possible to avoid being left with one chimpanzee if another died. Friends of Washoe and I urged the university to implement some other minor portions of the project so we could begin introductions within months, but the university wavered in its commitment to housing chimpanzees on campus. As a result, in August 2013 Friends of Washoe decided to move Tatu and Loulis to the Fauna Foundation in Carignan, Quebec, where they have begun a new chapter in their lives.

The following excerpt from a eulogy I wrote for Dar and read at his memorial service expresses how I felt about sharing my life with my chimpanzee friends:

I watched him go from being a boy to a man. I came into his life in late morning. I was with him at high noon, early afternoon, late afternoon, and suddenly it was sunset. His sunset was like sunsets on the equator: they happen so quickly it's dark before you realize it. So I watched him age just as I've watched my friends, parents, former students, husband, and myself age. The difference is that he aged in one place. That's the hard part. It was very difficult to see someone I love dearly be so restricted. Dar's death was a relief. I saw him finally free.

While we did everything we could to make life as interesting as possible for the chimpanzees at CHCI, it was no match for them living where they were meant to be—free in the forests and savannas of Africa.

FRIENDS OR CAPTORS? MEMORIES OF MOJA AND OTHER CHIMPANZEE FRIENDS

Adriana Martin

Most people can recall the defining moment when their lives were changed by an event, a person, or a fellow animal. Peter Young, the activist prosecuted under the Animal Enterprise Terrorism Act who served two years in prison for his part in releasing eight thousand mink and foxes from fur farms, often uses the phrase "the point of no return," referring to an experience so powerful or eye-opening that afterward one cannot help but move forward in a different direction. For some people, such an experience leads to vegetarianism, for others veganism, and still others direct action.

Interacting with chimpanzees brought me to "the point of no return" and changed my life. Every choice I subsequently made—academic, philosophical, behavioral, and ethical—was influenced by all I had learned from my fellow apes. I cannot point to a particular incident but rather to a collection of moments I shared while spending three years with five chimpanzees, other caregivers, and my mentors Roger and Deborah Fouts.

In 1993, most people would have considered me an "animal activist." I was a paying member of the People for the Ethical Treatment of Animals (PETA), a vegetarian (now a vegan), and a sign-holding, petition-signing, slogan-wearing college student. To help meet my degree requirements, I volunteered to run behavioral experiments on captive birds and laboratory macaques. I had full access to the university's animal laboratories and had witnessed many things that most activists had only read about. I knew that keeping animals in captivity for any reason was wrong. But I hadn't always felt that way. Although I grew up around animals and had a particular affinity for stray dogs, as well as birds (chickens in particular), at that time I did not give much thought to animals in the food or biomedical industries other than buying into the idea that these were "necessary evils."

Later, after completing a bachelor of arts degree in psychology and anthropology at the University of Texas in Austin, specializing in primate behavior, I studied howler monkey vocalizations in Costa Rica, observed and cataloged chimpanzee behavior in zoos, and even applied to be a chimpanzee caregiver at the MD Anderson Cancer Research Center outside Austin. I was on my way to becoming a "real scientist," one who would never compromise her personal ethics. There was a line I thought I would never cross—vivisection, the invasive cutting into live animal tissue. I have since discovered that this line is often blurred by denial, peer pressure, ignorance, greed, and arrogance. I was lucky not to get the job at MD Anderson, where I believe this may have occurred for me. Many years later, while looking back at what I had thought was a missed opportunity, I saw it as a marked change of direction.

In 1996, I was accepted into the Experimental Psychology Master of Science Program at Central Washington University (CWU). I was ecstatic to learn that I would be studying under the program's codirectors, Roger and Deborah Fouts, and working with Washoe, Moja, Tatu, Dar, and Loulis, the five chimpanzees at the Chimpanzee and Human Communication Institute (CHCI) who communicated using American Sign Language (ASL). There is not a primatologist alive who has not dreamt of having conversations with chimpanzees on an equal level. I had read about Washoe, but I was not as familiar with the other four chimpanzees, having never read the book *Teaching Sign Language to Chimpanzees* by Drs. Beatrix T. and R. Allen Gardner, or Roger Fouts's autobiography, *Next of Kin*, which was not yet in print.

The following summer I moved to Ellensburg, Washington, to begin my studies and meet Washoe and her family. The famous chimpanzee matriarch Washoe, a central part of any primate behavior textbook, along with Kanzi, Nim, Koko, Chantek, and other apes, was legendary in the field. During my studies, I saw footage of baby Washoe signing to her human friends and teachers to open a door or open a briefcase.

There she was, a tiny chimpanzee in diapers, signing up a storm. The cute factor was through the roof, and the scientific implications were equally astounding.

Washoe, in her thirties when I met her, was the only one of the five chimps at CHCI who had been born in Africa. Born in 1965, Washoe had been captured as an infant by the US Air Force, perhaps to be part of the Space Program, but she had never been used. Instead, Washoe had been sold to Drs. Beatrix T. and R. Allen Gardner, an experimental psychologist and an ethologist, respectively, on June 21, 1966, and had become part of Project Washoe, one of the most famous and successful ape language research studies.

Baby Washoe had been cross-fostered—raised by one or more members of another species—in the Gardners' home. The Gardners and their graduate students had not used spoken language but instead ASL while interacting with Washoe during her normal daily activities of eating, playing, and potty training. Since chimpanzees in the wild communicate through a series of gestures, it had been determined that the gestural language of ASL would be the best means of communication with them. Earlier attempts to teach chimpanzees spoken languages had failed because chimpanzees lack the anatomical structures needed to produce consonants, so their speech could not be understood.

The Gardners had been very strict in their methodology, making sure that all signs Washoe learned were properly documented. (Their methods and results are described in detail, along with photographic evidence, in their seminal book *Teaching Sign Language to Chimpanzees*.) Washoe had learned signs quickly, her vocabulary increasing daily. As a result, she had the distinction of being the first nonhuman to acquire a human language.

One of Washoe's caregivers had been Roger Fouts, a graduate student at the University of Nevada under Allen Gardner. In 1970, Washoe had moved with Roger and his wife Deborah Fouts to the University of Oklahoma's Institute of Primate Studies, where Washoe met other chimpanzees for the first time in her life. Having been raised like a deaf human child, young Washoe had been traumatized by the transition to the institute and its other chimps. But she had proven to be a strong, resilient chimpanzee despite harrowing circumstances, such as being in a cage for the first time in her life, seeing chimpanzees with whom she could not communicate in sign language, and, in essence, being treated as an "animal."

Subsequently, the Gardners conducted a second language experiment. By then, Washoe had become well-known in the scientific community, generating skepticism about a chimpanzee using ASL. One of the most prevalent rumors was that if Washoe was indeed signing appropriately and engaging in conversations with humans—and not merely imitating caregivers—she had to be a "chimp genius" and, as such, Project Washoe could not be replicated. But with their second language experiment the Gardners did replicate Project Washoe, this time using Moja, Tatu, and Dar, three other cross-fostered chimpanzees. The only difference between the two study populations was that while Washoe had been wild-caught, Moja had been born at the infamously brutal Laboratory for Experimental Medicine & Surgery in Primates (LEMSIP); Tatu at the Institute for Primate Studies in Norman, Oklahoma; and Dar at the Holloman Air Force Base in Alamogordo, New Mexico.

The Gardners' second language experiment had been as revealing as Project Washoe. Moja, Tatu, and Dar had used ASL not only with humans but also with each other. This proved conclusively that Washoe was not a "chimp genius" and furthermore that when chimpanzees are given the appropriate language modality—based on hand gestures as opposed to spoken words—they succeed to an amazing degree in communicating with it.

Washoe, meanwhile, had lost two babies. After the death of her second baby, she became visibly depressed, signing BABY repeatedly. To console Washoe and give her a chance to be a mother, Fouts adopted Loulis, a chimpanzee born at Yerkes Regional Primate Research Center to a mother used in biomedical research. Thus began Project Loulis, an experiment devised to test the theory that a human language (ASL) could be passed on by one generation of chimps to the next. In this innovative experiment, Loulis learned his first fifty-five signs from Washoe, Moja, Tatu, and Dar. With the exception of seven signs—WHO, WHICH, WANT, WHERE, NAME, THAT, and SIGN—humans had used only spoken English in his presence. According to the results of the study, Loulis was designated the first nonhuman to learn a human language from nonhumans.

On my first day at CHCI I was immediately put to work gathering enrichment items for the chimps. I was surprised to learn that they got such items as clothing, shoes, plastic mirrors, toys, brushes, purses, and magazines on a daily basis. This was normal for them because as part of their cross-fostering experience they had been raised amidst all the comforts of a human home. They ate from plates and bowls, and used spoons and toothbrushes. Coming from a laboratory background, I had been trained to think that when objects were given to captive animals, including chimps, they would fight viciously for them and, rather than enriching their environment, the items would contribute to chaos and unsanitary conditions as they could not be retrieved for proper cleaning or sterilizing. I did not realize how heavily indoctrinated I had become in the ways of treating captive animals. After I voiced concern to my trainer, she said, "We don't call them animals." Up until that point, I had not known that *animal* was a bad word. However, I soon learned that a chimpanzee was called either "chimp," as in "Each chimp gets one bowl of soup," or by name, as in "Tatu did not take her vitamins today." I also learned that the chimps were not fed—rather, their food was served—and that we were not caretakers but caregivers. The chimps were not a research commodity for us to study; instead, we were there to help make their lives as interesting and complex as possible. The chimps' physical and psychological well-being, along with safety, was the top priority. CHCI's philosophy was "chimps come first," a phrase I would repeat countless times to others over the years.

After a few weeks, I had the routine down pat: empty the dishwasher, get clothes out of the dryer from the night before, put out new enrichment (e.g., burlap sacks, mirrors, magazines, brushes, toys), remove old enrichment, clean and disinfect enrichment, clean all enclosures, make lunch, and clean all enclosures again, always making sure there were five chimps present when entering and leaving a chimp area and always washing my hands with disinfectant. In addition, there were several key rules to remember: do not stare at the chimps; do not interact with the chimps unless trained to do so; use ASL when addressing the chimps (minimize use of spoken English in their presence); do not cross any red lines (red lines marked the areas where it was not safe for a human to cross because a chimp could reach out and grab, pull, poke, or drag a person of any size or strength); do not offer the chimps a treat that you cannot provide; only give what you have been permitted to give; and check the medical and behavioral log for the day.

The chimps were given choices daily, from the type of vegetable they wanted to eat to the blanket color they preferred or the paint colors and types of paintbrushes

Figure 92. Moja

they wished to use. We asked what they wanted for their meals by signing the question WHAT WANT EAT?—to which the chimps would answer by signing the name of a favorite dish, such as SANDWICH or MEAT. They ate a variety of foods, including fruit smoothies, fresh fruit, fresh vegetables, bean soups, oatmeal, celery with peanut butter, and granola bars. They usually got what they had requested, along with other nourishing foods. Allowing the chimps these choices was the least we could do for them after humans had taken away their freedom and everything that was natural to them.

I attempted to spend time with each chimp, engaging them in activities such as looking through picture books and identifying the images, brushing their hair (contrary to popular belief, chimps have hair, not fur), letting them groom my wrists or elbows through the holes in the enclosures, playing chase, painting, or just signing about everyday activities. However, as hard as we caregivers tried to remain neutral in our affections we invariably developed better chemistry with one or two of the chimps. We all had a favorite chimp, and the chimps had their favorite humans. As I spent more and more time with the chimps, I developed a very close bond with Moja.

Moja was a beautiful chimp by all accounts. Slender and graceful, she looked a lot like a young Washoe, another strikingly beautiful chimp. Moja's legs were very straight, as was her back. Her face was deep black, with hazel eyes and lips that were naturally pursed. Her pouty look made her a crowd favorite at the Chimposiums—weekend open houses held for community members, who paid a fee to spend one hour learning about chimps and chimp behavior. Moja would look into my eyes, and I would look into hers, with neither of us feeling threatened by the other, despite the fact that chimpanzees do not like to stare at each other because it is a sign of dominance or aggression.

Moja sometimes exuded a distinct musky odor like strong human BO, for no apparent reason. Usually only male chimps exude an odor, especially after a display when their hair becomes erect, making them look bigger while throwing, dragging, and beating whatever inanimate objects are available. In the wild, such displays can include large branches or even rocks. In captivity, chimps use objects such as toy phones, big purses, shoes, or anything else that will make noise when wielded effectively.

Every day for three years when I entered the chimp area, after first greeting Washoe—the group matriarch respected by everyone—and saying hello to all the chimps, I would sit down with Moja for an extended greeting. She would be so excited to see me and would sign HUG/LOVE many times, an interaction I admit was very flattering. There was a routine to greeting Moja. First, she usually wanted me to blow air on her face, indicating her desire by signing BLOW. So I would blow my breath in her face, and she would breathe it in and sign COFFEE? Indeed, I usually had just finished my coffee. Then she would point to the zipper on my fleece vest to indicate that she wanted me to zip and unzip it, while she stared at it with fascination. Next Moja would sign THAT, pointing to the Velcro zipper tag, then point to her ear in the sign for LISTEN, showing that she wanted to hear the sound of Velcro. I would happily oblige, knowing how much Moja loved Velcro. She also would often make a "tick tick" sound with her mouth and point to my watch. I would put my watch close to the cage so she could listen. Such a routine occurred hundreds of times, with variations prompted by Moja's different requests for the sights, sounds, and smells that she wanted to experience. Sometimes I would open my mouth and show her my teeth and tongue, and she would do the same for me. If I had a scab or a cut that was visible, she would sign HURT THERE, and I would allow her to inspect it from a safe distance. She always wanted to groom my scabs, but I did not let her as she could have easily hurt me or infected my wounds with her long fingernails.

Moja's favorite color was red. When it was time for me to hand out blankets, she would inevitably pick the red one from a pile of multicolored blankets, signing RED THAT. If there were no red blankets at sleep time, she would sign RED. I would answer NO RED, RED DIRTY, meaning that the red blanket was in the washer. She would then point to the enrichment closet and sign RED THERE, to remind me where I could get another red blanket. During the day, she would ask for red clothes to either wear or use for making nests. Moja would also stare at herself in the mirror and comb her long arm hair with a brush. She looked good in red, and I think she knew it.

One day Moja asked to groom the back of my hand. I offered the back of my wrist at a safe distance while tucking all my fingers into the palm of my hand for protection. But as Moja groomed me she suddenly struck my hand with one of her long fingernails and took some skin off. Instinctively, I pulled my hand away and gasped in pain. In disbelief, I signed MOJA YOU HURT ME. Moja had taken me by surprise, and that was a bad thing. We had been taught to never let a chimp surprise us and to always anticipate potentially dangerous situations. Moja looked mortified. She stared at my hand and signed GROOM. I signed NO YOU HURT ME. She kissed the tip of her long, black index finger and very gently extended it to me. Hesitatingly, I put my hand out again, and she gently touched it, rubbing the back of my hand with her soft fingertip without using her nail. It was obvious that she felt badly for having hurt me. Her empathy moved me; I felt ashamed for having made her feel guilty. I signed YOU ME FRIENDS. The grooming session continued without incident, and there were no hard feelings.

━━━ ━━━ ━━━

One cold winter night Moja did not want to come inside to her night enclosure. It was not safe for the chimps to sleep outside at night because no one was there to watch them; additionally, the nighttime temperatures in Ellensburg could drop below freezing. On nights when a chimp decided to stay out, one of us would sleep on a cot outside the enclosures until the chimp came in, and then close the door, an honor that fell to me three times—once with Loulis and twice with Moja.

On the memorable night that Moja refused to come inside, I could tell she was playing a game with me. She would come to the hydraulic door as if about to enter her night enclosure, but when I attempted to close the door she would run outside again. This went on for about an hour. I was getting frustrated, and when a human gets frustrated with a chimp the chimp always wins. I decided to ignore her instead of begging her to come inside—"please, pretty please" had never worked before anyway.

Deciding on a different approach, I took the cot from the enrichment room while Moja, who could see me from outside the sliding glass door, watched intently. (This door was used by caregivers to go outside and open the outdoor enclosure for cleaning.) I then took out some clean sheets, a blanket, and a pillow and made the bed, all the while avoiding eye contact with Moja, who was making raspberry noises with her lips and clapping to get my attention. I was doing my best to ignore her, which she found frustrating. I set the cot under the overhead tunnel that Moja was supposed to use to come back inside. I positioned the cot in such a way that I could see the outdoor enclosure through the sliding glass door and still be under the tunnel so I would know if she was inside or outside. Then I closed the hydraulic door, turned off all the lights, and got into bed, leaving Moja locked outside. I closed my eyes for a moment but had no intention of sleeping; I was worried that Moja would know I was bluffing, but decided to stand my ground anyway.

Moja could not believe her eyes, gasping when she thought I had given up on her. I watched as she stood in disbelief, staring at me. I closed my eyes. She started making raspberry sounds with more urgency than before. Acting as inherently stubborn as any chimpanzee, I still did not open my eyes. Moja clapped, to no avail. She then rattled the fence loudly. Finally, I opened my eyes and saw her frantically sign IN, IN, IN. I got up and opened the tunnel door, then Moja came partway in and lay down with half her body in the tunnel and the other half outside. Now I could not close the door. Moja had outwitted me! She fell asleep, victorious. I went back to my cot and slept below my hairy friend. The next morning Moja came all the way in as if nothing had happened. I closed the door behind her, and a brand-new day started.

I spent many moments like that with every one of the chimps. They each had a unique way of interacting with me, breaking down any barrier that separated us. I was amazed at the complexity of my interactions with them. Emotionally and semantically, we enjoyed true interspecies relationships.

Back then I lived and breathed chimpanzees. For three years, I easily spent seventy hours a week with them. I went to class to study chimpanzee behavior and evolution, went home to grab a quick bite and talk about chimpanzees with my friends, then returned to the institute for more time with the chimps. It was unfathomable to me that people outside the institute didn't think the world revolved around chimpanzees and their issues. When I dreamt about them—which I did often—what usually started as a pleasant dream invariably turned into a nightmare. The dreams repeatedly ended with the realization that somehow I had left the cages unlocked and the chimps had escaped. In the back of every caregiver's mind is the understanding that chimps who get out or hurt someone will ultimately be hurt as a result. The chimpanzees would be demonized in the press, or worse, campus police would shoot them before we could coax them back inside the building. To avoid such a scenario, the technicians carried walkie-talkies and keys to the enclosures at all times, aware that at any moment an impromptu "banana party" could take place due to a piece of fencing not holding up or a rake or shovel having been left in an enclosure after cleaning. The caregivers, too, were constantly vigilant while in the building, intent on keeping the humans and chimpanzees safe. Sometimes we could let our guard down just enough to enjoy the presence of our hairy friends at a safe distance, but any close interaction was charged with the possibility of an escape, an injury, or something else that would shatter the safe haven the Foutses had worked so hard to create.

My relationship with the chimps was extremely complex. On the one hand, I was a friend, food dispenser, and blanket supplier; on the other, a warden in their prison. Such ambiguous relationships cannot be maintained without one or both parties suffering mental trauma. One day I walked by Moja and she signed KEY THERE GIMME while pointing at my pocket. Moja knew I had the ability to free her, but I could not. What kind of friend was I? I fought back tears as I signed SORRY CAN'T. Eighteen years after leaving CHCI and over a decade after Moja's death, my relationship with her still haunts me. No chimpanzee should be in prison, and no human should be put in the position of serving as a prison guard for a good friend, a lose-lose proposition that takes a toll on both parties in unimaginable ways. This is a truth I still struggle with today.

※ ※ ※

I have not seen my chimp friends since 2000. Washoe, Moja, and Dar have died, and Tatu and Loulis have been relocated to the Fauna Foundation sanctuary in Canada. Many others remain captive through no fault of their own — at the mercy of a greedy species. Because of my interactions with all the individuals at CHCI, both chimpanzee and human, my understanding of the world has changed. I have learned that chimpanzees, like humans, vary in their capacity to deal with change, trauma, and loss. Washoe was a pillar of strength, for herself and others; both chimps and humans could rely on her for reassurance. However, Moja was fragile, emotionally and psychologically. She had been scarred by her experiences at LEMSIP and in Oklahoma, and at some point in her life had caused great harm to herself by self-mutilating, as captive chimpanzees tend to do after experiencing great stress.

When I first met the CHCI chimps, most were in their twenties and had already been through so much. Chimps in captivity are expected to live well into their forties, fifties, or even sixties, so long after I left CHCI the chimpanzees were still there. And now, nineteen years after leaving Washington—during which time I have attended law school to study animal law, lived abroad, moved to different states, and been twice married and divorced—Tatu and Loulis are still waking up behind bars. This certainly puts life in captivity in perspective. It's heartbreaking.

As much as I want the laws to change so chimps and other nonhuman animals are granted personhood, I know that those who are in cages now do not have time to wait for the glacial pace of the legislative process, or for future generations to gain sufficient awareness about the dwindling primate populations and care more about their fate. We have a duty now to make sure that not one more chimp is born into a life of captivity for *any* reason. Chimps do not belong to us, and they certainly do not belong to science.

PART III

ZOO LIFE:
MAKING THE BEST OF A CONFINED WORLD

All zoos, even the most enlightened, are built upon an idea both beguiling and repellent—the notion that we can seek out the wildness of the world and behold its beauty but that we must first contain that wildness. . . . Caught inside this contradiction are the animals themselves, and the humans charged with their well-being.

—THOMAS FRENCH, *Zoo Story*

Figure 93. Pancho at the Buenos Aires Zoo

AGAINST ALL ODDS: HELPING CHIMPANZEES AROUND THE WORLD

Hilda Tresz

I grew up in Budapest during the time when most people believed only men could work with large animals and a woman's place was to care for the babies. By age eighteen, I had a unique position as the keeper of Budapest Zoo's Small Mammal House. All the infant animals needing to be hand-reared were moved into the Small Mammal House, and I could not have been happier raising the European brown bears, Asiatic black bears, orangutans, lions, raccoons, foxes, martens, and many other small mammals.

Next to the Small Mammal House was the Primate House, where, when the chimpanzee keepers needed help at feeding time, they asked me to assist. I remember those days like they were yesterday. On my first day doing this the keeper was showing me the routine as the chimpanzees were lined up by the fence waiting for their morning milk to be handed to them in their metal cups. The next thing I knew, I was smacked on the head with a cup filled with a half-liter of milk. I decided I would never feed a chimpanzee again.

Then one beautiful sunny day I had to feed the chimpanzees by myself. I remember thinking, "I can do this. Nothing to it, right?" When I arrived, the chimpanzees looked relaxed. Susie, lying on her back with her legs crossed, reached her arm out for a banana. I gave her one, watched as she transferred it to her other hand, then her foot, and reached out again. I moved a little closer. In a flash, Susie sprang to her feet, grabbed my hair, and knocked me silly on the mesh that was separating us. Once I caught my breath, I noticed there were a few zoo visitors watching. I picked myself up, along with my shattered ego, and left. This time I swore I'd never trust a chimpanzee again in my life.

Years passed, and I forgot about the chimpanzees—or so I thought. I left the zoo, went to college, and married Zoltan, the supervisor of the Budapest Zoo's Primate House. After college we moved to Chicago, Illinois, where Zoltan worked for a construction company and I sold sausages at the European Sausage House. Lost without the animals, I cried like never before.

After the birth of our son, Kevin, we were ready to start a new life. At the library I found a book that contained the addresses of zoos, national parks, and other places where we could work with animals. Zoltan and I licked envelopes until dusk. The next day we mailed out two hundred letters with our résumés.

A week before Christmas 1990 we received the good news that both of us had been offered jobs to work with eighty-five chimpanzees at the Primate Foundation of Arizona (PFA) in Mesa, a privately owned breeding colony and behavioral research facility for chimpanzees who primarily had been pets or circus performers. Although biomedical research had not been conducted on its grounds, the PFA chimpanzees had been bred for medical research and were on standby to be moved to any biomedical research lab at the stroke of a pen. When the PFA closed in 2010, the chimpanzees were sent to the MD Anderson Cancer Research Center in Bastrop, Texas.

I was so excited about this new job that I forgot about my previous experience with the chimpanzees in Budapest—that is, until I started working with chimpanzees again. In the months that followed, working with the eighty-five chimpanzees was exhausting and stressful, an everyday emotional roller-coaster. I had never been covered with so much straw, urine, feces, and vomit. I remember waking up in the middle of the night sweating and asking myself how I would shift certain chimpanzees from one cage to another if six of them grabbed me at the same time, which could easily occur. Zoltan encouraged me to be patient and receptive to the chimpanzees, who, having spent years in circuses or private homes, had unique needs, as well as diverse personalities. He asked me to imagine myself in their shoes, like a child with a new teacher in school, stressing that the chimpanzees did not know me and had no reason to like me, that ordering them around or yelping at them would be met with aggression and distrust, while patience would help gain their trust.

These chimpanzees were very smart and, as a new keeper, with the lowest rank, constantly enjoyed testing me. Susie took pleasure in flipping me off when I asked her to move into her inside cage, a behavior learned from her previous owner. Patty would hold open the shifting door that connected her cage to the next one with her foot and send her baby to steal food from the other cage. Nahagio tried to grab me every time I was about to open her door, once scratching my hand and leaving a scar. Kukui patiently waited for me with liquid fecal matter in his mouth and then spit it on me to see if I would jump. Akimel enjoyed regurgitating on the top of my head if he was upset. He was upset a lot. Simba liked to snatch the shifting door out of my hand and bang on it for what seemed like an eternity. Their skilled teamwork was astonishing—like organized crime.

Needing to better understand chimpanzee behavior very quickly, I read books by Dr. Jane Goodall and Dr. Frans de Waal while also searching the internet for online articles. However, these materials helped me only in theory; the most useful guidance came from my husband. As a result, I learned, listened, and changed my behavior. Now when Akimel regurgitated on me I left, hosed my hair, changed my clothes, and then walked right back to the cages again. When Kukui began mixing fecal matter with water in his mouth, I walked away before his attack. If he spit on me before I could get away, I stayed calm, never yelping or threatening him, and acted as if nothing had happened. When Kukui found that boring and stopped, I then stoically suffered through the next phase of his testing, which involved throwing handfuls of sawdust, vegetables, water, and anything else he could find until he finally ran out of options. Eventually he gave up this behavior, and we became good friends.

Several times a day I gave the chimpanzees little presents, such as bread or fruit to eat, or newspapers and telephone books to use in building nests for comfort while looking through colorful magazines. I talked to the chimpanzees who were responsive to me (while they didn't understand what I said, they appreciated my attempts at friendly communication) and stayed close to the ones who seemed to want more personal relationships. It was fascinating to watch the effects my behavior had on the chimpanzees. Some of my human characteristics are very similar to those of chimpanzees—for one thing, my facial expression always reflect my emotions. When I'm happy, I smile. When I'm sad, I cry. If I like someone or don't, they will know it. Being an open book worked well with the chimps because they were able to easily gauge my emotions. In the beginning, they sensed my fear and tested me, but later, as they felt my growing confidence and began to feel safe in my presence, some changed their behaviors toward me. Eventually, genuine trust and friendships began to develop between us, which was especially beneficial for the chimpanzees who were picked on or ostracized, sitting in the corners of their cages isolated from the group.

Initially, my lack of knowledge about chimpanzee behavior resulted in a big fight among the young males. One day Gisoki, a male chimpanzee about six years old, was being chased and came to me for help. I looked at his attackers and told them to stop. They listened to me, but Gisoki took it as a sign to restart the fight. I believe Gisoki thought I had taken his side and would help chase his attackers away, but I couldn't do anything to back him up because of the mesh separating us. As a result, Gisoki ended up being chased all over the place. Experience has taught me not to interfere in conflicts among the chimpanzees unless I can follow through on my promises to them.

I also learned not to intervene between adult chimpanzees and their offspring. For years, Ann watched her mischievous four-year-old daughter, Kia, cause trouble, such as grabbing me through the bars, seizing and breaking my cleaning tools, and throwing them at me, but Ann never stopped her. Any impish behavior Kia could conjure up was fair game for her. It would have been unwise for me to react in any way if Ann was not doing anything about it herself, and it could have jeopardized our relationship.

Though a chimpanzee mother will naturally support her children regardless of what they do, when it comes to humans her children are always right. However, I once witnessed what seemed like an exception to this instinctive behavior. Ann's baby, Hakid, became sick with valley fever, a serious fungal disease of hot, dry climates that attacks the lungs and other parts of the body. Medicating him with Kia in the same cage was difficult. I would ask Ann to sit close to the mesh, holding baby Hakid in her lap while I spoon-fed him the medicine mixed with yogurt and Ann and Kia ate their own servings of yogurt. Kia generally ate her yogurt with lightning speed and sometimes grabbed Hakid's mixture out of my hand, usually spilling it on me and hitting me on the head with the spoon. On the day in question, I was almost finished medicating Hakid when I saw Kia fly toward me, and then, amazingly, Ann caught Kia's arm in midair and threw her on the ground just before she could grab me. Kia threw a hissy fit, screaming and hurling herself on the ground like a human child having a temper tantrum. Kia couldn't believe what her mother had done, and neither could I. Although there was no way to be sure about Ann's motivations, I believe that she protected me from her daughter.

About two and a half years after I began working at the PFA, my husband and I accepted positions as keepers at the Phoenix Zoo. After several different promotions, I became the behavioral manager, in charge of developing and implementing enrichment, training, and research programs for the animals. Even though I loved all the animals under my care, being with them didn't compare to being with chimpanzees, which unfortunately the zoo did not have because of their susceptibility to valley fever. I longed for the strong bonds and friendships, the humor, cunning personalities, and constant level of activity I had experienced with chimpanzees.

It was a happy day when, in 2007, Dr. Virginia Landau, director of ChimpanZoo (CZOO), asked me to be a mentor for the Jane Goodall Institute. ChimpanZoo is a global research association that was founded in 1984 to help people better understand chimpanzee behavior, improve chimpanzee habitats in zoos, and increase public awareness about them. I have been working with the Jane Goodall Institute, helping chimpanzees around the world, ever since.

For the first three years, my global rescue work was done via e-mail and Skype with various staff members of zoos, developing plans for basic husbandry, enrichment, dietary issues, behavioral problems, and infant care. During the past eleven years, I have traveled to zoos in Asia, Africa, the Middle East, and South America thanks to generous donations from individuals and advocacy groups. Initially, my main purpose was to introduce singly housed chimpanzees into group settings, organize their basic husbandry, and design and implement enrichment programs. Now I try to improve the lives of all the animals I can during my short visits, as well as educate zoo staff.

My first priority is always to make changes for the chimpanzees who are living alone. Whether they have been separated because of social and emotional issues or limited physical capabilities, there is always a way to get them out of isolation and introduce them to at least one other chimpanzee. My second priority is to put babies who have no parents together with adults who can serve as surrogate parents so the young ones can learn species-appropriate behaviors.

Many zoos work hard to change the lives of their chimpanzees. In one case especially close to my heart, Canadian tourists Zofia and Stan Kurylowicz were visiting the Buenos Aires Zoo in November 2008 when they were shocked to find that a fifty-year-old male chimpanzee named Pancho, who had arrived at the Buenos Aires Zoo as a young adult in 1973, had been living alone for thirty-five years. After the Kurylowiczs contacted Dr. Landau looking for options to improve Pancho's life, I received an e-mail with an attached photograph of Pancho from Erica Grimm, Dr. Landau's assistant, asking if I would help. The expression on Pancho's face broke my heart. Realizing that we were nearly the same age, I wondered if I would still be in my right mind had I been in solitary confinement for nearly my entire life and found it hard to imagine how he had survived all these years. I read the e-mail again and again, then unclenched the mouse and went for a walk to process the information. I do that a lot; it keeps me from reacting immediately, which is a good thing in my profession. By the time I got back to my office, I was able to reply: "Of course I will help. I wish I could have helped much earlier." From that moment on, all I could think about was Pancho sitting by himself, day after day, with his forehead pressed to the window.

Seven months later the work began. Pancho's keeper, Pablo Gomez, and Santiago Ricci, a Buenos Aires Zoo intern, were well prepared and assisted in implementing the changes. Santiago and I thought alike in many ways; the minute he got the case we proceeded with lightning speed. Skype allowed us to have long brainstorming sessions regarding crucial decisions despite the distance and language barrier.

Pancho lived in a 320-square-foot heated exhibit with a 6-meter glass wall, an artificial tree, and a hammock. Despite its acceptable size, his exhibit was a closed, indoor area that didn't allow him to breathe fresh air, feel the rain or sunshine on his body, or experience grass and soil under his feet. To my relief, I learned that the keepers indeed cared about Pancho and had tried to enrich his life. Pancho had arrived at the Buenos Aires Zoo in 1973 as a young adult. The keepers had been afraid to put him with the other chimpanzees because his right hand was injured, restricting his mobility, and he had limited vision due to being cross-eyed. They had also been fearful that the other chimps would harm him since he'd had no social interaction with other chimpanzees for over four decades. But almost every day Pancho had been given enrichment that included plastic balls, paper bags, paper boxes, rags, leather gloves, and clothes, as well as items with different smells and tastes, like honey and mint. In the summer, he had enjoyed iced fruit and juice; in the winter, *mate cocido*, a common South American tea. Pancho had been taken care of better than I had originally thought.

Figure 94. Pancho in his zoo enclosure

Yet, despite the Buenos Aires Zoo's best efforts, Pancho was still miserable and unable to exhibit species-appropriate behaviors because he was living in isolation. And although enrichment was critically important, it had its limitations. I knew that social enrichment should be a priority for such a socially oriented species as chimpanzees, and so I requested to immediately find Pancho a companion.

While looking for a suitable companion for Pancho, we evaluated his enrichment program so we could upgrade it to include more species-appropriate enrichment. One such change was to add browse and substrate to allow Pancho to forage and build nests. The bare floor in his concrete enclosure had no browse, such as indigenous edible green leafy branches, grasses, and plants, or substrate, such as dry leaves, shredded paper, hay, or straw, so Pancho was not able to forage or build nests—natural behaviors for chimpanzees. This also meant that he spent most of his time on a hard floor, which was very uncomfortable and could cause physical problems. In addition, because the exhibits were hosed down in the mornings it took a long time for the floors to dry, forcing Pancho to stand on a damp floor or in puddles of water for half of each day.

Lack of substrate and browse is the number-one problem I address in most of my rescue work. Adding browse, the easiest and most versatile enrichment, is always my first choice if I cannot immediately provide social enrichment. Browse is the most multifunctional enrichment because it's easily used as both substrate and food, as it is a great source of dietary fiber, is low in calories, and is full of vitamins and minerals. Sometimes browse is better than regular substrates because it has enough moisture to make it practically impossible to set on fire, an advantage in countries where people smoke and tend to throw their cigarette butts into the animals' cages.

In captivity, it's important to give chimpanzees the opportunity to search for their food rather than simply presenting food they will finish in a few minutes, leaving them bored for the rest of the day. In the wild, they are challenged to regularly forage for food. So we scattered seeds in the substrate and browse, which gave Pancho the opportunity to spend time looking for the seeds before he ate them, engaging him in both a physical and mental activity. We also increased foraging duration by chopping his food into smaller pieces and adding more feeding times. In addition, Pancho was given paper and fresh grass, enabling him to build nests for the first time in more than forty years. An important behavior in the wild, chimpanzees can make up to two nests a day—their usual nighttime nest and an occasional day nest.

I was now satisfied with Pancho's new environmental enrichment, but his social enrichment still needed to be addressed. I periodically bombarded everyone involved with e-mails reminding them of Pancho's condition, and finally, through the collective effort of Santiago and the Jane Goodall Roots & Shoots coordinators, we were finally able to move forward with a social enrichment plan.

Living together near Pancho's enclosure were four chimpanzees: Martin, a forty-year-old male; his eight-year-old son Gombe, whose mother had died when he was only two; Sasha, a twelve-year-old female; and Kangoo, her one-year-old son. When I asked the zoo officials why Pancho was kept in solitary confinement when four chimpanzees lived so close to him, they told me that introducing Pancho to a group of chimpanzees was too risky because, having been alone for such a long time, he lacked the necessary social skills to safely interact with these other chimpanzees and that he had special needs. Of the four, it seemed that Gombe, because of his age, would be the best choice for a companion. Although it could be tiring for Pancho to deal with a "teenager" at his age, I thought it would lift his spirits, knowing that many older chimpanzees live longer when youngsters are around to keep them engaged, like humans with grandchildren.

Soon I developed an introduction protocol to put the two males together. At the time, there was no funding available for me to fly to Argentina, so I conducted the introduction using Skype and e-mail. In October 2009, Pancho and Gombe were

" "

Many older chimpanzees live longer when youngsters are around to keep them engaged, like humans with grandchildren.

Figure 95. Pancho (left) enjoying his daily browse while Gombe (right) watches

Figure 96, 97. Pancho (right) and Gombe (left) playing

slowly and successfully introduced, a long-awaited happy event for Pancho, who could finally live in the company of another chimpanzee. Following the introduction, the keepers said that Pancho was more active than ever and seemed twenty years younger. When I received pictures of them playing, I was thrilled. That night when I went home I opened a bottle of red wine, put my feet up on a table, and smiled for a long time.

Pancho and Gombe lived together until Pancho passed away in December 2010 from complications of old age, at which time Gombe, then ten, was transported to the National Zoo at the Parque Metropolitano de Santiago in Santiago, Chile, and introduced to Yudi, an older widowed female chimpanzee, with whom he has lived ever since.

Making positive changes for chimpanzees in countries where there are cultural and religious differences or a lack of basic primate knowledge can be especially challenging. Often I am viewed as an outsider—and understandably so, because I am a white woman from an American zoo who doesn't share the local religion, customs, or language. Initially, distrust, doubt, and fear are evident when I suggest things different from established routines and acceptable standards, such as covering concrete cage floors with substrate or asking people not to smoke in the animal cages. Even with an invitation and advanced notice of my arrival I usually have to spend the first three or four days negotiating about how I plan to put chimpanzees together or improve enrichment because institutions or keepers can be skeptical about what I suggest can be done, such as that huge male chimpanzees be put together with infants. Willingness to communicate with me and allow me to see the conditions in which their animals are living are often the first steps that lead to beneficial changes. And, once I start to work, they see that I am not there to judge but to help them, leading to other positive changes that no one ever thought could take place.

Many employees at the zoos where I work are scared of making introductions. When chimpanzees are first put together, it can sometimes look like Armageddon, with screaming, chasing, hitting, grabbing, and throwing, which can be alarming. While introducing chimpanzees, I have seen zoo directors hold their heads and, staring at the floor, rock back and forth, thinking the animals were killing each other when actually they were playing. Afterward there are a lot of happy tears, and the people usually say they can't believe they didn't do the introductions earlier.

The last time I was at the Alexandria Zoo in Egypt I found Meshmesh, a male chimpanzee, sitting by himself, which, in my understanding, he had been doing for about a decade, even though the zoo had two other adult male chimpanzees—Oscar and Fatuta. All three chimpanzees were singly housed next to each other. Oscar and Fatuta had outside cages, but Meshmesh was in a dark room without windows or fresh air. Because the keepers were afraid to put three male chimpanzees together, all Meshmesh could do was stare at the walls and listen to the outside noises. Other than the keepers delivering food or cleaning, there were no visitors. The staff were unaware of their impact on him. Meshmesh lived in the most horrible conditions I have encountered to date.

After assessing the situation, I introduced Meshmesh to Oscar and Fatuta. They smiled, played, hugged, tickled, somersaulted, and laughed, something for which the staff was not prepared, believing the chimps might injure or even kill one another. The chimpanzees' husbandry program was also changed, including adding substrate so they did not have to be on concrete. Watching the delight the animals exhibited, and the surprise and happiness of the people observing, was incredibly gratifying.

These three chimpanzees were best friends for about a year, until Oscar and Fatuta died of a mysterious illness, leaving Meshmesh alone again. After several months, I arranged to have Meshmesh transported to the Giza Zoo, but shortly after, civil war broke out in Egypt and the zoo had to temporarily close. The staff wanted to take care of their animals, but they had a hard time getting to work. Eight months later Meshmesh became severely ill and died in July 2013. Something in me also died that day as I realized that despite my having rescued Meshmesh twice he had still passed away. Meshmesh remains the chimpanzee closest to my heart. He suffered for so long and for no reason. I felt helpless and hopeless, wondering whether I should continue working with chimpanzees. *What's the use?* I'd ask myself. Nevertheless, I would soon resume my work.

My work in countries with different religions and cultures has constantly required me to do research and acquire new skills to avoid suggesting culturally insensitive changes to chimpanzee care. The phrase "knowledge is power" perfectly describes my work in a Middle East zoo helping a young female chimpanzee who was not being introduced to a male chimpanzee because it was believed she was a different subspecies. When I brought up birth control as a solution to the problem, a few of my friends told me that Islam was against birth control and advised me not to suggest it or I would be considered ignorant and imprudent. I then sought advice regarding proper etiquette in relating to Arabic people and asked a friend to compose a template letter showing me how to properly address Muslim staff members so I could establish respectful communication. I was advised to start my letter by asking about the person's health and family and in the middle of the letter say something about Allah. Not knowing what I was supposed to say about Allah, I educated myself by consulting with Muslim people. I also learned more about Islamic culture and beliefs regarding birth control by

Figure 98. Left:
Meshmesh on the floor
of his windowless room
before rescue

Figure 99. Below:
Meshmesh building a nest
for the first time

reading all the pertinent parts of the Koran and the Sunnah. Interestingly, I found that preventing conception was accepted in the teachings of Mohammed Prophet (Peace Be Upon Him); his followers were able to practice azl or "coitus interruptus." Warm feelings went through my heart; I had good ground to present my case now. After my presentation, the zoo staff was speechless. I ended up not using birth control with the female chimpanzee because DNA tests showed that she was, after all, the same subspecies as the other chimpanzee. Ultimately, the chimpanzees were introduced and have been living together happily ever since.

When I work to help improve conditions for chimpanzees in various countries, I also focus on educating staff at the facilities to provide a broader perspective for their own future animal care. Though quite a few countries mate chimpanzees from different subspecies, I explain the importance of maintaining the integrity of the individual species and the use of birth control. I educate the staff about the subspecies of chimpanzees in the wild, and they are often surprised to learn how the cultures, behaviors, and physical attributes of chimpanzees differ. Additionally, I talk about the use of substrate, browse, and three-dimensional spaces, as well as explain how to grow grass in harsh environments and how to build self-sustaining gardens to provide a sufficient food supply. I spend a lot of time talking about the similarities and differences between chimpanzees and humans. Most people genuinely care about improving the circumstances of their chimpanzees, and generally admit they had not known the things I shared with them and had never thought they were harming the chimps.

※ ※ ※

In most cases, there is insufficient funding to make even the smallest of changes, so I have to get very creative and use what is available at practically no cost. Because most chimpanzees need immediate help—as they live in horrid conditions with only the lucky ones having perhaps a wooden bench or tire—I don't write protocols anymore but simply assess the situations and make immediate changes with whatever resources are available.

At times I have been asked to visit potentially dangerous places to assess the living conditions of captive chimpanzees and try to help them. In one country, a civil war was just over, but the people were still living on the edge, with little food and few supplies. The zoo I was assessing was in a catastrophic state, with no food available for the animals. After seeing a female chimpanzee with an infant in her arms but no food, I suggested I buy some milk powder for supplemental food. The zoo worker looked at me in disbelief and said, "Madam, why are you so concerned with feeding the animals? Shouldn't you worry about us? Why would I give milk to the chimpanzees when my son has not had milk in six months?" He was right. I was so concerned about the starving chimpanzees that I'd become blinded to the dire circumstances of the local people. Taking the zoo worker's words to heart, I ran off and purchased milk powder for the chimpanzees and the entire staff as well.

I quickly reassessed the animals' situation. Discovering an entire "jungle" of edible trees around them, I taught the keepers how to cut branches without destroying the trees, how much food they needed to chop for the animals, and which tree branches would be best for them. I worked from dusk till dawn chopping down branches for food and gathering wheelbarrows of leaves for substrate. The chimpanzees were fed.

After all these years, I still follow up on all the animals' lives. I always try to have an inside person or an outside liaison stay in contact with me and the zoo staff so I can make sure things stay the way I left them. However, it is extremely difficult to follow up and ensure continuous improvements from the other side of the world. Many times after I leave a zoo, a new situation arises that the staff does not know how to handle, and instead of asking me for help they simply put the chimpanzees I rescued back the way they were. When situations like this occur, it's hard for me to remain hopeful; I have seen so much suffering that it floods my mind like some great biblical tidal wave.

I am very aware that it's our homocentric bias to assume that we know what is best for captive chimpanzees. We put them on feeding schedules and choose their food. We select the chimpanzees for them to breed with, introducing and separating them. We clean their exhibits, medicate, and euthanize them. These chimpanzees seldom have control in their environments. It has become increasingly clear to me that all I can really do is patch things up. But this is still an important task because it matters to the individual chimpanzees whose lives I enhance or save—who, due to my help, no longer suffer in dirty, empty cages going quietly insane. For them, I keep on going, like the Energizer Bunny. There is a lifetime of work ahead to help chimpanzees in need. I'm rolling up my sleeves and waiting for the next call so I can get to work.

CAPTIVITY: THE STORY OF HOLLY AND LUIS

Jayne Weller, DVM

My wide-brimmed hat had mesh on the sides of the crown, and the torrents of water from the black clouds above had poured through the holes down my face, down the back of my neck, and inside my already heavy oilskin coat. I was soaked. A mixture of water and sweat was unpleasantly sticking my shirt to my torso as I raked the meerkat enclosure until there were no footprints in the sand. I had been told that the "industry" was concerned about how natural the enclosures looked to the public, and footprints were unnatural. Staring in disbelief at the very unnatural wire mesh enclosure around me, I wondered if I was the only one who understood the meaning of irony.

This was my first day as a zookeeper at a private zoo in Sydney, Australia. Sitting down for a minute on a mock rock, looking at the empty meerkat enclosure around me, with five enclosures yet to clean in the next hour, I wondered whether the volume of water from the pouring rain could come close to filling the engulfing emptiness within me and drown the uncertainty I was feeling about what I was doing at this place. Then, while looking up to watch the large droplets falling from the sky, I felt Kora, a meerkat who had quietly entered the enclosure, scratching at my bare leg, pulling my sodden sock over my boot as she squinted up at me. Looking at her, I asked her what she was doing. Kora looked straight up at me, her eyes blinking against the heavy drops, her coat drenched and parted down her back, and made short, deliberate grunts as only meerkats can. I half chuckled, half scoffed at this little creature trying to comfort me.

Climbing into my lap, Kora reached up to touch my face with her nose, communicating to me with her grunts and touch. The love and understanding I received from her was something I could not only appreciate but also reciprocate. Suddenly, I knew I was where I was supposed to be—part of a greater family of sentient beings.

Over the course of that day in the rain, I received messages from all the animals—meerkats, monkeys, cats, bears, red pandas, apes, and otters—telling me exactly why I was there: for them. I was their caregiver, their savior, their friend, their mother. The constant struggle for mutual understanding I had often felt in the human world was now contrasted with a feeling of compassion and acceptance from these beings, which gave me a sense of purpose and joy in life. Unlike human beings, who can be selfish and closed to both their own and other species, the animals around me weren't, and I suddenly felt contentedly connected to their worlds.

After this day of revelation, I spent every spare minute listening to, and communicating with, all the members of my new family, discovering their worlds and my relationship to them. Learning the ways of the animals, I knew when they were sick before they showed signs, when they were happy, and when they were not. We existed not as human and animal but as a finely tuned ecosystem of species working together.

When zoo management asked me to be a backup keeper for two new chimpanzees, Holly and Luis, a brother and sister who had spent twenty-five years suffering in tiny living quarters, mainly alone, I was honored and excited. I was given strict instructions to stay away from the mesh, because Holly could fit her hands through and grab me, and Luis could thrust his fingers out trying to reach me and scratch me with his sharp fingernails. While awaiting my first encounter with them, I read about chimpanzee behavior, talked to experts, and watched others work with chimpanzees, but nothing prepared me for actually meeting the pair. I felt a heavy nervousness, like having a large rock in the depths of my stomach, concerned about what would happen if they didn't like me.

When the day finally came to meet Holly and Luis, the heavy door to the night den was opened for me, and I stepped into the corridor outside the double-meshed rooms where they slept at night. I knew not to stare straight into the chimpanzees' eyes for any length of time because, as with other primates, it would be very threatening. So I lowered my eyes, glancing up briefly to see Holly racing toward me from the other side of the den. She then climbed to the platform that allowed her to sit precisely at the height of my head.

Scanning the room, I saw Luis sitting with his body half turned away from me. He glanced up and then quickly looked the other way, turning his back again, showing no interest in me. Holly, however, was shaking with excitement, grunting and wringing her hands to get my attention, staring at me with expectation—her eyes wide and bright, her eyebrows raised, and her lips pursed. Looking away, I began talking, asking if she liked her new home. From the corner of my eye, I saw her push a stick toward me. Having heard that both Holly and Luis enjoyed trading, I asked the keeper next to me if I should offer to take the stick even though I had nothing to give in return. She told me to be careful because chimpanzees sometimes offered things in order to grab a hand.

When I looked at Holly, she held my gaze without malice, as if I were a long-lost friend. I felt safe and decided to reach out and accept the stick. I stared at her, my hand with the stick outstretched in front of me, frozen in disbelief at such a gift of trust. As I said thank you, she looked down, grooming her hand while drawing air through her teeth. Humbled by the gesture, I smiled calmly with the knowledge that we had a connection.

Soon I began working with Holly and Luis two days a week when the other keeper was off, but most days I spent part of my lunch break and any other spare time visiting them. Holly responded to me the most, and we gradually built a very strong friendship. She loved sitting around, chatting, and grooming me through the bars, eventually allowing me to groom her. We read picture books and flipped through magazines. She gave me rocks and sticks and sometimes tried to push her blankets through the bars for me. I was always thinking of new and inventive presents for her as well. Some days we laughed hard when Holly tried to stand on her head or made ridiculous faces in the mirror. Eventually Holly, Luis, and I began communicating readily about our wants and feelings—not through spoken words but through gestures and expressions that came easily while present with one another.

Life for Holly and Luis was now much better than they had ever experienced. Every time I watched Luis carefully groom Holly, or gently play and tickle her, I was ecstatic, knowing that life for them had greatly improved from the years when they had been imprisoned in tiny shipping-container enclosures.

Holly and Luis had been raised to be circus performers in the 1980s. Luis was only three when he had been made to work in the world of entertainment. At a time when

Figure 100. Holly (left) and Luis (right)

he should have been with his mother, he was learning to drink tea from a cup, ride small ponies, dress up in funny clothes, and walk bipedally next to a person from whom he only wished love. Before Holly had been old enough to perform, the circus had closed due to increasing insurance costs and diminishing public interest in performing animals. The circus owner had kept all the animals in caged enclosures except for Holly, who had been raised as a human child for the first seven years of her life. Too hard to handle during her adolescence, she had been moved to a cage near Luis. For five years, Holly and Luis had lived in separate cages, where they could see and touch each other but not properly interact, or even move around normally, as the cages were no larger than toilet cubicles. They had been fed whatever food was available, usually just bread, and their keepers had not spent any time with them.

Life had improved slightly when a new keeper decided they should be housed together in a larger space. A new makeshift home was then built out of two shipping containers joined by a two-meter-square mesh area. Holly and Luis had endured another five years of living in these substandard conditions waiting for a proper home—no other zoos wanted to adopt two related chimpanzees who might be difficult to integrate into an already established troop.

Not until Luis was twenty-five years old and Holly eighteen were they moved to the more spacious enclosure at the zoo where I worked. The staff had carefully designed Holly and Luis's new home to encourage climbing, swinging, foraging, and nesting, allowing the chimpanzees to travel around without ever touching the ground. The enclosure had climbing structures, ropes, and tires; grass and other substrates like woodchips and sand in which to forage; and different types of materials from which to build nests, such as branches, leaves, blankets, shredded paper, and hessian sacks. While captivity is never ideal, Holly and Luis had finally been given a home where they could become better-adjusted chimpanzees and hopefully live happily.

At the zoo, unlike the circus, enrichment was an integral part of Holly and Luis's lives. Compared with life in the wild, captive environments are usually spatially limited, and lack both novelty and complexity, allowing the inhabitants little control. The function of enrichment is to encourage captive chimpanzees to display their natural behaviors and allow these behaviors to influence what they need.

The hanging ropes and tires helped Holly and Luis regain strength in their bodies by climbing and swinging. Luis spent long periods of time testing his abilities. He enjoyed checking his good looks in the mirror but mainly liked noisy, active, and food-oriented activities such as playing with balls, water bombs, eating condiment smears on the walls, sultana fishing, using his fingers and tongue to get food out of the plastic bottles strung above the wire roof of the enclosure, and playing tickle tag with Holly. Holly's favorite activities included dressing up in old clothes, especially things she could put on her feet, looking at picture books and magazines, painting, chasing bubbles, rummaging through heaps of hessian sacks and cardboard boxes, and looking at herself in the mirror.

The friendship I formed with Holly was not always smooth sailing. One day the other chimp keeper and I were chatting near the enclosure, not paying attention to Holly. While this frustrated her, Holly managed to cope well until we gave each other a goodbye hug. She was so jealous of the alliance I had made with the other keeper, with whom she was also close, that she screamed, ran for the largest stick she could find, and threw it at me. For weeks afterward, when I was near her enclosure she threw whatever she could find at me, especially sticks. Eventually, she forgave me, once again pant-hooting and screaming with excitement when she spotted me from a distance as I headed toward her enclosure.

At one point, Holly and Luis began working together to test our intelligence and patience. Every afternoon we placed their dinner in the den so they would enter their night enclosures. One night after placing their dinner inside, I opened the hydraulic doors for them to enter. As soon as the doors opened, Luis ran in first, as he usually did. Holly, however, didn't follow him and instead grabbed three hessian sacks and a large stick to place on the tracks of the hydraulic door. Excited, she then sat in the doorway screaming while Luis grabbed almost all the food in his hands, feet, and mouth and ran back out of the enclosure, dropping some of the load for Holly to pick up as she followed him. I wasn't sure if I felt silly for having been tricked, angry that I wouldn't be getting home at a reasonable time that night, or ecstatic that Luis had actually involved Holly in his plan and then shared some of his prize with her.

Working with Holly and Luis was both joyous and heart wrenching. Luis had beat Holly on a regular basis when they had been at the circus because he had no other way to deal with his boredom and frustration. As a result, Holly's skull had been fractured more than once. The skin on her head, shoulders, and buttocks had burst into gaping wounds with the force of Luis's strikes, and her fingers were still crippled and scarred. Although Luis had fewer aggressive episodes under our care, when his rage did emerge it became increasingly difficult for me to witness since I felt powerless to stop it. My heart would break as Holly cried for help and ran toward me with an outstretched hand, her body awkward and battle-scarred and a fear grin splitting her face. Had I separated them, Luis would have seen me as Holly's ally, so, since I had to maintain an easy relationship with him as well, they had to be left to work it out themselves. But I could never shake the feeling that I had betrayed my closest friend by not protecting her when she needed it.

After every beating, Holly would try to placate Luis by grooming him and offering her hand in peace. Luis showed obvious repentance, but this didn't mean he would refrain from attacking Holly again when his frustration and rage returned. Amazingly,

Holly never held it against me for not protecting her; instead, she would come to me for comfort after an attack by Luis. At such times, I was the only one she would allow to groom her; using a long stick, I would closely examine her wounds to ensure that they were healing properly.

※ ※ ※

The year I spent with Holly and Luis I cried a lot. But I also laughed and learned more than I could have imagined about the art of listening, openness, patience, and tolerance. Most importantly, I learned how similar we are to our primate cousins and how tragically dissimilar our life circumstances are. Unlike Holly and Luis, I had choices. I was white, Western, and privileged. I could choose what and how much to eat and drink, talk on the phone, watch plasma screens, and use computers. I felt undeserving of my freedom, which I had only because I belonged to the species *Homo sapiens*. I was the captor, free to live how I chose, and Holly and Luis were captives, destined to spend their lives behind bars.

Although during that time I started to lose the youthful idea of being able to change the world, I desperately held on to the notion that I could make important differences—a belief that still provides inspiration to continue my work. There is much to be done, and I want to feel worthy of my free, privileged life on this side of the bars.

The day I left the chimpanzees, Luis turned away from me, so we ended our relationship in the same way it began. Holly screamed, and I looked into her eyes for a long time, asking her to forgive me for leaving, for not having saved her sooner, and for being part of a species that imprisons and enslaves. She reached her whole hand out to me, and I touched my fingertips to hers. Then she gently squeezed my fingers.

IRREVOCABLE BONDS

Erna Toback, PhD

I fell in love with chimpanzees before I could even tell the difference between a chimpanzee and a gorilla. It happened over a two-day period in the early 1970s while I was entranced by Jane Goodall's account of her eleven-year journey with the chimpanzees of Gombe, conveyed in her book *In the Shadow of Man*. When I finished the last page, I closed my eyes, imbued with the fantasy of walking the forest paths surrounded by the amazing community of chimpanzees whom Jane had brought to life. By the time I reached Africa some thirty-five years later, old Flo and David Graybeard, the first chimpanzees to touch my heart, had long since passed away. Although my dream of observing life amongst free-ranging chimpanzees in their natural habitat was not to be, I am grateful to, and humbled by, the captive chimpanzees whose resiliency and generosity have enabled me to manifest my fantasy in other ways. While all their stories are worthy of mention, I will share a few that have especially touched my heart.

In 1985, I joined the Jane Goodall Institute's ChimpanZoo program at the Los Angeles Zoo, where I was fortunate to work with Cathy Granholm, who had been involved there for several months. The focus of ChimpanZoo was to collect long-term behavioral data on captive chimpanzees housed in zoos across the country and around the world. The group of nine chimpanzees at the Los Angeles Zoo consisted of two adult females, two adult males, one sub-adult female, and several infants and juveniles.

My first couple of weeks in front of the chimpanzee enclosure were spent learning to distinguish one individual from the next. Yet even after my countless hours of observation and data collection, the chimpanzees appeared to be largely unaware of my presence. Then one day as I approached the enclosure after completing the strenuous hike up to the chimpanzee exhibit, Andy, a five-year-old juvenile male, turned toward me—momentarily distracted from the "chimp politics" that were unfolding behind him—and attempted to carry out a typical adult male chimpanzee greeting display: he stood up on two legs, began a bidpedal run, stomped his feet, shook his head, vocalized, then presented a play face in my direction. I was stunned. Andy had acknowledged my presence, welcoming me into his day; I felt honored.

Andy's greeting displays became part of our daily routine, and his enthusiasm was contagious. Soon other chimpanzees followed suit, acknowledging my presence with their own unique greeting displays. I responded with my version of chimpanzee facial and manual gestures, awestruck by our burgeoning human-chimpanzee relationships; I had actually become a social counterpart outside their enclosure. Once greetings were exchanged and everyone settled down, I recorded behavior for the ChimpanZoo program.

Andy was engaged in the initial phase of securing his future place in the male hierarchy, yet he continued to seek his mother Pandora's attention, which had recently shifted to his new infant sister. Interestingly, this did not stop him from seeking my attention, probably because I had become a novel distraction! Over the next few months, I grew to depend on Andy's engaging antics because they punctuated the long, quiet afternoons with whimsy while the adults napped lazily nearby. The constancy of his routine reinforced a sense that I was now completely immersed in the everyday rhythm of the chimpanzees' lives, especially Andy's.

Months later I arrived at the chimpanzee enclosure and found several groups of dozing chimps dispersed around the habitat, but I could not find Andy. I was dumbfounded when Cathy told me that Andy had been transferred to a Chinese zoo the night before. Sadly, there had been no chance to say goodbye. Andy was gone—just like that. I began to visualize him on the airplane, waking from his tranquilized state alone in a dark crate, dazed and wondering why his beloved caregivers, who had placed him in the crate, had disappeared. I wondered how Andy would recover from the abrupt separation from his family and companions, and how his mother, Pandora, would respond to his absence. I was heartbroken. It was the first time I grieved for a chimpanzee.

During the following weeks, Pandora withdrew from group activities, spending much of the day sitting on a rock at the top of the exhibit, gazing blankly into the

Figure 101. Pandora

distance. While I can only surmise Pandora's emotional state, her behavior was strikingly similar to that observed in wild chimpanzees after the death of an infant or other group member. In the wild, chimpanzee mothers often groom their dead infants, carry them around for a day or two, and eventually give them up, placing the infant on a rock or the ground and walking away. Sometimes it takes a while before the mother becomes actively reengaged in her normal daily routine. Like chimpanzees in the wild, Pandora slowly regained the normal rhythm of her life. Cathy and I wrote to the Chinese zoo inquiring about Andy, but to no avail. I still think about Andy and wonder what became of him.

Shortly thereafter, Cathy and I attended a ChimpanZoo conference where we met a Chicago-based animal caregiver who had created an environmental enrichment program for captive apes. Enrichment involves enhancing a captive animal's habitat with interesting objects, novel materials, textures, and food in order to encourage species-typical social and nonsocial behaviors, thereby reducing the boredom and routine of captive life. In the case of chimpanzees, enrichment often mimics a particular feeding tradition found in the wild, such as an artificial termite mound, which requires them to use a tool to extract food embedded inside. Other forms of enrichment mimic their wild habitats by providing tall wooden structures and hanging fire hoses that encourage them to climb, swing, and engage in play with social partners. Many chimpanzee enclosures have concrete floors that can be softened with blankets, leaves, branches, paper, and bales of hay. These novel items stimulate nest building, provide a comfortable place to relax, and encourage nonsocial play. Chimpanzees also engage with these objects by throwing or dragging the shreds of hay, bits of paper, or blankets around the enclosure to gain the attention of their social counterparts, solicit play, or incorporate them into a behavioral display.

When Cathy and I returned from the enrichment conference, we met with Jennie McNary-Becker, the head chimpanzee keeper at the time, to discuss the notion of incorporating enrichment into the chimpanzees' daily routine. Jennie wholeheartedly agreed that enrichment would significantly enhance the chimpanzees' lives. Without explicit permission from the zoo's director, and well before the behavioral enrichment program had been formally established there, Jennie supervised and assisted while we habituated the chimpanzees to our presence in the foyer of their indoor night cages. Once that was accomplished, we began filling those cages with a variety of materials and objects. Soon after, the zoo maintenance crew created an artificial termite mound, an iron contraption mounted on the outside of the indoor night cage bars and fitted with several solid rectangular containers that could be filled with enticing foods. A small opening in each container faced the inside of the cage, enabling the chimpanzees to insert sticks or other objects to extract foods such as ketchup, mustard, or applesauce. The containers were evenly spaced, providing an opportunity for several chimpanzees to use the device at one time. The chimpanzees went wild over this device and were fairly good at waiting their turns to participate. Observing their positive response to the various forms of enrichment we provided, I had no doubt that, particularly when rotated and unpredictable, it created novelty and stimulation that were vital to the chimps' sense of physical and social well-being.

We were ecstatic when our enrichment efforts were welcomed by the director of the zoo. He expressed great pleasure in the initiative we had taken. He also understood that our physical contact with the chimpanzees through the cage bars of their bedrooms provided social enrichment, nourishing the bonds developing between us. At the time, wild animal facilities had not yet addressed the potential danger inherent in physical contact between humans and captive primates. Unlike today, few rules or policies were in place governing such contact, or even considered part of the professional protocol.

Over time, the chimpanzees' enthusiastic response to our presence became more pronounced. During each visit, we were greeted by a crescendo of cacophonous vocalizations that began while we were still out of sight around the corner or down the road from the exhibit. Once the group settled down, several individuals routinely solicited our attention by gesturing toward their bedroom foyer in the back of the enclosure. Following their signals, we would join them there for personal time—chasing, tickling, and grooming eyelashes or fingernails between the bars. Whenever I wore sandals, Toto, an older adult male, would beg to groom my toes. Evidently, he was enthralled by the sight of bare human feet—something most captive chimpanzees never get to see! The "girls," on the other hand, enjoyed sitting and holding our hands through the bars while we gazed into each other's eyes.

Although these moments of physical contact were profound, new rules established to protect our safety eventually abolished such proximity between non-staff members and the chimpanzees. Sadly, it took a long time for the chimpanzees to realize that their attempts to solicit close contact with us through their manual and facial gestures and vocalizations were not going to elicit the results they expected. During their adjustment to this new reality, some chimpanzees threw tantrums, others "flipped us off" with hand gestures, while some simply gave up, turned their backs, and walked away. Cathy and I also endured a period of adjustment as we were obliged to refrain from physical contact with the chimpanzees. In response, we bolstered other aspects of our communication to ensure continuity and trust. The social bonds we shared with the chimpanzees continued to grow over the years, resembling, in some aspects, the lifelong bonds that develop between wild chimpanzee companions who belong to the same community.

"

Upon my return,
I was astonished
when two-year-old
Jamal greeted me
as if he had just seen
me the day before.

Figure 102. Baby Jamal

During graduate school, I was abroad for a year. Upon my return, I was astonished when two-year-old Jamal greeted me as if he had just seen me the day before. Amazingly, this captive-born youngster was displaying species-typical behavior found amongst his wild counterparts, who will routinely recognize and reengage with a returning community member after a long absence.

This species-typical behavior is a positive adaptation observed among primates and other animals who live in a fission-fusion community, a dynamic social structure in which a large stable parent population "fissions" (separates) into small temporary subgroups to forage, hunt, or patrol the territorial boundary together during the day or over many days, and "fuses" (merges) with the parent population to reestablish social networks and sleep within the safety of a larger group at night. Under these conditions, the ability to recognize familiar group members, distinguish them from strangers, and retain this memory from an early age provides a survival advantage, particularly to infants and youngsters. I believe that the bonds established between Jamal and I had been etched in his memory, a remnant of an evolutionarily stable strategy passed biologically and culturally from parent to child that contributes to their survival.

Although I was initially drawn to the infant and juvenile chimpanzees in the zoo's social group, I became increasingly attached to the adults. The "toe groomer" Toto, a middle-aged, wild-caught former circus chimp, had a playful, gregarious personality.

Figure 103.
Toto

He always acknowledged my appearance with long, elaborate greeting displays, which I returned with great enthusiasm, unhindered by zoo patrons observing the event. Even when it was obvious that I had not arrived with treats for an enrichment session, Toto actively and persistently solicited my attention through gestures and vocalizations commonly observed during chimpanzee communication. Our interactions lasted well into Toto's old age, when his eyesight and hearing had become so poor he was unable to recognize me at a distance.

Bonnie, a middle-aged wild-caught chimpanzee, had a sweet, gentle, empathetic temperament. Despite having been raised by humans as a pet, Bonnie displayed the same species-typical behaviors observed in her wild female counterparts—those of an attentive mother, aunt, companion, and peacemaker. However, when it came to humans Bonnie was particular: she only solicited human attention from specific individuals. Thus, whenever she acknowledged my presence with her typically understated greeting displays I was flattered. Over the years, Bonnie's attention-seeking behavior increased in frequency and duration. She spent more and more time simply sitting in close proximity to me unless distracted by intense interactions between other members of her group. She aged slowly and gracefully, never losing her ability to connect with a greeting, even if it was only with a quick shake of her head.

Bonnie had an affinity for certain human males, whom she would greet with distinct bipedal displays, hand gestures, and vocalizations. She always greeted one particular male vet with loud vocalizations even before she could see him, which is how we knew when he was coming. And the few times Bonnie saw my husband Norman standing in front of the exhibit she stood up bipedally, extended her arm toward him with a pronated wrist (a friendly gesture), and then sat for a long time just staring at him. Some suggested that Bonnie's interest in human males stemmed from a human male bond formed while she was home-reared by humans during her childhood, but there is insufficient information to support this contention.

Pandora, who had been born at the zoo and raised in its nursery, was an intelligent, politically astute, dominant female, as well as a highly skilled parent. Her role as a disruptive negotiator during male altercations was an indispensable contribution to group harmony. During frustrated attempts to resolve social group issues, she often gestured and vocalized toward me, seeking comfort and reassurance through species-typical behaviors that temporarily obscured the fact that there was little I could do.

Figure 104. Bonnie

On calmer occasions, she would walk over to wherever I was stationed, sit in close proximity, and solicit me to open my purse so she could peek at its contents. Sometimes she simply approached, made momentary eye contact with me, and quickly rushed back to the activity she had just abandoned.

In subsequent years, long periods of time passed between my visits to the zoo. Pandora would still interact with me, but her enthusiastic greetings were replaced by a new routine that eventually developed into a sort of "reentry ritual" between us: when I came into sight she would sit down, turn her back, and ignore me. Initially, I wondered whether this overt unwillingness to engage or communicate was an intentional expression of displeasure at my long absence. Based on Pandora's next response in this ritual, I can only presume that my assumption was correct. After about ten minutes of soliciting Pandora with verbal pleas and attempting to console her with gestural apologies, I would signal that my portion of the routine was over. With a tone of resignation, I'd utter, "That's it, Pandora—I'm leaving," and I'd start walking away. A few steps into my slow but deliberate departure, Pandora would turn around, whimper, and try desperately to squeeze her arms through the mesh to reach me as I began walking back toward her. With no ability to reach each other, we could only gesture, necks strained, arms outreached, and gaze at each other longingly. I never failed to well up with tears during these touching encounters.

Each chimpanzee's unique approach to resolving issues gave me new insights. Jamal taught me that the effects of one-on-one social interactions are profound and last indefinitely, particularly when bonds are established with affection, humor, and benevolence. Toto's relentless interaction with other chimpanzees during disputes over dominance and access to females taught me that when there is nothing to lose but time, perseverance is often a successful strategy. Toto's lighthearted disposition and terrific sense of humor, which were vibrant well into old age, showed me the value of these traits as positive coping mechanisms in challenging social settings. His solicitation of play-chase from his younger companions and human allies underscored the importance of retaining the capacity to laugh, play, and have fun with others despite frustration, disappointment, or distress, particularly in later years.

Bonnie's gentleness and nonconfrontational style demonstrated many clever ways to resolve conflict despite the potential impact on social stature, which ebbs and flows over time in chimpanzee society, as it does amongst humans. As a result, I gained

Figure 105.
Toto holding
young Zoe's hand

knowledge of methods for conflict resolution and also began to sense that adjusting to the shifts in one's social status is often more beneficial than resisting in vain.

While confident and assertive, Pandora was also tender and fair. Her ability to acknowledge all of her offspring without bias and defend them under all circumstances reinforced my sense of effective child-rearing practices. Watching Pandora also taught me that overcoming fear in the face of adversity, even during dangerous and disturbingly aggressive altercations, requires courage, fortitude, and, most importantly, commitment.

Jamal, Toto, Bonnie, and Pandora are gone now. But the lessons I learned from them, and the rest of their group, will remain with me forever.

I came to know many other remarkable chimpanzees living in laboratories, zoos, and sanctuaries that I visited or worked at over the decades. Some of my most compelling experiences occurred while caring for infant and juvenile chimpanzees who were born in a biomedical research laboratory and moved to a facility that had not yet met the requirements for accreditation. All these infants and juveniles had been abruptly separated from their mothers shortly after birth and placed in cozy backpacks, their mothers' places taken by tall, white-clad masked beings devoid of facial expression, warmth, soft hair, pulsing heart, and familiar smell. Instead of waking up securely cuddled in their mothers' arms, these infants woke up terrified, anxious, bewildered, and traumatized. A human surrogate can never replace the sense of security or the other ties that bind chimpanzee infants to their mothers. For the infant, the cloaks and masks may eventually disappear, but the damage is a fait accompli. For the mother, the confiscation of her infant is equally traumatizing. Devastated to wake up finding her infant missing from her arms, she can only peer through the bars, similar to the way Pandora gazed blankly into the distance after Andy's disappearance, wondering why her offspring was suddenly absent.

Every day mutual bonds developed between me and the young chimpanzees. My unshakable commitment to being the best possible surrogate mother served as a catalyst for each decision I made. I drew on my academic knowledge of wild and captive chimpanzee orphans who had been successfully adopted by peers and adults and on personal experience with captive chimpanzees who had been reared by other chimpanzees or human mother surrogates. I called upon the expertise of others in the field and depended on my maternal instincts. And while I worried that I could never adequately replace the early life experiences missed by these precious individuals, I did my best.

Years ago, when I first read that young chimpanzee mothers often carry their dead infants for days before releasing them and moving on, I wondered whether these mothers were mourning their losses, expressing their grief. Today, evidence published by anthropologist Dr. Barbara J. King in her book *How Animals Grieve* suggests that indeed chimpanzees, as well as other animals, grieve the loss of relatives and companions.[1] Photographs of chimpanzees who have recently lost an infant or other group member suggest a story too difficult for some to accept or understand and irrelevant to many members of the biomedical research community for whom chimpanzees are "business and bread."

The well-worn notion that chimpanzees are in laboratories to serve the greater good of humans was eventually debunked, due to the small number of biomedical study protocols on chimpanzees that produced results relevant to human treatment, how few chimpanzees were actively used in research, and how many hundreds of chimpanzees were warehoused in laboratories solely because each one provided approximately sixty-five dollars per diem in government support. In 1997, the Institute of Laboratory Animal Research (ILAR) produced a report, entitled "Chimpanzees in Research: Strategies for their Ethical Care, Management, and Use," proposing that humans have a moral obligation to provide lifetime care to chimpanzees previously used in biomedical research. It also suggested that the government establish sanctuaries to accommodate retired chimpanzees for life. Growing public and private support for these measures eventually resulted in the CHIMP Act of December 20, 2000, amendments to the act, and a directional change at the National Institutes of Health (NIH) supported by its director, Dr. Francis S. Collins. The agency publicly acknowledged that housing chimpanzees in laboratories for biomedical research was unethical and unnecessary, and that it would no longer support invasive research.

I can still recall how I felt when NIH announced that all government-owned and -supported chimpanzees residing in biomedical research laboratories would be released and retired to Chimp Haven, the National Chimpanzee Sanctuary in Louisiana which currently cares for over two hundred chimpanzees. This would never have happened without the enduring passion and perseverance of animal welfare advocates, attorneys, legislators, academics, chimpanzee caregivers, veterinarians, volunteers, and some members of the biomedical community who worked tirelessly over the past several decades—and who continue to work—to ensure that every government- and privately owned chimpanzee living in a laboratory, home, roadside zoo, or entertainment compound will ultimately be able to experience the long-term benefits of an enriched quality of life in a sanctuary.

My abiding love and empathy for all the chimpanzees I have known in labs, zoos, and sanctuaries—as well as those I have yet to meet—sustain me. The face of every chimpanzee whose eyes have met mine is forever emblazoned in my heart. Although my dream of observing life among free-ranging chimpanzees in their natural habitats was not to be, I am grateful to all the captive chimpanzees whose resiliency and generosity have enabled me to serve their greater good.

UP CLOSE WITH PRIMATES

Kristina Casper-Denman, PhD

I had never imagined working with chimpanzees. Like most people growing up in the 1970s, I had worshipped Dian Fossey and Jane Goodall but felt that I could never do such things. First, I was not a fan of dirt or camping. Second, a former boss had told me that chimpanzees could not be trusted, that they were smarter than most humans and could redirect our attention in the blink of an eye.

As a teenager, however, I wanted to work with chimpanzees, but there were none in Massachusetts that I knew about, so I decided to work with monkeys. My first foray into primatology was at the New England Regional Primate Research Center (NERPC) in Massachusetts and involved lab research with monkeys. At sixteen, my heart had not yet evolved to the point where I was fully aware of all the implications of biomedical research on monkeys or other animals being used in experiments. In my own little corner of the world, I was cleaning the cages of marmosets and macaques, as well as feeding them. Not until much later did I realize these same precious babies were being used in medical experiments that harmed them. I did know that perception studies, some dietary studies, drug addiction experiments, and pharmaceutical research were occurring and that such research would not end well for the monkeys, but perhaps I was in denial about the extent of it. This work was a painful aspect of my life, and I still feel badly for having taken part in it.

Luckily, two researchers at NERPC were kind not only to me as a budding primatologist but also to the monkeys. Dr. Andrew J. Petto and Dr. Lyna Watson taught me the importance of using enrichment to provide mental stimulation and a sense of peace to captive primates. We tried our best to house the monkeys to benefit them socially because they needed the companionship of other monkeys for activities important to their well-being, such as grooming, playing, and cuddling. For the monkeys who were singly housed, enrichment was even more critical to help alleviate the stress of living alone. We provided them with pieces of fleece so they could groom, even if it was a solo activity, and puzzle feeders to stimulate foraging, giving them something to do to avoid boredom,

Years later, while I was at Arizona State University in the MA Program for Physical Anthropology, I accepted a work-study position at the Primate Foundation of Arizona (PFA) located in the desert outside Mesa. The PFA was home to dozens of chimpanzees who were retired circus performers, former pets, and research subjects. The foundation had originally been established for behavioral research and breeding; however, it had an agreement with the MD Anderson Cancer Research Center in Texas stipulating that the foundation's chimpanzees would be available for biomedical research at its Texas lab whenever needed.

In 1993, I arrived at the PFA to work with primate anatomist Dr. Mary Marzke as a research assistant tasked with measuring the growth and development of chimpanzee babies, comparing those raised by chimp mothers with those raised by humans in the nursery. I viewed the research assistantship as a great way to take a break from data entry while adding experience to my curriculum vitae.

Many of the chimpanzees at the PFA had once lived like humans and now were living in a confusing world—no longer as chimpanzees but certainly not as humans. They were living in social groups far different from those in the wild or during their early lives as pets. Yet these chimpanzees were fortunate to be cared for by a staff interested in enriching their lives both socially and environmentally. I discovered that the PFA had many social groupings that might not occur in other captive settings, such as bachelor groups and groups of mothers and infants; occasionally new infants were born, even though technically this was not supposed to happen. Chimps who could not be socialized lived alone but were able to see and hear other chimps, even though they could not touch them. One male chimpanzee lived by himself because he was too aggressive to live with others yet content to be within vocal and visual range of them.

There was something magical about hearing the chimpanzees vocalize to one another as I entered behavioral data about them while sitting in another building just a few hundred feet away. I longed to be with them, to understand them, and to have them accept me.

We took measurements when each chimpanzee had an annual health check under anesthesia. As I not only measured their fingers and toes but also their testicles, I learned about the importance of making sure metallic calipers are warm. The colony manager often assisted the veterinarian during these health checks. One time a large, handsome adult male chimpanzee came out of anesthesia a little early and was groggy. The manager was standing a wee bit too close to him, and the chimp grabbed his manhood. We all stood very still and held our breath until the chimpanzee unclenched his large, powerful hand and the manager was able to back away.

When we did health checks on the mothers, I held their infants, many just a few months old. Being nose to nose with baby chimpanzees was awe-inspiring. For those brief moments, I needed to be a chimpanzee, to pass myself off as someone familiar so the babies would feel soothed and secure. I had held dozens of human children through the years as a baby-sitter, but holding baby chimps was very different, requiring me to position them more upright than horizontal and to shift them around like chimpanzee mothers do without much fussing. The smell, touch, and texture of the infants' skin and hair were foreign to me. The babies were fragile and yet had the strength to cling to me if they chose to. Though it was a blessing to hold them, it was more of a blessing to return in the afternoon and see the babies with their mothers. The most gratifying part of my interaction with the chimps was knowing that my actions did not create fear or resentment and did not interfere with their social bonds.

Then there were the kinder kids, young chimpanzees who had been rejected by their mothers and raised by human caregivers. When the kids were together, they stayed in close contact by creating a long, fuzzy chimpanzee locomotive, with hands placed on each other's backs and walking in a shuffling bipedal gait. At first, I was taken aback, but the more I saw them the more I realized how this alloparenting (being taken care of by someone other than their mothers) allowed them to thrive, playing, eating, and fighting as if they lived in a normal social group.

Of course, there is no way to create a fully "normal" social group of chimpanzees in captivity. In the wild, fifty to one hundred chimpanzees live together in the forests of Central Africa in groups ranging in age from babies to elders. They are free to roam, enjoy many foods, and live with family members and friends. Although no captive setting could ever replicate that fully, the PFA did create a setting where the chimpanzees could engage in natural primate behaviors like foraging, grooming, and playing. It is virtually impossible to raise chimpanzees in the United States and then find a destination for them in tropical Africa that would suit their needs and be safe.

I worked at the PFA until 1995. In 2010, it closed, sending its remaining chimpanzees to the MD Anderson Cancer Center in Texas.

※ ※ ※

From 1997 until 2009, I volunteered at the Sacramento Zoo for the Jane Goodall Institute research program called ChimpanZoo (CZOO), which studied chimpanzee behavior in zoos and other captive settings so that the lives of chimpanzees could be improved. It has always been difficult for me to understand zoos, but recognizing that chimps would likely be around for a long while, I knew it was important to make a difference in how they were cared for. While teaching part-time at American River College in Sacramento, I had been introduced to the local CZOO coordinator, Dr. Patrice Gibson, who taught a class associated with the program. It was an honor to subsequently be trained by her in the art of behavioral research. While studying with her, I was introduced to four geriatric (over age thirty-five) chimpanzees: Sam, Judy, Joey, and Josie. Sadly, Judy died of a congenital heart defect soon after I began work as the CZOO co-coordinator. Patrice and I observed the chimpanzees and recorded their movements and interactions for hours at a time. It was challenging to learn the ethogram—four-letter codes that CZOO created to help identify activities—yet it was a breakthrough for me to be able to write down what I saw with little hesitation as I attempted to understand what the chimpanzees were experiencing.

Most visitors at zoos who view a chimpanzee exhibit tend to walk away quickly when they don't see action, assuming nothing is happening. But if they quietly observed for a few moments, they would see subtle interactions among the chimpanzees. For example, Joey would groom Josie, poking her eyes and teeth, and pulling her arm to get her to move closer to him. Josie would tolerate this behavior for minutes at a time but eventually become frustrated, scream, and run away. Chimpanzees would keep track of one another by pant-hooting, a long, seesawing technique of communicating that starts as a whisper, grows to the roar of a thunderstorm, and ends with a scream.

We are not supposed to have favorites in science, but I loved Josie best. She would come to the glass windows, arms crossed in front of her; nod when she recognized someone; and tap herself on the head when she was extremely excited. Josie always connected with me by making eye contact. When there were fights, she would run to the glass to find comfort and companionship from me. On Easter, when the chimpanzees received carved watermelon baskets filled with goodies like strawberries, Jell-O eggs, and sprouts, Josie promptly removed the sprouts then, grasping the handle of the watermelon basket, carried her bounty to the corner of the enclosure, where she

"

Josie would come to the glass windows, arms crossed in front of her; nod when she recognized someone; and tap herself on the head when she was extremely excited.

Figure 106. Josie

would not need to share her goodies, and sat daintily gnawing her fruit until it was all gone. Joey liked to bite into the Jello eggs, squishing each one in and out of his teeth, showing visitors his Easter treats.

The eldest chimpanzee involved with our CZOO observations was Sam, handsome and quiet, with graying hair, a pouty lower lip, a sweet potbelly, and a broad back. It's difficult to know the exact biological ages and full life histories of wild-caught chimpanzees, but we knew that Sam had been wild-born and that he had not suffered in medical research labs or the entertainment industry before living with several chimpanzees at the Sacramento Zoo. Sam and Josie enjoyed a lovely courtship. On various occasions, Sam would gaze at Josie, the only female when I started observing the group in late 1997, show his erection, and beckon to her. She would oblige, moving slowly to him. Sam would gently groom her face, her head, maybe her back. Then their coupling would last only a few moments before they separated again. This could go on all afternoon. Parents would flee the exhibit horrified, teenagers would gawk, and I would continue to collect data. People tell me not to anthropomorphize, that chimpanzees do not feel the same emotions as humans or that we cannot know what they are feeling. However, after twelve years working with CZOO I truly believe Sam's heart skipped a beat when he saw Josie hanging upside down by the waterfall in the sunshine, soaking up the afternoon rays.

Sam's patience, gentle touch, and habit of making sure everyone came in for afternoon feedings made him special to me. He was there when Maria, the first chimpanzee born at the Sacramento Zoo, entered the world. Maria's mother, Amelia, had been transferred from Zoo Miami and introduced into Sam's group in 1999, shortly before Maria's birth. As baby Maria grew into a firebrand, Sam was her faithful playmate. Maria, who loved to tease him, would swing into him from the ropes above his head and kick at him, just to entice him to chase her. Sam would engage with her each time, often playfully swatting at her or poking her with his fingers. When Maria wanted Sam to tickle her, she would place her hand on that spot and laugh quietly. Often his tickle was not enough, and Maria would try to tickle herself.

Sam even took good care of Pablo, also introduced into the group in 1999, sharing food with him and letting him sit by his side for social interaction despite how difficult the introduction of new males usually is. When there were problems in the group, Sam would hug the other chimpanzees. His relationship with the chimps in his group still impacts them today, especially in the confidence reflected by the now eighteen-year-old Maria.

Sam passed in 2005, while in his fifties, from heart-related issues. He was the first chimpanzee I had known well, and I mourn his loss to this day. It was even harder when Josie passed in 2012. I still look for them when I come to the enclosure to observe with a primatology class and when I simply visit my chimpanzee friends.

Today, the lives of the Sacramento Zoo chimpanzees continue with the addition of a young male, Dougie, who was transferred from the Jackson Zoo in Jackson,

Figure 107. Sam (right) sharing a quiet moment with Pablo (left)

Mississippi. Dougie brings a vibrancy to the group, especially when playing with Maria and bonding with Pablo. I miss observing my friends on a regular basis, and I especially miss Sam and Josie, but I know that the docents and keepers continue their excellent educational and enrichment work with all the chimpanzees.

Over the course of forty years, I have evolved from being a child feeling ill-equipped to work with chimpanzees to an adult yearning to be with them. Both at the PFA and the Sacramento Zoo, seeing powerful chimpanzees in such vulnerable states made me want to protect them, honor them, and ensure that they and their wild cousins remained safe. I now know that to care for them was to care about myself and humanity.

PART IV

FROM ORDINARY TO EXTRAORDINARY:
EVERYONE CAN MAKE A DIFFERENCE

Solutions to the numerous challenges in our lives are not usually delivered by
a thousand warriors marching to a hundred drums and led by a grand general.
Effective responses are often small and immediately appropriate—
the acts that we as individuals are entirely capable of undertaking.

—MICHAEL NICOLL YAHGULANAAS, *Flight of the Hummingbird*

Figure 108. Harry playing his guitar for Sam (left) and Kodua (right) at the Center for Great Apes

THE PEOPLE OF THE FOREST: SHARING MUSIC WITH GREAT APES

Harry Hmura

I have met more than a hundred captive chimpanzees, each with a traumatic past due to years of abuse as a medical research subject, entertainer, or household pet. Chimpanzees used in biomedical research have been subjected to decades of torment living in unnatural, stark environments and enduring unimaginable suffering through cruel experiments, social isolation, and poor diets consisting mainly of hard biscuits. As a result of my personal experiences with these sentient relatives, I have a much broader perspective on what it means to be a human. I have experienced the wild beauty chimpanzees possess, together with with their fragility, strength, and will to overcome adversity.

My awakening began on a Sunday night in 1999. While working on a recording project in my Chicago studio, I decided to take a break. I turned on the television, and a PBS special, *The Wisdom of the Wild*, was airing. Linda Koebner was talking about the chimps who had been moved from the Laboratory for Experimental Medicine & Surgery in Primates (LEMSIP) in New York to Lion Country Safari in Palm Beach County, Florida. Linda had worked with these chimps at LEMSIP and accompanied them on their journey to Florida. My heart sank in disbelief as she described how reluctant the chimps had been to leave their transport cages when they had first arrived at the safari park. Having lived in small steel cages with metal bar floors in research facilities for so many years, the chimpanzees were fearful about stepping onto grass—something they had never experienced. Linda was coaxing a few of them out of their transport cages with food, with no luck. Finally, the chimps summoned the courage to take their first steps toward freedom, feeling the earth underneath their feet and seeing the sky overhead without bars in front of their eyes. The story continued when Linda came to visit them eighteen years later and paddled over to the island where they were with Terry Wolf, the wildlife director at Lion Country Safari. Three of the chimps were still alive—Doll, Swing, and Sparky. Doll and Swing recognized Linda immediately, bobbing their heads and stretching out their arms, as Linda also did, joyful with tears as they hugged each other. It was especially touching to watch Linda comforting Sparky, who had cancer and died a few days after their reunion. The recognition and emotions of both Linda and the chimps brought tears to my eyes. I was amazed that the chimpanzees remembered her after almost two decades. It was clear to me that these beings shared the same bonds and memories as humans do. The documentary was a revelation for me. Although it captured moments of joy, it was painful to watch the torment and abuse that chimpanzees are forced to endure in medical research laboratories. In truth, I was stunned.

A few days later I introduced myself to Linda over the phone. She said that Doll and Swing were still living at Lion Country Safari. Thrilled to hear this, I told Linda that I had upcoming gigs in Florida and asked if it would be possible to meet the chimps. She put me in touch with Terry, and I made plans to visit the park.

My initial visit to the park was a numbing experience. I had to stay in my car, so I could only see the chimps from afar. There were the chimpanzees who had been through so much now living with others of their own kind, roaming freely on three different islands. I kept yelling, "Doll, Swing," hoping I might be able to recognize them.

A few nights after my gigs I sat under the Florida moon with my guitar and began to find the rhythms and melodies that fit my overwhelming emotions, eventually composing the song "Feel the Spark" as a tribute to Sparky's life—celebrating his spirit and remembering all he had had to endure. I finished the song when I returned home, and put it on my first album, *Passion*, which is dedicated to his memory and to Linda Koebner. The credit notes on the album say: "A creature whose bravery I'll never know. Whose will and courage goes far beyond words."

In the documentary, Linda mentioned that it was a dream of hers to open a sanctuary for chimpanzees used in research. I told her I would like to support the chimps. From its beginning, Linda was involved with Chimp Haven sanctuary, which opened in April 2005. At the grand opening, I had the opportunity to play "Feel the Spark" for Linda and others.

I continued to reach out to chimpanzee sanctuaries, offering to play my guitar for fund-raising and awareness events. Virginia Landau, the director of ChimpanZoo at the time, invited me to play at a cocktail party on the eve of a 2004 ChimpanZoo conference at the Lincoln Park Zoo in Chicago. There I met Gloria Grow, the founder and director of the Fauna Foundation, and one of Fauna's volunteers, Rachelle Hansen. Gloria had rescued fifteen chimpanzees from the dreadful LEMSIP, who were now living at her sanctuary outside Montreal. I heard the disturbing personal stories of the chimps. When it was time to share my music, I played "Feel the Spark," which connected me to Gloria and the Fauna chimps. I was thrilled when Gloria extended a gracious invitation for a visit, which led to a few performances in Canada at fund-raising events for the Fauna Foundation, including one with noted blues/rock guitarist Jeff Healey at his club in Toronto, Ontario. I helped out at two Toronto events, playing at Fauna Foundation exhibit tables to draw people in, which was where I, for the first time, saw photographs and videos of the Fauna chimpanzees.

The following year I had the opportunity to meet the Fauna chimpanzees—Jeannie, Pepper, Tom, Billy Jo, Sue Ellen, Toby, Binky, Rachel, Regis, Yoko, Chance, Petra, and Jethro. When I arrived at Fauna, my emotions were running in every direction, and I had no idea what to expect. I wondered how the chimpanzees would react to me, the same type of being who had caused them decades of misery.

While being escorted into the chimp house by Gloria's partner, Richard Allen, I was reminded of how important it was to obey all the rules, especially to stay in the safe areas, which were designated by a painted line on the concrete floor. I could smell and hear the chimps. We then came to a large open area where the kitchen was, and, looking up, I saw all the chimpanzees looking down at me. I felt the world stop. The horror of their past lives became all too real.

※ ※ ※

Lunch in the chimp house was a menu of fresh fruits and vegetables. After serving lunch, I went back to the guesthouse to fetch my guitar, and then Rachelle took me to the chimp house playroom so I could play guitar for Toby, who by chance was the only chimpanzee there. One of the newest chimps at Fauna, he had been rescued from a zoo. I knelt down and started strumming my guitar. Toby, who was sitting on a low wooden platform holding on to a rope, immediately started rhythmically swaying his head and body in time to my strumming and tapping on the guitar face. Then he opened his lips like the bell of a trumpet and let out a rhythmic sound. After playing for about five minutes, I walked to the front of the chimp house to play for Billy Jo, who was outside in an overhead walkway. Having been warned that he was not fond of men, I wondered how he would react. As I stood underneath the walkway and began strumming my guitar, with Billy Jo looking down at me, Billy Jo, like Toby, began to bob his head and sway to the rhythm of the smooth, medium-tempo melody, not taking his eyes off me and the guitar. Rachelle was surprised and said, "Oh my God, Billy Jo is enjoying this." The universal language of music had brought us together to share an unforgettable moment between species.

Later I played the role of head chef, planning a spaghetti dinner for the chimpanzees, one of their favorite meals. After picking fresh vegetables from the garden to make enough spaghetti sauce to go with pasta for thirteen chimpanzees at three helpings apiece, I simmered the onions, tomatoes, garlic, and veggies, delighting in the sounds and looks of the chimpanzees who could see the kitchen area from their indoor enclosures. While the sauce cooked, I played my guitar for them. I recall the staff commenting on how calm and quiet it was in the chimp house that afternoon. I was strumming and singing very quietly because I didn't want to disrupt the chimps, especially sweet Jeannie.

Jeannie was the first chimpanzee to steal my heart. After I witnessed Jeannie having one of her fits—spinning, slapping the ground, slapping herself—the result of what the biomedical research community had done to this beautiful soul, I was sick to my stomach. The staff immediately calmed her down, believing that perhaps my presence as an unknown male could have triggered her reaction, a conclusion that made sense since most of the people at the labs had been men. I'm amazed that after all the misery, pain, and fear inflicted on Jeannie and the other chimpanzees during their decades as biomedical research subjects, they have the resiliency to carry on—and even forgive people.

Pepper was the second chimpanzee to steal my heart. One afternoon I walked to the second floor and watched the gentle communication between Rachelle and Pepper. Standing behind Rachelle as she was giving Pepper grapes and a bottle of water, I was surprised when she said that Pepper was motioning for me to come closer. I gently approached her, offering soft-spoken greetings and asking Pepper if she was enjoying her grapes. I put a grape in my mouth and exaggerated my chewing to express the idea that the grapes were good. Pepper smiled as she watched me chew. We greatly enjoyed each other's company that day.

The day I was leaving the sanctuary I walked to the chimp house to say goodbye. It was late in the afternoon, and the only chimpanzee in the overhead walkway was Pepper. I looked up at her as she looked down at me. I told her how great it was to meet her, how much I loved her, and that I wanted to come back to see her another time. Then I said, "I wish you could give me something to go home with." Pepper immediately started shuffling through little bags and plastic bottles, and found a foot-long twig resting among the leaves. She gently pushed the twig through the grating, not breaking any of the tiny branches, and into my awaiting hands. I thanked her with all my heart, sent a kiss with a hand gesture toward her, and said goodbye. To this day, the twig Pepper gave me sits next to a photo of Pepper in my studio as a reminder of how amazing this exchange was on many levels. Pepper understood exactly what I had asked her, and she had searched for something that would fit through the small grating. Her awareness astounded me.

After this trip to the Fauna Foundation, I became increasingly involved in activities focused on chimpanzees. I watched countless videos and documentaries about chimpanzees in medical research. The reality of humans doing this to such exquisite creatures made me sick. In one interview that stayed with me, a scientist who worked at LEMSIP said, "Yeah, we pushed them [chimpanzees] to the limit—we had to do it because it was science," a perspective I found deplorable. Whenever I drove by universities where animal research was going on, I could not stop thinking about the primates suffering in tiny cages behind the walls. The more I found out, the more I couldn't stop thinking about the fate of all the animals in research. As a result, I broke down and went into a very dark place for many years—a state that ultimately led to my awakening.

Over the years, I have had many opportunities to perform at awareness-raising events sponsored by chimpanzee sanctuaries in North America. These performances started through my association with Linda Koebner, Terry Wolf, and Gloria Grow. Then other chimp advocates came into my life—like the late Carole Noon, founder of Save the Chimps; Patti Ragan, founder of the Center for Great Apes; and Lesley Day, founder of Chimps Inc.—as did the chimpanzees and orangutans living in their sanctuaries. I had an overwhelming feeling that I had to interact with, and help, these advocates.

When I first phoned the sanctuaries, I thought the directors would all wonder what kind of character I was and flatly say no, but instead they all said, "Yes, come on down." I have had the honor of playing for the chimpanzees at both the Center for Great Apes and Save the Chimps. The Center for Great Apes sanctuary is home to chimpanzees and orangutans, all former entertainers and pets; it was enchanting playing for the center's apes, who seemed content sitting or lying quietly, staring at my fingers strum the guitar, and occasionally glancing at me. It was the first time they had heard or seen a guitar up close. Their eyes, body language, and attention revealed a deep connection with the music.

I was a little nervous about playing at Save the Chimps because it was such a huge sanctuary—twelve three-acre islands that more than 250 chimpanzees called home. There were about twenty chimpanzees living on each island, and I was worried how playing to such a large audience would go. The staff took me to four outside fenced areas situated by each of the chimpanzees' indoor enclosures. When I sat on my side of the fence and started strumming the guitar, all the chimps in the area ran up to the fence, sat down, and listened to the music. It was a remarkable experience. One amazing moment was when Kiley moved her head back and forth in time to the music and then started clapping. Since no one around her was clapping, she wasn't imitating anyone.

As a musician, I am aware of the universal language of music that crosses all barriers, including those between species. Music goes beyond sensory enrichment and can touch the soul. Poet and artist Kahlil Gibran long ago wrote about music as the language of the spirit. I bring this feeling with me when I play for the chimpanzees, hoping to lift spirits, evoke joy, and stir up some fun.

Figure 109. Above: Kiley listening to Harry's music at Save the Chimps
Figure 110. Below: Arthur sounding in time with Harry's beat at Save the Chimps

Chimpanzees are magnificent wild creatures who don't belong in human homes, garages, trailers, commercials, photo shoots, and music videos. Using great apes in entertainment is unnatural, physically and psychologically damaging, and simply not acceptable. The cruel and unethical practices used by trainers—beating, humiliating, violating, and intimidating—to make chimps perform for financial gain are disgraceful. Responsibility for such practices lies with the breeders, trainers, and consumers who keep them as pets. Given our current knowledge, there are no excuses for such behavior.

All the chimpanzees I have met in sanctuaries have taught me more than they will ever know. They have become a part of my life. I treasure our similarities and our differences. I am humbled by the beauty they possess and the strength they have shown in overcoming adversity. These people of the forest deserve more than what we have given them. They are entitled to live out their lives in peace.

NOTES FROM A JUNIOR PRIMATOLOGIST

Micah Sparks

When I grow up, I want to be a primatologist. I have liked primates for six years, since I was two. I call them all monkeys for short because I did when I was two and I am used to it. I know that monkeys have tails and apes do not. I also know which primates are monkeys and which ones are apes.

I am a junior primatologist because I got a certificate from the American Society of Primatologists that says I am. They also sent me a National Primate Research Center coloring book.

Primatologists study primates by watching them live every day. They take pictures of monkeys and apes and make sure they are healthy. Primatologists live with primates in the jungles near the equator. There are a lot of primates in Africa because of the jungles. It is hot at the equator, and primates like that. Also lots of trees and plants grow where it is warm and wet because plants need water and sunlight.

I want to work in the Democratic Republic of the Congo in Africa. A lot of chimpanzees and other apes live there. I have read about it in my big ape books. My favorite books are *Planet Ape*, *Great Ape Odyssey*, and *Monkey Business*. I also love *Zoobooks* and *National Geographic Kids* magazines. I like all kinds of monkeys and apes, but my favorite ape is the chimpanzee. I like chimpanzees because they can do a lot of things I can do and are funny and smart like people. When I visit them at the zoo, they watch me and do what I do. I want to learn sign language to communicate with them for real.

Figure 111. Micah visiting the chimpanzees at the Rio Grande Zoo

Primates need to live in their natural habitat to be really healthy. If they are not healthy, they can die. Primates need fruits, leaves, nuts, and termites for healthy food. They have to live with other family or group members for protection and friendship. Some primates live in zoos. Zookeepers keep them healthy so they will not die. Primates in zoos have to have enrichment. Enrichment makes them forage, and that is good for their brains. Other primates live in people's homes as pets. They are not healthy because they are not supposed to be home animals like cats and dogs. These chimpanzees get in trouble because they are not in their natural habitats. They do things that are bad in homes but not bad in the jungle.

I help primates at the zoo by bringing them enrichment, like cardboard tubes and boxes, and paper books and magazines. Boxes can't have plastic or tape or be the kind used in fast-food places. I also collect clothes for bedding. I get all these things from my family and other people.

I signed a bushmeat pledge to help save the chimpanzees from poachers. Poachers kill primates for their meat. I tell people about bushmeat and not to buy things for my house from the jungle. I also sent e-mails to Congressman Steve Pearce to help save the chimps used in New Mexico for research. They are sick because they were used for science projects, and chemicals were put in them that can make them die. They need enrichment and doctors to take care of them. They cannot go back to the jungle because they do not know how to forage or live there. The jungle would make the chimps sick and die.

Animals are God's creation just like people are. They need to have the same value. If I had a magic wand, I would give rewards to all the people who bring chimpanzees used in entertainment, research, and kept as pets to sanctuaries.

WHY CHIMPANZEES? NOTES FROM THE MOTHER OF A JUNIOR PRIMATOLOGIST

Angela Sparks

My son Micah intends to become a primatologist. He has already been certified as a junior primatologist by the American Society of Primatologists. Why did this organization bestow such an honor on a six-year-old? Simple: Micah's passion for primates goes beyond his years. We do not know where it came from or how long it will last, but it does not seem to be fading.

Micah was barely talking when stories of Curious George sparked a glimmer in his eye. His second birthday party was focused on the theme of Curious George, with all the trimmings that commercialism could offer. Micah's Curious George collection grew to be so extensive that he had his formal two-year-old portrait taken with all of his "Georges." At the time, we thought it was just a fad.

For most of my six children, each year's birthday celebration is a new adventure based on a theme related to the current interests of the birthday child. But Micah's birthday celebrations for the last eight years have all revolved around primates, featuring such activities as having fun with Curious George; going "on safari" to look for monkeys through homemade binoculars; having cake at the zoo with chimpanzees; going with friends to see the movie *Chimpanzee*; making chimpanzee magnets; and decorating with chimpanzees and other apes. When his birthday approaches, Micah always asks, "What type of primate party will we have this year?"

As Micah developed from a toddler to a little boy, our library trips involved searching for every Curious George story we could find beyond our home collection. Always looking for more material on primates to satisfy his continuing interest, I introduced Micah to the "real Georges" in true stories about the great apes of Africa and other parts of the world. Micah soon learned, and was adamant about, the fact that his beloved Curious George was not a monkey but an ape, since monkeys have tails. Micah thought everyone should know this critical information and could not understand why the authors of the Curious George books apparently did not since they refer to tail-less George as a monkey. So my three-year-old soon educated everyone he met about primate classification facts, while others his age forgot about the animals as soon as library time was over.

Our move to the Albuquerque, New Mexico, area when Micah was almost four gave us an opportunity to become members of the Rio Grande Zoo. And since Micah has been homeschooled, with a flexible schedule, we were privileged to visit the chimpanzees and monkeys there regularly at all hours of the day. For us, there was no need to read the enclosure descriptions about each species. In just these few years, Micah had made it his mission to know the different types of primates, where they lived in the wild, and their classifications—monkey or ape. Even though at the Rio Grande Zoo the gorillas appeared first along the path, followed by the orangutans, siamangs, and a variety of monkeys in close proximity, no trip was complete without a jaunt across the zoo to the chimpanzees. Micah had to explore every window of their enclosure, pressing his hands to the glass, while making facial gestures and arm motions to get their attention in the hope that his friends would return the greeting. Micah was often the only zoo visitor who was successful. Maybe they sensed his heart. I had that experience only once, when I urged a crowd of people to step away from the window in front of a nursing chimpanzee mother to give her some space, then placed my hand to the glass, and she returned the gesture as if knowing that I was a mother, too.

After a few years of visiting the zoo, one spring day in 2010 we noticed an abundance of trash in the enclosures, as if purposefully placed, and found out it was actually enrichment material. That day Micah learned something that would give his life even more purpose—that primates in captivity must be challenged to forage and think to be happy and healthy, and enrichment materials serve this function. Enrichment items include food and treats hidden in boxes, between pages of magazines, in telephone books, or in cardboard tubes. Later that day we were fortunate to come across a caregiver in an enclosure with a six-month-old siamang named Noah, who had been rejected by his parents and was being hand-raised until he could be transferred to another zoo. The caregiver was explaining Noah's situation when Micah, who had just learned about enrichment, asked a burning question: "What do the babies use for 'richment?" The caretaker stated that the smaller primates used cardboard boxes and toilet paper tubes, which were in high demand. I thought nothing more about the subject—until Micah later discovered his mission.

The week following that zoo trip our family view of trash changed forever as Micah's mission became defined. In our house, chores are distributed among all family members based on age and ability, and at age five Micah was on wastebasket patrol, collecting trash from four bathrooms, a laundry room, and a school room. As the trash he had collected was being dumped into a larger bag, Micah screamed, "Stop! Don't throw away the monkey treats. My monkeys need them!" ("Monkeys," the pet name Micah had used for all primates before learning their distinctions, was the default name he used when overly excited.) Micah picked every discarded toilet paper tube out of the trash, and we later delivered a bag filled with them to the zoo. Micah had discovered his mission, and henceforth we always saved the toilet paper tubes from certain demise at a landfill or recycling center.

Our weekly homeschool co-op held a class on dinosaurs for kindergarteners. When Micah learned that people who study dinosaurs are called paleontologists, he asked his dad what people who study primates are called. His dad told him, "Primatologists." And Micah exclaimed, "Then I am going to be a primatologist." It has been eight years, and Micah has never expressed a different career goal.

During a field trip to the local fire department when Micah was six, there was a discussion with the fire chief about what each child would like to become. Most of the children gave the usual answers—a policeman, a football player, a teacher, a doctor— but Micah said, "I am going to be a primatologist and study apes in the Democratic Republic of the Congo." The fire chief replied with a chuckle, "Can you even spell that?" Micah sat up straight and said, "*P-R-I-M-A-T-O-L-O-G-I-S-T*," as if the fire chief were asking him to actually do so. "Wow!' was all the fire chief said in response.

After Micah had been pursuing his mission for a while, it expanded. Being the youngest and watching the successes of older siblings as they got their pictures in the

Figure 112. Angela and Micah getting ready to deliver a week's worth of enrichment to the Rio Grande Zoo

paper or interviews on television at a community event sometimes made Micah feel left out, and he'd say, "I want to become famous, too! Mommy, what can I do to become famous?" So one day I asked Micah if we should write about his toilet paper tube collecting for the Valencia Area Family Educators' newsletter. He thought the idea was hilarious, because everyone uses toilet paper, and agreed. His project and the article needed a name, and Micah came up with "Micah's Monkey Mission." I questioned the accuracy of the word *monkey*, but Micah insisted on it because it sounded better than anything he could imagine with the word *primate*. Subsequently, his article appeared on the "Kids Corner" page of the January 2011 edition of the newsletter. Micah continued collecting cardboard toilet paper tubes from our family, church friends, the homeschool co-op, and a local Girl Scout troop. Everywhere we went a grocery sack of such tubes was passed as frequently as a handshake. Those who were unaware of his mission raised an eyebrow until Micah explained his purpose, then they, too, began to save them, making toilet paper tubes no longer trash in many local households.

As Micah's mission grew in popularity after publication of his article, I thought maybe the Rio Grande Zoo should know about his efforts as well since they were a part of the story. So I sent the information in an e-mail, and before long *BioScape* magazine, a publication of the Rio Grande BioPark Society, wanted an interview with Micah for a magazine article.

With Micah dressed for the occasion in a safari hat and vest, toy binoculars, and a canteen, and with a huge bag of toilet paper tubes over one shoulder and a stuffed chimpanzee named George under his other arm, we headed excitedly to the zoo. When we arrived, Micah was given a tour by the primate manager that included the back of the ape house, the enrichment room where all donations were sorted, and the kitchen and night quarters for the apes. He learned about contact between primates and humans and about safety in moving and caging for feeding, sleeping, and providing health care for the primates. To Micah, this was as good as meeting Superman or Mickey Mouse at Disneyland.

The tour opened up for Micah a whole new understanding of the needs of primates. He learned that in addition to cardboard tubes the primates needed telephone books; kitchen boxboard; magazines and discarded paperbacks; and sheets, blankets, and recycled clothing for bedding. He was also told some fascinating facts like straw bedding makes the orangutans' hair fall out and that they like old soccer jerseys and nightgowns to use for nests. Micah also learned the requirements necessary for donating clothing and bedding—no zippers, snaps, ties, buttons, or embellishments. The staff told us that all materials donated were sorted and hazards removed by volunteers and students. Micah's new plan was to bring all materials prepped for use.

After Micah's second article, "Sparks of Enthusiasm: Six-Year-Old Enriches Primates," appeared in the summer 2011 issue of *BioScape* magazine, he stepped up his efforts collecting household items to be donated to the zoo. Now he began collecting all cardboard tubes, including those from paper towels, saran wrap, foil, ribbon, carpet, and wrapping paper. As a result, I became an expert at the tedious task of peeling the last remnants of paper and other commodities from cardboard tubes so they will pass his inspection, which is why I only buy brands that do not use glue to attach their rolls. Micah also started rounding up phone books, magazines, catalogs without staples, paperback books, and clean paper egg cartons without dried raw egg remnants. The primates can use all boxboard from kitchen and household items, with plastic windows and tape removed, except for freezer waxy boxes, fast-food boxes with oily stains and strong food smells, or any corrugated cardboard that may have stored foods in warehouses and thus might be tainted with pesticides or other chemicals. Items Micah began collecting for bedding included sheets, blankets, throw rugs, and soft clothing with all pocket grommets and zippers cut away, and buttons, ties, elastic, strings, and decorative elements like sequins or metallic fibers removed. This made sense to us, not only in terms of helping apes but for sustainable living. We never really thought of it as going green—for us it was going ape.

The chimpanzees like all the enrichment items. They enjoy fingering through the pages of magazines looking for a dab of peanut butter or a raisin. It looks to passersby as if the chimps are actually reading the pages until they intermittently eat a section or two. Like my children, the apes love to make periscopes and binoculars out of cardboard tubes, tooting them like horns, and are especially excited when a treat falls out of one end. They say that one man's trash is another man's treasure when speaking of the things we discard, but who ever thought that our trash could do so much for our zoo friends?

Micah's quest to become the best junior primatologist he can continues beyond the scope of "Micah's Monkey Mission." He has learned about the impact of the bushmeat trade on chimpanzees and has taken the bushmeat pledge at bushmeat. org, asking many adult friends and primate protectors to join him. Following Micah's awareness of the plight of chimpanzees used for research in Alamogordo, New Mexico, he wrote a letter asking Congressman Steve Pearce to support legislation to protect the chimpanzees and provide medical care for them in a sanctuary for the remainder of their days. Micah takes notice of any animal in captivity. Television shows about people who raise capuchin monkeys and chimpanzees as children bother him. Micah can tell any fellow viewer why it is wrong and what should be done. On a visit to the circus when Micah was eight, he noticed that the lion did not look healthy and pointed out that the size of his cage and schedule of performances in localities across the state prevented access to any enrichment and had likely led to his condition. This was an interesting discussion to have with an eight-year-old.

Micah has quite a stuffed ape collection, though to him they are not toys but friends. Each one has a name and a purpose. Micah explains that these stuffed friends are the only primates allowed to be kept as pets. His primate book collection is almost as vast as his stuffed ape collection. Although none of his books are at his current reading level, he asks about every word he does not know. Micah has become a self-proclaimed expert on the differences between foraging in the jungle and simulated foraging at the zoo. He can tell anyone he meets about chimpanzees' needs for enrichment, socialization, community, and family, as well as where they live, how they work together in groups, hunt, and gather. Micah's understanding of world geography includes the United States, Africa, Asia, and Borneo—he reads or looks at the pictures in his ape reference books with a globe at hand and can tell you in detail about the African jungle, though he has only a general idea about the rest of the world.

Many people think Micah is an odd little bird. They are taken aback when we make birthday party or Christmas gift suggestions of safari gear and ape reference books and do a double-take when bags and boxes of cardboard are passed among friends at events and activities. "Why chimpanzees and monkeys?" they ask. Such a question is always a great story starter about the mission of a very unique child—my son Micah, the budding primatologist. Each of our children has unique gifts, interests, and talents, but never did I dream that Micah's love for primates might one day land him in the Democratic Republic of the Congo! That is his plan. We look forward to the postcards.

AFTERWORD

C himpanzees were listed as a threatened species three years after the US Endangered Species Act of 1973 (ESA) became law. In 1990, the ESA changed the classification status for wild chimpanzees from threatened to endangered but, taking advantage of a loophole, kept captive chimpanzees classified as a threatened species, resulting in the continued warehousing and use of thousands of captive chimpanzees in invasive research. Fortunately, the tide has now turned for captive chimpanzees in the United States, due to public outcry as more people have learned about the complex emotional lives of chimpanzees and their suffering in captivity.

The final effort to end the split classification began in December 2010, when the National Institutes of Health (NIH)—which had by then funded hundreds of millions of dollars a year in chimpanzee housing, maintenance, and research over several decades—requested an analysis of the use of chimpanzees in biomedical research from the National Academy of Sciences' Institute of Medicine (IOM). A year later, the IOM concluded that the use of chimpanzees in biomedical research was no longer necessary. On June 26, 2013, the NIH cut all funding for such research and agreed to retire about four hundred government-owned chimpanzees, leaving fifty others on standby in case they were needed. (By contrast, many other countries had long before either banned or significantly limited the use of chimpanzees in medical research.) Subsequently, the US Fish and Wildlife Service (FWS) changed the classification of captive chimpanzees from threatened to endangered under the US Endangered Species Act, a modification that went into effect on September 14, 2015. Two months later the NIH announced that it would "retire" the remaining fifty chimpanzees.

The endangered classification, in extending to captive chimpanzees the same protections afforded to their free-living counterparts, put an end to invasive research on chimpanzees in the United States. However, an exceptions clause in section 10 of the ESA stated: "The secretary may permit any act otherwise prohibited by section 9 for scientific purposes or to enhance the propagation or survival of the affected species."[1]

This clause, allowing for the taking of chimpanzees for scientific or conservation purposes, left a major loophole impacting the protection of chimpanzees in captivity. In 2016, FWS, taking advantage of this loophole by exercising extensive liberties in its interpretation of the exceptions clause, issued a special permit to Yerkes National Primate Research Center allowing for the transfer of eight chimpanzees from its research facility in Georgia to the Wingham Wildlife Park in the United Kingdom, some 4,200 miles away. The New England Anti-Vivisection Society and other plaintiffs legally challenged Yerkes to prevent the chimps from leaving the country, but lost the case.[2, 3] Meanwhile, Yerkes had turned down offers from five US primate sanctuaries eager to permanently retire the chimpanzees. As a result, instead of living out their days in a peaceful sanctuary seven of them (one died before the transfer) are on permanent display in a primate exhibition, having none of the protections they would have been given under US law. Even with their newly granted endangered status the chimpanzees' best interests did not prevail.[4]

Currently there are 1,476 chimpanzees in the United States. Of those, 427 remain warehoused in federally funded and privately owned biomedical research laboratories, 10 are in entertainment compounds, 25 are being kept as pets or are living with sellers or breeders, 237 live in accredited zoos, 613 live in accredited sanctuaries, and 164 are in unaccredited facilities.[5] It's a race against time to retire the chimpanzees still waiting to put their feet on the earth, as many are old, sickly, and fragile. Even young chimpanzees have been weakened by the conditions in which they live. The most pressing issues now are to get research laboratories to release the remaining chimpanzees into existing sanctuaries; to raise funds for additional housing and lifetime care at the sanctuaries; and to grant legal rights to captive chimpanzees so they are no longer considered things but persons.

Many individuals and organizations in the United States, from animal rights activists and animal welfare and rescue groups to members of the scientific community, are vigorously addressing these issues. They are working hard to support chimpanzees living in sanctuaries and expedite moving research, entertainment, and pet chimpanzees into sanctuaries. Steven Wise, president of the Nonhuman Rights Project, for one, has been laboring unremittingly on groundbreaking cases to provide chimpanzees with legal rights to body liberty, protection from further exploitation, and transfer to accredited primate sanctuaries where they can live enriched and healthy lives.

Chimpanzee advocates in Africa are also hard at work. Among much else, they are rescuing chimpanzees who have been poached for the exotic pet and entertainment trades, building new primate refuges for the orphaned chimpanzees, looking after chimps in existing sanctuaries, and developing long-term education and conservation projects in home-range countries.

The advocacy taking place on behalf of chimpanzees is vital to their survival and future well-being. Advances in animal welfare, as a whole, are happening as bans on using animals in circuses now exist worldwide; Hollywood is increasingly turning to animatronics and CGI imagery in films; the number of roadside animal exhibits has decreased; discussions about repurposing zoos as sanctuaries are occurring with increased frequency; many fashion designers worldwide have pledged to stop using fur on their apparel; and more people are embracing plant based diets, eschewing animal products altogether. Clearly, public perception of animals is transforming: once viewed only as food, entertainment, and commodities, animals are more frequently beheld as sentient beings deserving of rights and freedoms. And still there remains a staggering amount of work to be done to fight the injustices and suffering that continue every day in the nonhuman world.

ACKNOWLEDGMENTS

Captive chimpanzees have broken open my heart; I have felt their pain, and in so many ways they have helped heal mine. We owe them a great debt. This book is my gift to them.

Many people who make the world a better place for animals have been a source of enlightenment and inspiration to me. Among them are the contributors to this book, who gave selflessly of their time and energy to share their personal stories in these pages. From my heart to yours, thank you.

To the research professionals whose primate vivisection work in laboratories was too painful to recount for publication in this book: I hope one day you will find the courage to share your stories.

I am indebted to Teri Micco for the years of conversation we shared about the suffering and beauty in the world, and for her many creative contributions in the early stages of this book.

I owe a debt of gratitude to my friends who believed in this book from the first seed of an idea through its myriad stages of gestation and birth, and who supported me in countless ways. Thank you, Kaye Burr, Frances Kean, Donna Gordon, Lesley Rubin Diamond, Michael Nunnally, Ellie Gray, Pauline Sargent, Callian Meran, Martin Rutte, Forouz Jowkar, Patricia Johanik, Judy "Guma" Tretheway, David Labiner, Maya Youngblood, Jann Rudd, and my sister, Sandra Lenore.

My gratitude goes out to Diana Lightmoon for her enduring friendship, especially during my period of intense grief while descending into the world of captive chimpanzees almost two decades ago; Willow Murphy, for continually reminding me to hold to my deepest intentions and keep going, no matter how difficult the material; Lin Reams, for spirited pep talks when the road to completion seemed so long; Adriana Martin, for her steady encouragement; and Tom Aageson, for his unwavering trust that this book would see the light of day.

My heartfelt thanks to Corine Frankland for her insights into my soul connection with chimpanzees; Lisa Blair, for her inspiring encouragement to get this book into the world; and Ruby Gibson, for understanding the importance of sharing these stories to help alleviate future suffering.

Ellen Kleiner, founder of Blessingway Authors' Services, has been my anchor in a sea of publishing ideas over the past eight years. I am grateful for her wise counsel and seasoned editorial assistance, which has helped improve this book in many ways. Thanks also to Lora Lisbon, concept editor at Blessingway, for reading the first draft of the manuscript and believing in its message from the very first story.

I am most grateful to Dr. Theodora Capaldo, president emeritus of the New England Anti-Vivisection Society, and Erika Fleury, program director for the North American Primate Sanctuary Alliance, for their insightful suggestions for the introduction and afterword; and to Judy Rosenman, Dax Riner, Kaye Burr, Ann Mason, Rita Gentry, and Cinny Green for their editorial reviews during the manuscript's early stages.

I was incredibly lucky to collaborate with a team of creative individuals who resonated with the heart of this book. Deep appreciation goes to the esteemed photographer Wendy McEahern, who edited the photographs into a cohesive collection (no small feat with images so wildly varied in quality); gifted artist and book designer Janice St. Marie, who skillfully guided my design visions into being and made the long months of page production a joyful experience; and master book designer David Skolkin, who graciously made time in his busy schedule to consult on the cover design.

My appreciation to Magdelyn Brennan for creating the first *Chimpanzee Chronicles* video; Willow Murphy, Rose Driscoll, Monica Morris, Tom Alexander, and Laura Bonar for their support at my early manuscript reading; and Ben Allison for his sage counsel during the planning and development of this book.

A deep bow of gratitude to my mother, Lois Rosenman, who was supportive of me and this book up until her last years of living with Alzheimer's disease. I wish she and my father could be here to hold this book in their hands. They would be so proud.

I want to acknowledge the teachers, principals, and schoolchildren of Santa Fe, New Mexico, who participated in my chimpanzee compassion projects. Today's children are tomorrow's leaders and activists, and it is my profound hope that together they will build a future rooted in empathy, tolerance, and courage to always do the right thing, even when it is not easy.

Finally, I want to express my deepest appreciation and heartfelt gratitude to all the Indiegogo supporters whose donations launched the publishing of this book. A most special thank you to Jean M. McNeill, Golden Champion of Chimpanzees; David Rosenman, Super Champion for Chimpanzees; and Theodora Capaldo, Donna Gordon, Elizabeth Reego, Annette Osnos, Callian Meran, and David Labiner, Champions for Chimpanzees.

ACKNOWLEDGMENTS

RESOURCES

BOOKS AND DVDS

BOOKS

NONFICTION

Among Chimpanzees: Field Notes from the Race to Save Our Endangered Relatives by Nancy Merrick

The Animal Manifesto: Six Reasons for Expanding Our Compassion Footprint by Marc Bekoff

The Animals' Agenda: Freedom, Compassion, and Coexistence in the Human Age by Marc Bekoff and Jessica Pierce

Beautiful Minds: The Parallel Lives of Great Apes and Dolphins by Maddalena Bearzi and Craig B. Stanford

Beyond Words: What Animals Think and Feel by Carl Safina

Bonobo Handshake: A Memoir of Love and Adventure in the Congo by Vanessa Woods

Brutal Kinship by Michael Nichols and Jane Goodall

Captive by Jo-Anne McArthur

The Chimps of Fauna Sanctuary: A True Story of Resilience and Recovery by Andrew Westoll

Eating Apes by Dale Peterson

The Emotional Lives of Animals: A Leading Scientist Explores Animal Joy, Sorrow, and Empathy—and Why They Matter by Marc Bekoff

Great Ape Odyssey by Dr. Biruté M. F. Galdikas

How Animals Grieve by Barbara J. King

In My Family Tree: A Life with Chimpanzees by Sheila Siddle

In the Shadow of Man by Jane Goodall

Kindred Beings: What Seventy-Three Chimpanzees Taught Me about Life, Love, and Connection by Sheri Speede

Monkey Business: A History of Nonhuman Primate Rights by Erika Fleury

Next of Kin: My Conversations with Chimpanzees by Roger Fouts with
  Stephen Tukel Mills
Nim Chimpsky: The Chimp Who Would Be Human by Elizabeth Hess
Opening Doors: Carole Noon and Her Dream to Save the Chimps by Gary Ferguson
Phoenix Zones: Where Strength Is Born and Resilience Lives by Hope Ferdowsian
Rattling the Cage: Toward Legal Rights for All Animals by Steven M. Wise
Significant Others by Craig Stanford
Visions of Caliban: On Chimpanzees and People by Dale Peterson and Jane Goodall
We Animals by Jo-Anne McArthur
When Elephants Weep: The Emotional Lives of Animals by Jeffrey Moussaieff Masson
  and Susan McCarthy

FICTION

A Beautiful Truth by Colin McAdam
Flight of the Hummingbird: A Parable for the Environment by Michael Nicoll Yahgulanaas

CHILDREN'S BOOKS

Chimp Rescue: True Life Stories by Jess French
A Chimpanzee Tale by Karen Young
The Chimpanzees I Love: Saving Their World and Ours by Jane Goodall
The Eagle and the Wren by Jane Goodall
Hurt Go Happy by Ginny Rorby
Rickie and Henri by Jane Goodall

DVDS

Chimpanzees: An Unnatural History by Allison Argo
Jane Goodall's Wild Chimpanzees by Stephen Low and David Lickley
One Small Step: The Story of the Space Chimps by David Cassidy and Kristin Davy
Project NIM by James Marsh
Unlocking the Cage by Chris Hegedus and D A Pennebaker

CHIMPANZEE SANCTUARIES IN NORTH AMERICA AND AFRICA

NORTH AMERICA

Center for Great Apes, Wauchula, Florida, www.centerforgreatapes.org

Chimp Haven, Keithville, Louisiana, www.chimphaven.org

Chimpanzee Sanctuary Northwest, Cle Elum, Washington, www.chimpsanctuarynw.org

Cleveland Amory Black Beauty Ranch, Murchison, Texas, www.fundforanimals.org

Fauna Foundation, Carignan, Quebec, www.faunafoundation.org

Primarily Primates, San Antonio, Texas, www.primarilyprimates.org

Primate Rescue Center, Nicholasville, Kentucky, www.primaterescue.org

Project Chimps, Morganton, Georgia, www.projectchimps.org

Save the Chimps, Fort Pierce, Florida, www.savethechimps.org

Wildlife Waystation, Sylmar, California, www.wildlifewaystation.org

AFRICA

Ape Action Africa, Yaounde, Cameroon, www.apeactionafrica.org

Chimfunshi Wildlife Orphanage, Zambia, https://www.chimfunshi.de/en

Chimp Eden, the Jane Goodall Institute South Africa, South Africa, https://www.chimpeden.com

Chimpanzee Conservation Center, Guinea www.projectprimate.org

Chimpanzee Refuge Project, Gambia, www.friendsofanimals.org/chimpanzee-refuge-project/

Help Congo—Habitat Ecologique et Liberté des Primates, Congo, www.help-primates.org

J.A.C.K. (Jeunes Animaux Confisques au Katanga), Democratic Republic of the Congo, www.jacksanctuary.org

Liberia Chimpanzee Rescue & Protection, Liberia, liberiachimpanzeerescue.org

Limbe Wildlife Centre, Cameroon, www.limbewildlife.org

Lwiro Primate Rehabilitation Centre, Centre de Rehabilitation des Primates de Lwiro, Democratic Republic of the Congo, https://www.lwiroprimates.org

Ngamba Island Chimpanzee Sanctuary; Chimpanzee Sanctuary & Wildlife Conservation Trust, Uganda, https://ngambaisland.org

Parc de la Lékédi, www.parcdelalekedi.ga

Sanaga-Yong Chimpanzee Rescue Center, IDA Africa, Cameroon, www.ida-africa.org
Sweetwaters Chimpanzee Sanctuary, Kenya, www.olpejetaconservancy.org
Tacugama Chimpanzee Sanctuary, Sierra Leone, www.tacugama.com http://
    tacugama.com/
Tchimpounga Chimpanzee Rehabilitation Center, Congo, www.janegoodall.org.uk/
    our-programmes/tchimpounga-chimpanzee-rehabilitation-centre

ORGANIZATIONS CONCERNED
WITH CHIMPANZEE WELFARE

American Anti-Vivisection Society, www.aavs.org
Animal Protection of New Mexico, www.retirethechimps.org
Ape Action Africa, www.apeactionafrica.org
Arcus Foundation, www.arcusfoundation.org
Born Free Foundation, www.bornfree.org.uk
Chimpanzee Sanctuary Fund, www.chimpstosanctuary.org
Endangered Species International, www.endangeredspeciesinternational.org
Friends of Animals, www.friendsofanimals.org
Friends of Washoe, www.friendsofwashoe.org
Global Federation of Animal Sanctuaries, www.sanctuaryfederation.org/gfas/
Great Apes Survival Partnership, www.un-grasp.org
Humane Society of the United States, www.humanesociety.org
In Defense of Animals, www.ida-africa.org
Jane Goodall Institute, www.janegoodall.org
Kibale Chimpanzee Project, www.kibalechimpanzees.wordpress.com
National Anti-Vivisection Society, www.navs.org
New England Anti-Vivisection Society, www.neavs.org
Nonhuman Rights Project, www.nonhumanrights.org
North American Primate Sanctuary Alliance, www.primatesanctuaires.org
Pan African Sanctuary Alliance, www.pasaprimates.org
Project ChimpCARE, www.chimpcare.org
Project R&R: Release & Restitution for Chimpanzees in US Laboratories,
    www.releasechimps.org
Wild Chimpanzee Foundation, www.wildchimps.org

338

NOTES

INTRODUCTION

1. D. Stiles et al., eds., "Stolen Apes—The Illicit Trade in Chimpanzees, Gorillas, Bonobos and Orangutans," *A Rapid Response Assessment* (Arendal, Norway: United Nations Environment/Programme, GRID-Arendal, 2013).

2. David Shukman and Sam Piranty, "The Secret Trade in Baby Chimps," *BBC News,* January 30, 2017, http://www.bbc.co.uk/news/resources/idt-5e8c4bac-c236-4cd9-bacc-db96d733f6cf.

3. "Anthrax: A Hidden Threat to Wildlife in the Tropics," *Max-Planck-Gesellschaft,* August 2, 2017, https://www.mpg.de/11415814/anthrax-chimpanzees.

4. Fabian H. Leendertz et al., eds., "Anthrax Kills Wild Chimpanzees in a Tropical Rainforest," *Nature* 430 (July 22, 2004): 451–52.

5. Great Apes Survival Partnership (GRASP), *Ebola & Great Apes,* https://europa.eu/capacity4dev/unep/documents/grasp-ebola-great-apes.

6. Robert M. Yerkes, "Provision for the Study of Monkeys and Apes," *Science* 43, no. 1103 (February 18, 1916): 231–34.

7. Yerkes National Primate Research Center, "History," http://www.yerkes.emory.edu/about/history.html.

8. Project R&R, "The Beginnings," www.releasechimps.org/research/history/beginnings.

9. Project R&R, "Air and Space," http://releasechimps.org/research/history/air-space.

10. National Aeronautics and Space Administration, "A Brief History of Animals in Space," https://history.nasa.gov/animals.html.

11. *One Small Step: The Story of the Space Chimps,* a film by David Cassidy and Kristin Davy, 2008.

12. National Aeronautics and Space Administration, "Brief History," https://history.nasa.gov/animals.html.

13. Project R&R, "Air and Space," https://releasechimps.org/research/history/air-space.

14. Project R&R, "History of Use," http://releasechimps.org/research/history.

15. G. A. Bradshaw, PhD, et al., "Building an Inner Sanctuary: Complex PTSD in Chimpanzees," *Journal of Trauma & Dissociation* 9, no. 1 (2008): 9–34, doi: 10.1080/15299730802073619.

16. Jarrod Bailey, "Lessons from Chimpanzee-Based Research on Human Disease: The Implications of Genetic Differences," *Alternatives to Laboratory Animals-ATLA* 39, no. 6 (2011): 527–40.

17. Jarrod Bailey, "An Assessment of the Use of Chimpanzees in Hepatitis C Research Past, Present and Future: Validity of the Chimpanzee Model," *Alternatives to Laboratory Animals-ATLA* 38, no. 5 (2010): 387–418.

KEY OUT: A CHIMPANZEE'S PETITION FOR FREEDOM

1. Matthew Fox, *Meditations with Meister Eckhart* (Santa Fe, NM: Bear & Company, 1983), 14.

IRREVOCABLE BONDS

1. Barbara J. King, *How Animals Grieve* (Chicago: University of Chicago Press, 2013), 80–83.

AFTERWORD

1. US Fish and Wildlife Service, *Endangered Species Act of 1973 as Amended through the 108th Congress* (Washington DC: Department of the Interior, 1973), 28.

2. Project R&R, "Stop US Fish & Wildlife Service from Making Another Mistake," http://www.releasechimps.org/resources/article/stop-u.s.-fish-wildlife-service-from-making-another-mistake.

3. New England Anti-Vivisection Society v. US Fish and Wildlife Service and Yerkes National Primate Research Center, Civil Action No. 16-cv-149 (September 14, 2016).

4. Timothy Pratt, "Precious Cargo: The Endangered Species Act and the Case of the Yerkes Chimps," *Undark,* https://undark.org/article/precious-cargo-the-endangered-species-act-and-the-case-of-the-yerkes-chimps/.

5. Lincoln Park Zoo, "Chimpanzees in the US," *ChimpCARE,* www.chimpcare.org/map.

CONTRIBUTORS

ALLISON ARGO has made documentary films for twenty-five years that advocate for the just treatment of nonhuman beings. She is known for her emotionally charged and deeply personal films, particularly her intimate portraits of endangered and abused animals. Her films, which she writes, edits, produces, directs, and often narrates, have won six Emmys, a DuPont Columbia award for journalism, and over fifty awards internationally; all have been broadcast on TV by PBS and National Geographic. Her Emmy award-winning film *Chimpanzees: An Unnatural History,* which gives a sobering glimpse into the world of chimpanzees in North America, was broadcast in 2006, capturing the hearts of viewers around the world. Allison has traveled the globe searching for chimpanzees in the mountains of Tanzania, combing the Amazon for endangered frogs, and exploring the underbelly of Bangkok looking for displaced elephants. Her latest film, *The Last Pig,* continues her mission as a filmmaker to speak out for the voiceless and inspire compassion for all living beings. (www.ArgoFilms.com)

SARAH BAECKLER DAVIS is a primatologist, lawyer, nonprofit fund-raiser, and bridge builder. She has worked with and for chimpanzees since 1997, the year she met Washoe, the famous sign language chimpanzee. Sarah has a graduate degree in primatology from Central Washington University and a JD from Lewis and Clark Law School. She served as executive director of Chimpanzee Sanctuary Northwest for its first five years, helping it evolve from infancy to an established and respected member of the chimpanzee sanctuary community. She then spent a year and a half leading the North American Primate Sanctuary Alliance, which she cofounded in 2010, along with six other sanctuary directors. In 2014, she founded Project Chimps with the mission to retire nearly three hundred chimpanzees. Presently, Sarah is the executive director of Humane Society Naples.

MARK BODAMER, PHD, worked with chimpanzees for more than two decades, including chimpanzee sign language studies with Washoe, Moja, Tatu, Dar, and Loulis at Dr. Roger and Deborah Fouts's primate facility at Central Washington University. Mark received his PhD in experimental psychology from the University of Nevada-Reno, studying under the pioneering chimpanzee comparative psychologists Drs. R. Allen and Beatrix T. Gardner. Mark's work helped shed light on the continuity between species and the ethical issues regarding the long-term care and psychological well-being of chimpanzees. As an associate professor of psychology, he taught Introduction to Psychology, Research Methods, and Comparative Psychology at Pacific University in Forest Grove, Oregon, and Gonzaga University in Spokane, Washington. Mark is vice president of the board of trustees for the Chimfunshi Wildlife Orphanage Trust in Zambia, where he has spent fifteen summers leading his students and colleagues in chimpanzee research, educational outreach, and humanitarian aid projects.

KRISTINA CASPER-DENMAN, PHD, is a professor of anthropology and history at American River College in Sacramento, California, where she also teaches a class in zoo primatology. She was co-coordinator of the ChimpanZoo program at the Sacramento Zoo and the northwest regional volunteer coordinator until 2009. Kristina has observed capuchin and howler monkeys in Costa Rica; worked with a variety of monkeys, including several species of marmosets and macaques; and interned at the Primate Foundation of Arizona, doing research on growth and development, while earning her MA in physical anthropology at Arizona State University. She has presented research papers at the Southwest Anthropology Association, the Sacramento Anthropology Society, the American Society of Primatologists, and ChimpanZoo conferences. Kristina earned her PhD in Native American studies at the University of California, Davis, in 2013.

DEBBY COX began her career in chimpanzee captive management at the Taronga Zoo, Australia, in 1986, visiting over a hundred zoos worldwide to review the management and facilities of great apes. In 2003, she volunteered in Burundi at the Jane Goodall Institute's (JGI) halfway house for confiscated chimpanzees and returned as codirector the following year. After translocating the chimps to Kenya, Debby established the

Ngamba Island Sanctuary at the request of JGI and the Ugandan government. While acting as project director of the sanctuary and director of JGI Uganda, she received a master's degree in environmental sciences from Australian National University. In 2004, she turned over the directorship of the sanctuary to a Ugandan national in order to focus on chimpanzee conservation and welfare programs for JGI Uganda. Debby served as a consultant for JGI within the Africa Program countries from 2009 to 2016. She has also been vice president of Captive Care for the International Primatological Society and an advisor for the Pan African Sanctuary Alliance, as well as on its Captive Care Committee. Debby has returned to her homeland in Australia and is currently working with Indigenous Rangers in Northern Australia.

EILEEN DALLAIRE, executive director of the Primate Rescue Center in Kentucky, manages the care of nearly fifty primates and directs the various departments of the sanctuary and staff. Eileen graduated magna cum laude, with a BA in psychology, from the University of Kentucky in 2003. She has participated in the Primate Training and Enrichment Workshop at MD Anderson Cancer Research Center in Bastrop, Texas (2008), the Chimpanzee Husbandry Workshop at the Kansas City Zoo (2011), the Leadership Development for Animal Care Managers at Chimp Haven in Shreveport, Louisiana (2012), the USDA Nonhuman Primate Symposium (2017), the Chimpanzee Species Survival Plan Conference at Chimp Haven (2017), and the North American Primate Sanctuary Alliance Workshops (2013–2018).

LESLEY DAY is the founder of Chimps Inc., a Bend, Oregon–based nonprofit sanctuary for chimpanzees and big cats. Topo, the first chimpanzee to find refuge there—and the one featured in her story—arrived in 1995. Lesley's first rescue was a snow leopard in 1991, a year after obtaining her United States Department of Agriculture license. She is a founding member of the North American Primate Sanctuary Alliance.

JOHN DEBENHAM, PHD, DVM, graduated with a degree in veterinary science from the University of Sydney in 2011 and in 2015 completed his Certificate in Zoological Medicine from the University of Edinburgh. In 2017, he received his PhD in Intestinal Protozoa in Wildlife from the Norwegian University of Life Sciences. During his veterinary studies, he cofounded Survive Australia, which supported conservation projects around the world, including the Lwiro Primate Rehabilitation Centre and Roots & Shoots Nepal. Currently, John works as a lecturer and clinical veterinarian at the University Animal Hospital, associated with the Norwegian University of Life Sciences, and is head veterinarian at the Tangen Zoo. He gained experience in great ape medicine working at Lwiro Primate Rehabilitation Centre in 2006 and Tchimpounga Chimpanzee Rehabilitation Centre in 2012. John's goal is to combine clinical work with continued research in wildlife diseases, furthering his training as a veterinarian and conservation biologist.

JENNY DESMOND is an animal welfare and conservation consultant living in Liberia. She holds a master's degree in social work from the University of Denver. She and her husband, Jim, cofounded Liberia Chimpanzee Rescue & Protection (LCRP) in West Africa and its US affiliate, Partners in Animal Protection and Conservation. As an NGO, the goals of the LCRP are to provide lifelong care for orphaned chimpanzees, work with local governments and international organizations to enforce anti-poaching laws for abolishing the bushmeat and wildlife trafficking trades, and help drive dynamic strategies in the conservation of wild populations. Jenny has consulted with a wide array of animal conservation organizations on projects ranging from strategic planning to establishing animal care protocols, fundraising, and marketing campaigns. Her clients have included the Jane Goodall Institute, Pan African Sanctuary Alliance, Great Ape Survival Project, Smithsonian Institution, Orangutan Foundation International, Harmony Fund, and EcoHealth Alliance.

AMY FULTZ is the director of behavior and research at Chimp Haven, which she cofounded in 1995 and where she welcomed the first chimpanzees in 2005. Amy brings extensive professional experience to Chimp Haven after many years of behavioral work in zoo, sanctuary, and research facilities. Responsible for socialization of the chimpanzees and overseeing the enrichment and training programs, she also conducts observational research on the chimpanzees as they adjust to their new lives at the sanctuary. Working with primates since 1986, and specifically with chimpanzees since 1992, she specializes in introductions, having introduced hundreds of chimpanzees at Chimp Haven alone. Amy is passionate about chimpanzee conservation issues and has published and presented scientific papers based on her research.

ROSA GARRIGA, PHD, DVM, is a veterinarian with almost two decades of experience working with wildlife. She has supervised the health care of over 250 orangutans at the Orangutan Care Centre and Quarantine in Borneo, Indonesia, and more than 100 orphaned chimpanzees at the Tacugama Chimpanzee Sanctuary in Sierra Leone. Serving as a field veterinarian and technical advisor, she has worked as an animal handling and facility improvement consultant for hospitals, sanctuaries, and rescue and rehabilitation centers in Guatemala, Gambia, India, and Lebanon. Rosa received her PhD from Universitat Autònoma de Barcelona in human-chimpanzee coexistence in nonprotected areas of Sierra Leone, West Africa, in 2018; her degree in veterinary science in 1994, also from the Universitat Autònoma de Barcelona; and a master's degree in wildlife medicine from the University of London in 1999. Since 2011, she has been helping the Tacugama Chimpanzee Sanctuary develop and implement research projects for the conservation of wild chimpanzees in Sierra Leone, focusing on their coexistence with humans in nonprotected areas that have been highly degraded by human activities.

DIANA GOODRICH has worked for nonprofit organizations since 1996. She has master of science degrees in psychology and in animals and public policy. Her early career focused on working with children with special needs, managing volunteers, leading research projects on gestural communication in chimpanzees, and coordinating outreach efforts for a nonprofit film production company. She spent three years as a caregiver and executive assistant for the Fauna Foundation, a sanctuary in Canada for chimpanzees who have been retired by laboratories and zoos. Her passion for animal protection has led her to volunteer for numerous organizations, including several involved in emergency response during Hurricane Katrina. Diana began working for Chimpanzee Sanctuary Northwest as the director of outreach before the Cle Elum Seven chimpanzees arrived, and now serves as codirector of the sanctuary, along with her husband, J.B. Mulcahy.

GLORIA GROW, born in Montreal, is the founder and director of the Fauna Foundation, the first and only sanctuary for chimpanzees in Canada. Accredited by the Global Federation of Animal Sanctuaries, Fauna cares for chimpanzees and monkeys who spent years in research, the pet trade, and zoos. Over the last twenty years, Fauna has been home to 23 chimpanzees, 7 monkeys, 230 farm animals, and many dogs and cats. Before finding her calling for rescuing chimpanzees, Gloria attended the Nash

Academy of Animal Sciences and for fifteen years operated a dog grooming company. A founding member of the North American Primate Sanctuary Alliance, she is a trustee of the American Fund for Alternatives to Animal Research, sits on the board of advisors for the Laboratory Primate Advocacy Group, and is co-chair of Project R&R: Release and Restitution for Chimpanzees in US Laboratories. Gloria has coauthored two papers on the psychological effects of captivity and research on chimpanzees.

HARRY HMURA, international blues and jazz guitarist, founded Musicians for Apes, which grew into I AM, I AM, a project that supports great apes who have been used in biomedical research, entertainment, and kept as household pets, as well as the many sanctuaries that care for them. He has toured with Grammy Award–winning artists and performed at blues and jazz festivals in the United States, Canada, Europe, and Mexico. Harry has performed on radio, national TV commercials, and a wide range of network and cable television shows; written and produced two solo albums; and performed in the world-renowned Halo video game series Halo, Halo 3ODST, and Reach. His latest CD, *I AM, I AM,* features great ape vocalizations and sounds that were recorded at sanctuaries and indigenous habitats around the world. (www. iam-iamproject.com. www.harryhmuramusic.com)

MARY LEE JENSVOLD, PHD, is a primate communication scientist, associate director at the Fauna Foundation, and senior lecturer in the Department of Anthropology and Museum Studies at Central Washington University. She has worked with the Chimpanzee and Human Communication Institute family of chimpanzees since 1986. In 1985, she received a BA in psychology from the University of Oregon, in 1989 an MS in experimental psychology from Central Washington University, and in 1996 a PhD in experimental psychology from the University of Nevada-Reno. Specializing in ethological studies of apes, animal intelligence, communication, language, and culture, Mary Lee has published material about conversational behaviors, private signing, phrase development, chimpanzee-to-chimpanzee conversation, imaginary play, and artwork with chimpanzees. She also researches caregiving practices, zoo visitor effects, and public education about chimpanzees. Active in improving conditions for captive chimpanzees, Mary Lee is on the boards of the Animal Welfare Institute, Friends of Washoe, and the Fauna Foundation. She is a 2013–2015 Sigma Xi distinguished lecturer.

ASAMI KABASAWA received a doctorate in Asia and Africa studies in 2009 from Kyoto University, Japan; an MSc in primate conservation in 2003 from Oxford Brookes University, UK; and a BA in anthropology from Hunter College, City University of New York in 1996. During her undergraduate studies, she joined the volunteer program at the Laboratory for Experimental Medicine & Surgery in Primates (LEMSIP), New York, to improve the psychological well-being of captive chimpanzees, baboons, and other primates. In 1996, Asami worked with Janis Carter to set up a sanctuary for orphaned and confiscated chimpanzees under the Chimpanzee Conservation Project in the Republic of Guinea, West Africa. From 1997 to 2001, she worked with retired LEMSIP chimpanzees at the Wildlife Waystation in California, and from 2001 to 2005 she continued her work with captive chimpanzees at the Tacugama Chimpanzee Sanctuary in Sierra Leone. In 2006, Asami worked as a site manager at Kyoto University Primate Research Institute, Bossou Research Station in Guinea.

ADRIANA MARTIN, a native of Mexico, has an MS degree in experimental psychology from Central Washington University, where she first met the five signing chimpanzees at the Chimpanzee and Human Communication Institute (CHCI). Additionally, she obtained a JD from the University of New Mexico School of Law, where she was president of the Student Animal Legal Defense Fund. Now a researcher at Washington University School of Medicine, Adriana continues to advocate for ending all use of animals in research and for a vegan ethic. She lives in St. Louis, Missouri, with her three rescued cats—Malachi, Monster, and Evey—and her best canine friend, Bronwyn.

NANCY MEGNA is an animal advocate, activist, and caregiver who has been working with, and on behalf of, animals most of her life, including studying and observing primate behavior in labs, zoos, and in the wild. Nancy gained firsthand knowledge while caring for primates in two laboratories—New York University's Laboratory for Experimental Medicine & Surgery in Primates (LEMSIP) and Yerkes National Primate Research Center. This work compelled her to become a founding member of the Laboratory Primate Advocacy Group. As a program specialist and advisory board member for the New England Anti-Vivisection Society, Nancy has shared information about the inhumane practices and living conditions in labs that are hidden from the public due to closed-door policies. Currently, she works as a behaviorist with emotionally and intellectually disabled individuals. Nancy is committed to retiring all lab chimpanzees and ending the use of all animals in biomedical research.

PATTI RAGAN is the founder and director of the Center for Great Apes, the only sanctuary in the United States for chimpanzees and orangutans. She began her career as a teacher on the Miccosukee Indian Reservation in the Florida Everglades. Later she owned a successful staffing business in Miami, before volunteering as a docent at the Miami Metro Zoo and serving on the zoo's board of directors for six years. In 1984 and 1985, she volunteered at an orangutan rehabilitation center in Borneo, run by primatologist Dr. Biruté Galdikas. In 1993, Patti founded the Center for Great Apes, where, with a staff of dedicated employees and volunteers, she continues to manage the rescue, rehabilitation, and permanent care of great apes.

ANGELA SPARKS is the mother of six children (aka "the Sparkstribe") who range in age from fourteen to twenty-two. She holds a bachelor's and master's degree in social work from the University of Kentucky. Angela began her career in child protection and family crisis work and later shifted to foster and adoptive parent training and program administration, before leaving the workforce to raise her children. Homeschooled for the past eighteen years, her children have been active in everything from sports and church groups to the arts, scouting, and community service activities, inspired by their mother's willingness to make their dreams a reality. Angela, her husband Kimothy, and the rest of the Sparkstribe live in Los Lunas, New Mexico.

MICAH SPARKS, who wrote his story at age eight, is on a mission to educate every child and adult he meets about the plight of captive chimpanzees and their need for enrichment, socialization, community, and family. He received a Junior Primatologist Certificate from the American Society of Primatologists when he was five years old. *BioScape* magazine, a publication of the Rio Grande BioPark Society in Albuquerque, hearing that he had been gathering enrichment items for the zoo's chimpanzees, interviewed him for a feature story, "Sparks of Enthusiasm: Six-Year-Old Enriches Primates," which appeared in the summer 2011 issue. Micah's enrichment project is now in its ninth year.

JACQUELINE STEWART is a pseudonym for a biologist and former primate research laboratory employee who wishes to remain anonymous. She has worked in various facilities with many species of nonhuman primates and other wildlife, but chimpanzees remain especially close to her heart. She resides in a small town with her husband and family.

ERNA TOBACK, PHD, was born and raised in Boyle Heights, a multicultural working-class community in California. She attended California State University, Northridge, where she received a bachelor's degree in cultural anthropology with a focus on ethnomusicology and folklore, and a master's degree in physical/biological anthropology. She was awarded a PhD in primatology from the University of Stirling in Scotland. Erna has collected chimpanzee behavioral data at the MD Anderson Cancer Research Center, New Iberia Research Center, and the Los Angeles and Edinburgh Zoos. Additionally, she has created husbandry, behavioral, socialization, and environmental enrichment protocols for chimpanzees retired from biomedical research; taught physical/biological anthropology at Santa Monica College for fifteen years; and been a consultant for the Humane Society of the United States. Currently serving on Chimp Haven's board of directors, she continues her involvement in activities related to the humane care of captive chimpanzees and the retirement of biomedical research chimpanzees to sanctuaries.

HILDA TRESZ was the behavioral, enrichment, and international welfare coordinator at the Phoenix Zoo. She had twenty-eight years of experience working with chimpanzees and other exotic species around the world. An active mentor for the Jane Goodall Institute, Hilda traveled the world helping chimpanzees who were living in solitary confinement in zoos find new lives through the addition of basic husbandry, enrichment, and assistance with diet, behavioral, and medical problems. She also taught zoo staff how to improve animal welfare by employing free or inexpensive techniques. A Hungarian citizen with permanent residency in the United States since 1989, Hilda died unexpectedly at age fifty-six, while on assignment for the Jane Goodall Institute, as this book was about to go to press.

JAYNE WELLER, DVM, has always had a passion for animals and the natural world. After graduating in 2003 from the University of New South Wales with a science degree in zoology and an arts degree in music and English, Jayne became a senior keeper in a private Australian zoo. While working at the zoo, she became increasingly aware of the plight of captive animals and the importance of educating the public about their conditions and needs. In 2008, she cofounded Survive Australia, a nonprofit organization committed to supporting conservation projects worldwide through fundraising, providing needed supplies, and sharing expertise. Jayne received a Degree of Veterinary Science from Sydney University in 2011, and she successfully acquired a postgraduate certificate in Zoological Medicine from Edinburgh University in 2015. She is currently the veterinarian for the National Zoo and Aquarium in Canberra, Australia.

PHOTO CREDITS

COVER © Chimpanzee Sanctuary Northwest. **FIGURE 1** © Chimpanzee Sanctuary Northwest. **FIGURE 2** © Jenny Desmond | Liberia Chimpanzee Rescue & Protection. **FIGURE 3** © Chimps Inc.; photographer unknown. **FIGURE 4** © Mark Bodamer. **FIGURES 5, 6** courtesy of Fauna Foundation. **FIGURE 7** courtesy of Fauna Foundation; photographer Maggie Gillis. **FIGURES 8, 9** courtesy of Fauna Foundation. **FIGURE 10** courtesy of Fauna Foundation. **FIGURE 11** © Argo Films | www.argofilms.com; photographer Cici Clark. **FIGURES 12, 13** courtesy of Fauna Foundation. **FIGURE 14** courtesy of Jane Goodall Institute | Burundi; photographer unknown. **FIGURE 15** © Debby Cox. **FIGURE 16** © Nicole G. Sharpe. **FIGURES 17, 18** © Andy Nelson | www.andynelsonphotos.com. **FIGURES 19, 20** © Asami Kabasawa. **FIGURES 21–26** © Jenny Desmond | Liberia Chimpanzee Rescue & Protection. **FIGURES 27–30** © Center for Great Apes. **FIGURE 31** © Primate Rescue Center. **FIGURE 32** © Center for Great Apes. **FIGURES 33–39** © John Debenham. **FIGURES 40–44** © Rosa Garriga | Tacugama Chimpanzee Sanctuary. **FIGURE 45** © Nancy Megna. **FIGURE 46** © Mark Bodamer. **FIGURES 47–49** © Nancy Megna. **FIGURE 50** © Steve Winter | National Geographic Creative; www.stevewinterphoto.com. **FIGURE 51** © Save the Chimps. **FIGURE 52** © Sarah Baeckler Davis. **FIGURES 53–59** © Chimps Inc. **FIGURES 60–64** © Primate Rescue Center. **FIGURES 65–71** © Chimpanzee Sanctuary Northwest. **FIGURES 72–78** © Chimp Haven. **FIGURES 79–86** © Mark Bodamer. **FIGURES 87–92** © Friends of Washoe. **FIGURE 93** courtesy of Leandro Barrios | Buenos Aires Zoo. **FIGURE 94** © Stan and Zofia Kurylowicz. **FIGURES 95–97** courtesy of Santiago Ricci | Buenos Aires Zoo. **FIGURES 98, 99** © Hilda Tresz. **FIGURE 100** © Jayne Weller.

INDEX

ABOUT DEBRA ROSENMAN

DEBRA ROSENMAN, a writer, educator, workshop facilitator, and healer, has worked as an advocate for captive chimpanzees for almost two decades. During that time she developed a children's educational program that fosters deep respect and empathy toward chimpanzees while inspiring actions that make measurable differences in their lives, and created workshops that explore sacred relationships between humans, other species of animals, and the earth, encouraging participants to further cultivate their hearts of compassion. Debra is a Rubenfeld Synergy and Somatic Archaeology practitioner specializing in healing from trauma, compassion fatigue, ecological grief, and companion animal loss. She is also a Wisdom Healing (Zhineng) Qigong teacher and visual artist. Earlier in her career, Debra founded a New York City–based event planning company that became well known for its culinary and theatrical events nationwide.

Debra lives in the high desert of New Mexico with her recently adopted elder dog, Freida Heart. Her pioneering voice for animals in peril continues to raise awareness of the rights of nonhuman animals. To learn more about her work, visit www.chimpanzeechronicles.com.

Figure 113. Ngamba Island Chimpanzee Sanctuary